LUCAN
NOT GUILTY

LUCAN
NOT GUILTY

SALLY MOORE

FONTANA/Collins

*To truth and justice – and those who fight for them,
against the odds*

First published in Great Britain in 1987 by
Sidgwick & Jackson Limited
First issued in Fontana Paperbacks 1988
Second impression November 1988

Copyright © Sally Moore 1987

Printed and bound in Great Britain by
William Collins Sons & Co. Ltd, Glasgow

CONTENTS

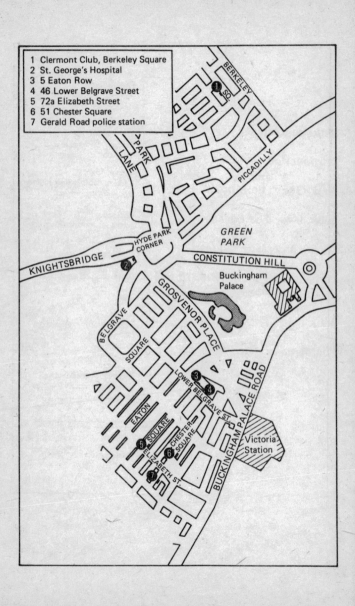

1 Clermont Club, Berkeley Square
2 St. George's Hospital
3 5 Eaton Row
4 46 Lower Belgrave Street
5 72a Elizabeth Street
6 51 Chester Square
7 Gerald Road police station

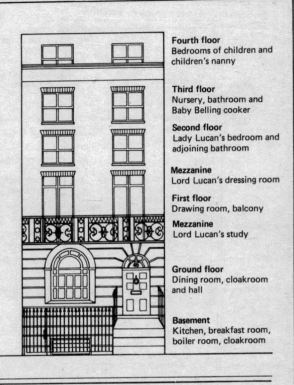

Fourth floor
Bedrooms of children and
children's nanny

Third floor
Nursery, bathroom and
Baby Belling cooker

Second floor
Lady Lucan's bedroom and
adjoining bathroom

Mezzanine
Lord Lucan's dressing room

First floor
Drawing room, balcony

Mezzanine
Lord Lucan's study

Ground floor
Dining room, cloakroom
and hall

Basement
Kitchen, breakfast room,
boiler room, cloakroom

Rough plan of the layout of 46 Lower Belgrave Street

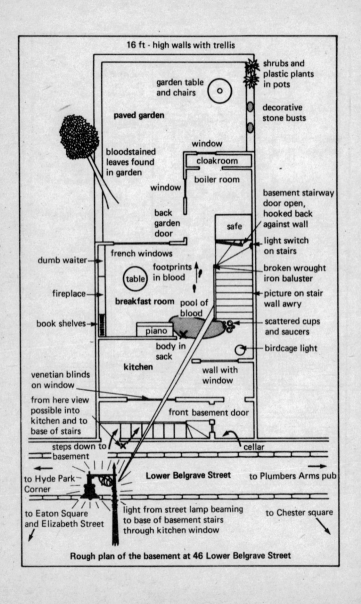

Rough plan of the basement at 46 Lower Belgrave Street

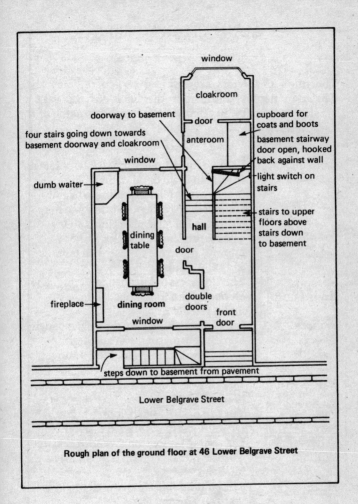

window

cloakroom

doorway to basement

door — cupboard for coats and boots

four stairs going down towards
basement doorway and cloakroom

anteroom — basement stairway
door open, hooked
back against wall

window

dumb waiter

light switch on
stairs

dining
table

stairs to upper
floors above
stairs down
to basement

hall

door

fireplace — dining room

double
doors

front
door

window

steps down to basement from pavement

Lower Belgrave Street

Rough plan of the ground floor at 46 Lower Belgrave Street

MAIN CHARACTERS

The main characters are referred to generally by their Christian names throughout the book for the sake of brevity and clarity. Bingham is the family surname of the Earls of Lucan.

John (Lord Lucan)	Richard John Bingham, 7th Earl of Lucan, Baron Bingham of Castlebar, Baron Bingham of Melcombe Bingham and a baronet of Nova Scotia; known to his family and old friends as John, to his gambling friends as Lucky, Luke or Johnny, and in his Coldstream Guards days as Arthur
Veronica (Lady Lucan)	The Countess of Lucan, née Veronica Duncan, John's estranged wife, nicknamed V
Frances	Lady Frances Bingham, their elder daughter
George	Lord Bingham, their son and heir
Camilla	Lady Camilla Bingham, their younger daughter
Kait (Kaitilin)	The Dowager Countess of Lucan, John's mother
Pat	The 6th Earl of Lucan, John's father
Jane	Dr Jane Griffin, John's elder sister
Sally	Lady Sarah Gibbs, John's younger sister
William	The Reverend William Gibbs, Sally's husband
Hugh	The Honourable Hugh Bingham, John's younger brother
Christina	Christina Shand Kydd, née Duncan, Veronica's sister
Bill	Bill Shand Kydd, Christina's husband

INTRODUCTION

No one hired me to take on this work. I had never met Lord Lucan, his family or his friends. I had to persuade people to talk to me, and I funded the work from my own pocket. The reasons I began my investigation, and the conclusions I eventually reached, were entirely my own.

What fired me in the summer of 1975, after the inquest held into Sandra Rivett's death, were three factors. A belief that the letters written by Lord Lucan on the night of the murder rang true. A sense of unease about some of the evidence which emerged at the inquest. And outrage at the injustice of a man – *any* man – being found 'guilty' without trial.

At the time I worked as a journalist for the *Daily Mirror* in London. Towards the end of the inquest, I was sent to try and get the first interview with Lord Lucan's mother, the Dowager Countess of Lucan. My requests were politely refused. I tried again after the shock of the inquest jury's verdict, which branded Lord Lucan a 'killer' in his absence. Lord Lucan's side of the story had never been told and I suggested to his sister, Lady Sarah Gibbs, that his family might try to redress the balance by using the *Daily Mirror* as a platform. Again they refused. The prejudicial publicity against Lord Lucan had been massive, and his family and friends had learned to be wary of the Press: they were not opening up to anyone.

My anxieties about the case, however, would not go away. From the newspaper reports of evidence from the inquest, it seemed to me there were points which did not tally. Was there more to the case than had so far met the official eye?

I rang Lord Lucan's mother. I apologised for approaching her yet again, having already been turned away, and pointed out that I was putting myself in jeopardy by doing so since she could, if she wished, now report me to the Press Council for intrusion. I said I was telephoning this time not as a journalist after a story, but as a private individual concerned about justice. I asked if she would allow me to come and outline to her points from the evidence which I thought were curious, in case this might be of help. She considered for a moment, said reasonably that it would be difficult for her to hear me out without making any comment herself, and suggested I rang her daughter. There was no reply when I rang Lady Sarah, so for the moment I gave up.

But my anxieties would still not go away. Colleagues who had covered the murder from the start did not dispel them. They seemed convinced that the whole matter was an 'open and shut case', and suggestions on my part that there might be some doubt seemed laughable. So I took the only other route. Assuming that the police knew all the answers, and would soon allay my doubts, I rang the murder headquarters at Gerald Road police station in Belgravia. I said I was thinking of writing a book on the Lucan case and would like to visit the station. A detective agreed to see me.

We met that August. Though he refused to be quoted by name, he couldn't have been more willing to talk, and offered more help than I had originally requested. The detective said he would go over the evidence with me, and show me the police photographs and Lord Lucan's letters. We could even, he said, hear secret tape recordings Lord Lucan had made of his wife, and he agreed to fix a joint lunch with the head of the murder squad, Detective Chief Superintendent Roy Ranson, once he returned from leave. I couldn't believe my luck. If this didn't lay my doubts to rest, nothing would.

But I was in for a few surprises at Gerald Road. I had gone there with a list of twenty-nine questions. But the detective's answer to several of them was that the police didn't know. And the replies he gave to some of the other questions turned out later to be inaccurate. In addition, my initial inquiries had shown that there had been an earlier crime at the house where Mrs Rivett was killed. Yet the detective seemed to know nothing about it.

At the end of August 1975, I then interviewed the head of the murder squad, Detective Chief Superintendent Roy Ranson, at his base at Cannon Row police station. I liked and respected him and his attitude. Even at this stage, after the inquest jury had delivered its verdict, he was prepared to question evidence with me. But, though he was convinced that Lord Lucan was the killer, some of my questions appeared to stump him. He also seemed to know nothing of the earlier crime at the scene of the murder. For two hours we talked across Ranson's desk, re-examining evidence, trying to solve at least one apparently insoluble puzzle in the case.

The Chief Superintendent was very helpful, but by the end of our session I was worried. So, I suspect, was he. I had expected to take him to lunch immediately after our interview, but Ranson said he'd 'take a rain-check' on that because he had other meetings. As we parted in the cobbled courtyard at Cannon Row, he said with conviction: 'You'll be back.' But as things turned out, it was not to be.

A few days later, I rang the famous pathologist on the case, Professor Keith Simpson, at Southwark mortuary. For the first time, in answer to my questions, I learned that Professor Simpson's opinion of how Sandra Rivett's death had occurred did not coincide with that of the detective at Gerald Road. Professor Simpson went into detail at a meeting we had together later. Far from my initial doubts being swept away, they were now increasing with every interview.

But who on earth were the two so-far-unnamed characters mentioned in one of the letters Lord Lucan wrote on the night of the murder – the alleged 'crooked solicitor and [the] rotten psychiatrist' whom Lucan claimed had 'destroyed' him 'between them'? I had asked the detective at Gerald Road who the solicitor was. The answer he had suggested turned out to be incorrect.

Trying to check on this point, I rang Lady Sarah Gibbs'

number in Northamptonshire. Her husband, the Reverend William Gibbs, answered. I asked who the solicitor was and he told me I'd better ring Bill Shand Kydd. I rang Bill Shand Kydd's country house in Leighton Buzzard. His wife Christina, Lady Lucan's younger sister, answered.

I told her that I was worried about the evidence, that I thought Lord Lucan might be innocent and that I was planning to write a book. To my surprise, she told me to ring her husband and gave me his London office number. Typically, Bill Shand Kydd took the bull by the horns and suggested we meet.

Shortly after, I found myself sitting in the drawing room of the Shand Kydds' London house in Cambridge Square with Mr Shand Kydd and one of his male business colleagues. They were clearly wary. While I tape-recorded them, they tape-recorded me. But an hour and a half later, when we parted, I felt I might have gained an ally.

Because I had not attended the inquest itself, and no official court transcript had been made of the four-day hearing, I had written to the coroner, Dr Gavin Thurston. In a reply dated 3 September 1975, he wrote: 'I regret that as the case of Mrs Rivett is still *sub judice*, I could not discuss the matter with you. The same situation applies to supply of copies of the depositions.' How could evidence which had already been given in open court, and reported in the newspapers, be '*sub judice*'?

Chief Superintendent Ranson had also said I couldn't see the police notes taken at the inquest, which one of his colleagues had denied even existed. So the police agreed to arrange interviews for me with forensic experts to check the evidence they had given in court. The arrangements were made through the Press Bureau at New Scotland Yard.

First on my list was Dr Margaret Pereira, the blood analyst on the case.

In mid-September I was shepherded up through tight security to her office at the Yard's forensic science laboratory on the south side of the Thames Embankment.

I had hardly begun the interview when, to my amazement, in walked the burly figure of Tom Gibson from the Press Bureau at the Yard.

'I thought I'd just pop over,' he said cheerfully, as if the idea had just entered his head. 'I missed the inquest myself. I was on holiday. And I'd be interested to hear all about it.'

As the interview progressed, Tom Gibson became more than just a listener. Dr Pereira had said that she could only tell me what she had told the inquest. Other information from her report to the police, which had not emerged at the coroner's court, was off-limits. Since I hadn't been at the inquest, I didn't know then what was forbidden territory and what wasn't. But whenever I came too close for comfort, pursuing a point which it turned out Dr Pereira had not been asked about in court, Tom Gibson pulled me back. In fact Dr Pereira herself, a top professional, was perfectly capable of saying: 'I'm sorry but I can't discuss that particular matter.' Which made Tom Gibson's unexpected presence even more intriguing. He was obviously there for a purpose, doing his job. And that seemed to include keeping me within bounds.

The Shand Kydds were going off on holiday to the Seychelles. I wanted to get whatever they could, or would, tell me on tape before they left London. Late in September, at Cambridge Square, I met Christina Shand Kydd for the first time. She was elegant, confident and extremely intelligent, a good foil for her husband. On the previous visit there, I had done most of the talking. This time Mrs Shand Kydd held the floor. But she had a tricky problem.

'The point which you must understand,' she told me, 'is that we are in a very difficult position. I mean our interest basically is entirely for [Lord Lucan's] children, which is all it can be. And actually, right from the very beginning of the [Lucans'] marital arguments, we tried to make it quite clear to both of them that although we might sympathise with what both of them said about each other, that really the last thing we wanted to do was get involved in their marriage, because you can't do that. But that any way we could help with the family, we'd be very happy to do. Well, the children are now in a ghastly position where their father – who they absolutely adored – has disappeared and has been branded as a murderer . . .' Although Christina was convinced of Lord Lucan's innocence, she was anxious about the effect of the whole affair on the children.

But it would hardly help Lord Lucan's three young children to grow up hearing far and wide that their father was a murderer if he wasn't. It was not easy. Let sleeping dogs lie, despite the injustice? Or go for the truth, wherever it led? I knew my answer.

One thing was clear from the start. The Shand Kydds knew basic information which I needed to be told. They also knew other people who might, with their encouragement, agree to see me.

Perhaps it was an omen but at 9.15 p.m. that evening, we heard a bomb explode somewhere nearby. The bombers had been busy on the night of the murder too. By 1.15 a.m. when I drove away from Cambridge Square, I felt shell-shocked myself. The torrent of new facts emerging about the Lucan affair – showing a picture totally at variance with the publicly known 'facts' to date – made my head reel.

The co-operation of the Shand Kydds acted as an open sesame. Through Christina, I was put in touch with Miss Lilian Jenkins, a nanny who had worked for the Lucans for years. She loved the Lucans' children, and memories of events and incidents during her service with the family before the Lucans separated remained fresh in her mind. She had also kept diaries. Nanny Jenkins was to help me for years. Her belief in Lord Lucan's innocence was total. In quick succession I had interviews with Susan Maxwell-Scott, the last person to see Lord Lucan before he disappeared, with Lady Sarah Gibbs and her husband, and – at last – with Lord Lucan's mother. The family was now behind me, and more than a hundred interviews with relatives and friends followed as time went on.

But any hope that I'd get all the help I wanted from Lord Lucan's solicitor fell flat. He had acted for Lord Lucan since the marriage broke up, when Lord Lucan went to court to try and get custody of the children in wardship proceedings. The solicitor's files must have been filled with relevant documents, all of which I needed to see. But the custody battle had taken place *in camera* and if the solicitor showed me material relating to it, I was told, he would be in contempt of court. So much for that.

It was by a bitter-sweet circumstance years later, through another source, that I finally came across revealing private letters and other material from Lord Lucan's own personal files, which are reproduced in this book complete with errors.

Some time had elapsed since I had asked Tom Gibson at New Scotland Yard to arrange interviews for me with the next forensic people on my list. In November 1975 I rang the Yard and walked slap-bang into a brick wall. Tom Gibson, no longer sounding so cheerful, told me there was 'no joy' getting the interviews because 'Ranson's not at all keen on you interviewing operatives in the case because of the *sub judice* angle and he feels there may be future legal proceedings in the case'. But Ranson had told me himself that he thought Lucan was dead. If he was right, there would never be a trial. Unless of course someone else was caught for the murder – but the police weren't looking for someone else. Gibson went on to say that Ranson also wasn't keen on anyone interpreting the evidence which had already been given at the inquest. He claimed it wasn't a block on me personally, but I found that hard to believe.

A few days later, I started getting calls from newsmen on other papers asking me for interviews. One of them said the police had told him about my book. I stayed silent. In order to get all the interviews I needed, the last thing I wanted was publicity. Despite that, two stories were published: one in a gossip column, the other in *Private Eye*. The latter was clearly intended to ridicule me. Who could possibly believe that Lord Lucan was innocent?

Regarding the inquest, a colleague lent me several books

of notes he had taken at the hearing. I also gained independent notes from elsewhere, and bought a copy of the reports on the inquest put out by the Press Association. Together with newspaper cuttings of the proceedings, and other material, I was able to piece together the evidence heard for the chapters in this book on the inquest.

Lady Lucan refused to see me, though her side of the story has been well publicised. Of those I approached, all Lord Lucan's relatives, and almost all his friends, gave me their help. Most of them tell their story for the first time in this book. A few gave me interviews on the understanding that their names would not be revealed, a condition which naturally I respect. I am grateful to them all.

I lost my father just before Lord Lucan's children lost theirs, and my mother in 1981. My commitment to the truth comes from them.

I would like to dedicate this book to their memory, and also to the memory of Kait, the Dowager Countess of Lucan, and Miss Lilian Jenkins, who have both sadly died. Like my parents, they were remarkable people whom I admired very much, and I should like to record my gratitude for their faith in me, their trust and their support in a very long uphill struggle. Others without whom this book could not have been written, and to whom special thanks are due, are: Bill and Christina Shand Kydd, The Reverend William and Lady Sarah Gibbs, Hugh Bingham, the Honourable John Edward Bingham and his wife Dorothea, and Dr Jane Griffin. Although I felt it was not proper to approach Lord Lucan's children while they were still children, I did eventually meet Lady Frances Bingham, and I am most grateful to her for agreeing to see me.

In addition I should like to extend special thanks to Freda Shand Kydd, Susan Maxwell-Scott, Michael Hicks Beach, Stephen Raphael, Madeleine and Charles Florman, who are now divorced, John Wilbraham, Caroline Hill, Robin Hill and his wife Juliet, who has sadly since died,

Lady Zinnia Judd, Professor Keith Simpson, who has also, alas, died, Dr Margaret Pereira, former Detective Chief Superintendent Roy Ranson, who has since retired from the force, and Dennis Gilson.

For their help I thank the Earl Alexander of Tunis, John and Jennifer Lowther, the Earl of Suffolk and Berkshire, Michael Stoop, Charles Sweeny, Charles Benson, Greville Howard, Dan Meinertzhagen and Andrina Colquhoun. I thank Henry Bedingfeld, Rouge Croix Pursuivant of Arms, of the College of Arms, who arranged the heraldic artwork showing the full achievement of the armorial bearings of the Earls of Lucan and the Earl's coronet. And Harry Dempster, and other former colleagues in Fleet Street, who gave me their help.

I should also like to thank Frank Field, Labour MP for Birkenhead, and Lord Longford for their help and advice midway through my labours. Through the kindness of Michael Druitt I was able to visit 46 Lower Belgrave Street, the house where the murder was committed. Victor Lownes generously made me a member of the Clermont Club, while it was owned by the Playboy organisation, and several members of his staff were kind enough to talk to me.

To my great regret, one employee I met there refused later to have anything to do with this book. I was particularly distressed by this because, like other staff at the Clermont, he had been very courteous to me and what he had originally told me turned out later to be significant. As recently as spring 1987, however, he asserted that Lord Lucan did not commit the murder. And he repeated the significant part of what he had originally told me – that he had seen Lord Lucan on the doorstep of the Clermont Club at about 9.00 p.m. on the night of the murder. 'Actually,' he added, 'it was at five past nine.' This meant that Lord Lucan *could not* have committed the murder. Unfortunately the man demanded that his name should not appear in this book. In the interests of justice I could not exclude his evidence. But on legal advice I have had to omit his name.

Naturally, since my conclusions are my own, they should not be taken to reflect the views of all those who aided me.

Though I have remained independent throughout, Lord Lucan's family and the Shand Kydds have now helped me for over twelve years. They supplied information, they assured others when necessary that I could be trusted, and they checked my material when the first full draft of this book was completed in 1980. Despite approaches from other journalists, they bore with me through the seemingly endless search to find the right publisher, and through my long and expensive struggle to make the manuscript publishable, despite the stringent British libel laws. I wish to place on record my gratitude for their continued trust in me through these trials and tribulations, without which all might have been lost.

I should also like to thank the libel lawyers I have consulted over the years, and the Society of Authors and the Writers' Guild for their advice; and my editor Jo Edwards.

My original manuscript was more than twice its current length. Although I had shortened it before I approached Sidgwick & Jackson this spring, publishing economics required a further cut of 40,000 words, and additional legal cuts required by the publisher later further reduced the content by a considerable degree. Book Two and some of my questions about the evidence raised particular problems, but I can only assure the reader that, within the confines of the libel laws, I have done all in my power to bring as much out into the open as is presently possible.

I have the deepest sympathy for Sandra Rivett and her family, and hope they will understand that my intention has not been to cause further distress, but to try and right what I believe to be a tragic and classic injustice.

For their personal encouragement, my heartfelt thanks go to Leslie Jackson, Zena and the late and much-loved Valentine Davis, Peter and Pauline Halliday, Jim and Bettilou Allen, Robin and Marianne Wellesley, Sandra

White, Wayne E. Smyth and my bank manager, Mr M. R. Kelland, who kept me afloat financially when things got tough.

For his unstinting support, help and advice, I should like to express my gratitude to my former husband Roger Todd, who sustained me for the first six years of research and writing. His uncompromising honesty, integrity and strength of character still inspire me.

Finally I could not have weathered the last half of the battle, which coincided with one of the darkest and most difficult periods of my life, without the help, support and comfort of Dr Jonathan Miles Brown, my dearest friend. He has stood by me through prolonged illness, unemployment and financial and other crises. He is an exceptional person of many talents, and without him I would never have been able to bring this book to publication. If it succeeds in clearing Lord Lucan's name, part of the credit will be due not only to all those who have helped me, but to him for keeping me going.

Quotations have been reproduced by kind permission of the following sources: the Press Association, *Daily Express*, *Daily Star*, *Daily Mail*, *Daily Mirror*, *The Sun*, *The Times*, *The Guardian*, *The Daily Telegraph*, *News of the World*, *You*, the *Mail on Sunday* magazine, *The Sunday Times* and its *Magazine*, *Sunday Mirror*, the London *Evening Standard* and *Evening News*, *Reveille*, and ITN. I also thank David A. Yallop for permission to refer to a passage in his excellent book *Deliver Us From Evil* (Macdonald Futura Publishers, 1981) and Norman Lucas for a brief quotation from his book *The Lucan Mystery* (W. H. Allen, 1975). If I have inadvertently left anyone out, I apologise. If you let me know, I will happily include your name in any future edition. To all those who have contributed, advised or eased my path in any way over the past twelve years, I extend my most grateful thanks.

Sally Moore
London 1987

BOOK ONE

The Murder

1

Out of sight in the bedroom, Veronica heard the water gush as John turned on the taps in the adjoining bathroom, deafening other sounds.

In seconds, she made up her mind.

She leapt from the bed, sprang through the bedroom door and ran in darkness down the thirty-five stairs to the hall.

Then she flung herself out through the front door into the chill night air of Lower Belgrave Street.

Outside, she was briefly illuminated by the glow of the street lamp which stood opposite the elegant Regency townhouse at number 46, just off London's fashionable Eaton Square and a stone's throw from Buckingham Palace.

Her face and hair were red with blood. Her shoes and tights had blood on them. The neck and sleeves of her brown jumper were heavily bloodstained and more blood was scattered over her green pinafore dress.

There was a gruesome smear at the back of her dress which looked, to a forensic expert later, as if a 'bloody hand' had reached out to grab her.

At the bottom of the steps to the house, she turned left and ran towards the lights of the Plumbers Arms pub, thirty yards down Lower Belgrave Street.

John came out of the bathroom to find the bedroom deserted. He went further upstairs, calling: 'Veronica, where are you?'

At the top of the six-storey house, the Lucans' eldest child, ten-year-old Lady Frances, was in bed in her pyjamas, reading a book. When she heard her father calling, she crept silently out of her room, moved to the banister rail and peered down the well of the stairs.

John had reached the third floor, immediately beneath her. She watched as he walked out of the nursery and crossed the landing into the nursery bathroom. Finding no one there, he went back down the stairs.

John recalled later the sound of the front door slamming shut, and his wife out in the street screaming 'Murder!'

His blood must have run cold.

Who would believe him *now?*

In the basement in a bloody scene of indescribable horror, there was 'something terrible' on the floor. Outside Veronica was running down the street, and he was certain she would accuse him. Upstairs, hopefully asleep in their beds, were the three children he loved above all else and was now powerless to protect. Reeling with shock, he did not pause to kiss them goodnight or goodbye before he fled.

From upstairs shortly after, Frances heard a noise, a sort of 'banging'. She did not know what it was. But it sounded as if it came from way down in the basement or out in the street. Could it mean, after her parents had both left the house, that *another* person had run up from the basement and out into the street?

At the Plumbers Arms public house, where a motto over the bar read 'Justice and Peace', a handful of customers sat quietly enjoying their drinks.

At about 9.50 p.m., the door was flung open and Veronica ran in.

The head barman, Arthur Whitehouse, who went to her aid, testified later in court: 'She was head to toe in blood, but it was crusted. She was quite all right for a few minutes. Then she started shouting: "Help me, help me, help me! I've just escaped from being murdered! My children, my children! He's murdered my nanny! He's murdered my nanny!"'

She did not name the killer, he said.

When newspaper reporters swarmed to the pub, they quoted Mr Whitehouse as saying: '[Lady Lucan] was just in a delirious state . . .' '. . . I could not get much sense out of her and she was in such a state of shock that eventually she went completely silent. Her head injuries were quite severe. She had been hit four or five times.'

At the local Metropolitan Police station in Gerald Road, Belgravia, the first message in the case was logged. It read: 'Person assaulted. Ambulance called. 10.07 p.m. Distressed female.'

Those words signalled the start of a massive police inquiry, a man-hunt which stretched around the world, and a desperate new chapter in the chequered history of the 7th Earl of Lucan. For Veronica, those words also marked the end of one era and the beginning of another. The days when the Lucans were a 'golden couple' had gone forever.

For two girls brought up in what Veronica later described as the 'grinding poverty of the middle classes' at their stepfather's country pub, Veronica and her younger sister, Christina, had made dazzling marriages.

Christina, the bright, socially confident brunette, had 'married a millionaire' – so the myth went.

In truth, Bill Shand Kydd – whose half brother, Peter Shand Kydd, is the stepfather of the Princess of Wales – had actually inherited £500,000 from the family wallpaper fortune. But his money was only part of his appeal. Bill combined an aggressive, macho personality with a forthright manner and a high-voltage sexual magnetism which could have powered the national grid.

After attending Stowe, one of the top-notch British public schools, he had joined the Household Cavalry and done his National Service fighting terrorists in Cyprus before he became a businessman. Bill lived life at breakneck speed – hunting, racing, powerboating, bobsledding and dicing with death on the terrifying Cresta Run in St Moritz, where he first became friends with John. Each year he had a wager with his fellow National Hunt jockey Chris Collins, the Goya heir. The prize for whichever of them rode most winners in a season was a slap-up dinner, paid for by the other, at any famous restaurant of his choice in the world.

Through the Shand Kydds, Veronica, the blonde, shorter sister, met and married into the British aristocracy.

John was then Lord Bingham and the heir to an earldom which dated back to 1795. The Lucans could lay claim to royal blood through an ancestor who was an illegitimate child of King Charles II. The family tree was linked to that of the Princess of Wales, and there were other connections with British royalty. It was part of family lore, and a matter of some amusement, that, as an infant, John's mother Kaitilin (Kait) had been dandled on Queen Victoria's knee. Her aunt had been a lady-in-waiting to the Duchess of Albany. Her mother had been a woman-of-the-bedchamber to Queen Mary. And Princess Alice, Countess of Athlone, who was Queen Victoria's longest-surviving grandchild, was one of Kait's friends. John's great-grandfather, the 4th Earl of Lucan, had taken part in the coronation of King Edward VII. His grandfather, the 5th Earl, had been a lord-in-waiting to King George V. And his cousin, Jennifer Lowther, under her maiden name Bevan, had been a lady-in-waiting to Princess Margaret.

Everyone saw John as 'a typical English lord and gentleman'. He was tall, dark and handsome, he had perfect manners, and he was known to his family and friends for his gentleness, kindness and generosity. With his straight-backed aristocratic bearing and his moustached poker face, he could seem 'awesome'. But he had an engaging 'twinkle' which wrinkled his eyes and nose when he laughed. As a bachelor with a title, John had been a prize catch. Girls had found him a glamorous escort, who ordered champagne and caviar at the most elegant nightspots at a time, said one, when 'every other young man was taking you to Lyons to eat scrambled eggs'. As a sportsman – racing powerboats, water ski-ing, bobsledding for Britain, competing on the Cresta Run – he was very dashing and brave. Whether he was driving his sports car at terrifying speeds through the Swiss Alps, or

28

playing for high stakes at the world's top casinos as a professional gambler, he thrived on excitement, challenge and risk. More than anything else, though, he epitomised *style*. The Italian film director Vittorio de Sica wanted to make him a movie star. So did producer Albert 'Cubby' Broccoli, who saw John as 'the absolute James Bond' and wanted him to play secret agent 007.

'He had it all – the looks, the breeding, the pride,' Broccoli said. 'I seriously wanted to test him for Bond, but all he'd say to that was "Good heavens!"'

As far as Veronica was concerned: 'I had been looking for a god and he was a dream figure.'

John opened the doors for Veronica to a life of indolent ease and luxury. As members of the international set, they jetted off to pleasure spots, mixed with the rich, famous and powerful, received invitations from the Aga Khan. They stayed as guests at huge country estates and the occasional castle and stately home. They frequented the best hotels, wined and dined lavishly at the most expensive restaurants, sipped champagne into the early hours at the most exclusive night clubs. They cruised on the Mediterranean in a chartered yacht, went powerboat racing in Miami, gambling in Monte Carlo, winter sporting in St Moritz. They graced events of the social calendar, raced their own horses. Veronica wore designer gowns and diamonds and emeralds worth thousands of pounds from Cartier. Though the Lucan family seat had long gone, they had the fashionable London townhouse in Lower Belgrave Street, filled with ancestral portraits and Georgian family silver. Veronica could stay in bed till midday while staff looked after the children and dealt with the chores. It was all a far cry from her days as a model and office 'temp'.

But the good days had passed. The Lucans had separated. A bitter battle had been waged for custody of the three children, which John had eventually 'lost'. And now, in one traumatic night, their nanny had met a brutal, tragic death and nothing would ever be the same again.

Police Sergeant Donald Baker and Police Constable Christopher Beddick were on mobile night patrol when the emergency call summoned them to 46 Lower Belgrave Street. They pulled to a halt outside the house shortly after 10.00 p.m. Sergeant Baker made his way to the Plumbers Arms on foot.

'I saw Lady Lucan on a couch in the bar,' he said later in court. 'From what I saw of her condition, I realised that she had been attacked. I gathered that there were some children at Lower Belgrave Street. I established that an ambulance was on the way.'

Leaving Veronica in the care of another police officer who had appeared on the scene, Sergeant Baker went back up the street to rejoin P.C. Beddick and investigate at the house.

The first problem was how to get in. Sergeant Baker descended the steps which led down beyond the railings from the pavement to the basement door, where the milk was delivered and the rubbish put out. It was locked. The basement window was shut. Through the venetian blind, its slats turned down at an angle of about forty-five degrees, Sergeant Baker saw the glow of a small red light in the kitchen. The rest of the room was in darkness. No entry from the basement was possible. He returned to pavement level and told P.C. Beddick to force open the front door. It gave way 'very easily'.

Inside, the house was almost in darkness except for a dim light which shone from a shaving mirror strip-light in the cloakroom at the far end of the hall. Sergeant Baker tried to turn on the hall light but nothing happened. The bulb was burned out.

Sending P.C. Beddick back to the patrol vehicle to fetch a powerful lamp, Sergeant Baker flicked on his small hand torch and ventured in alone. He walked past the dining room doors on his left, past the upward flight of stairs on his right. He continued along the narrow hall and down four steps towards the direction of the lighted cloakroom.

At the bottom of the steps, to his right, was the doorway to the basement. The door was wide open, hooked back. On the wallpaper opposite the doorway, he noticed fresh blood. He went through.

The steep staircase, which turned at a right-angle at the top, opened directly into the breakfast room. With the wall on his left, and a wrought-iron banister rail on his right, Sergeant Baker went halfway down the twelve stairs.

The basement of the house was shaped like an L in reverse. At the back, there was a lavatory or cloakroom, a boiler room and a narrow passage where there had once been a butler's pantry.

In the passage, opposite the back door to the garden, there was a large wall cupboard housing a safe which contained silver.

Beyond the passage, through an internal door, came the breakfast room. This had French windows looking out onto the garden, and the open staircase leading up to the hall. In one corner of the breakfast room was a dumb waiter which could be hoisted to the dining room above, and in another was a bookcase crammed with books. Nearby was John's upright piano, which stood against the back of the kitchen wall.

In the kitchen, at the front of the house, the window looked out at semi-basement level onto the railings and the pavement of Lower Belgrave Street.

From his position halfway down the stairs, Sergeant Baker faced the piano and the kitchen doorway, which was open.

'The area was all in darkness,' he said later in court, 'except for a small red light coming from the kitchen and some street lighting coming in through the [kitchen] window.'

The red glow turned out later to be a defective warning light on a kettle. The street lighting, from the lamp post opposite, cast a strong diagonal shaft of light to the base of the stairs. Inches away, in front of the piano, Sergeant Baker noticed a large pool of blood on the parquet floor. There were 'two or three footprints' in the blood. He glanced around for an assailant but saw no one.

Returning to the hall, he rejoined P.C. Beddick who had brought the powerful lamp from the patrol vehicle, and together they made a general search of the house for 'suspects' and for the children.

The first light they saw as they climbed the stairs came from Veronica's bedroom on the second floor. A bedside lamp was switched on. On the pillow lay a bloodstained towel.

Hearing noises from above, Sergeant Baker went up to investigate. In the nursery, a colour television was blaring loudly.

On the top floor, he found the children. In one room the Lucans' youngest child, four-year-old Lady Camilla, lay fast asleep. Frances stood protectively by her bed. In his own room, in bed, was John's son and heir George, Lord Bingham, aged seven.

'Where are Mummy and Sandra?' Frances kept asking the police that night. Sandra Rivett, twenty-nine, described by friends as 'a vivacious redhead who always liked a laugh', was the children's new nanny – and the latest in a long line. She had arrived at the house only a few weeks before, and some of her belongings had yet to be unpacked from her suitcase.

Satisfied that the children were safe and unharmed, Sergeant Baker left them with 'another police constable' who by then had arrived on the scene.

Returning to the ground floor, Sergeant Baker noticed 'an object' lying near the basement doorway in the hall.

'I thought it was a doll's leg,' he said later. 'It was white.'

He walked straight past it.

With P.C. Beddick, he went down to the basement. He tried a switch and a light came on. The sight was terrible. There was blood everywhere.

At the foot of the basement stairs, dirty cups and saucers were scattered on the floor, lying in a pool of blood. Sickening red blood splashes streaked wildly over the walls, the stair panelling and the parquet floor and spattered books on the shelves in the corner. A picture on the bloodstained stairway wall was knocked askew. Streaks of blood from the victim had shot up, over and onto the upright piano, which John had once made ring with the syncopated sounds of Scott Joplin rags.

Where the children had stood round their father at the piano at weekends in happier days – singing 'Onward Christian Soldiers', 'Baa Baa Black Sheep', and 'John Brown's body lies a'mouldering in the grave' – there were now ominous pools of blood.

Policemen who flocked to the house that night never forgot the horrific sight of Sooty, the black cat, crouched at the edge of one of the pools . . . lapping the murdered girl's blood from the floor.

But where was the body?

By the kitchen doorway to the left of the piano, Sergeant Baker saw what he thought was a tent bag. Fresh blood oozed out from the bottom.

'The top was folded over and there were bloodstains on the bag,' he recalled later in court. 'The cord was not drawn tight. The top was open. As I opened the bag I saw the top of a human thigh in black tights. I took out an arm from the bag. It was very white. I could feel no pulse.'

Sandra's body had been found.

In the official police photographs taken later of the scene of the crime, her black high-heeled shoes were shown in gruesome incongruity placed neatly side by side near to the bloodsodden sack.

A post-mortem the following morning revealed that Sandra had been battered to death with a blunt instrument and then bundled, bent double, into the sack.

For the first two uniformed officers on the scene, one discovery remained to be made. Where was the attacker?

One area which had not been searched was the back of the basement and the garden. Sergeant Baker crossed the breakfast room, careful not to tread in the blood, and went through the internal door to the passage where there had once been a butler's pantry. The safe in the wall cupboard was to his right, the back door to the garden immediately opposite to his left.

The back door, used on summer weekends in the past when the weather was warm enough to have lunch outside, was normally kept locked. Sergeant Baker found the door closed but unlocked. He went through.

The garden was mostly paved and had the same sad air of neglect and defeat as the house. There were some bushes in the thin strip of soil, several tubs containing forlorn plastic plants, a few stone busts, some garden furniture and a large tree. The walls surrounding the garden were partly painted pink, bore a rose trellis and were about 16-feet high – difficult to climb even by someone prepared to be spotted by neighbours from overlooking houses. Nevertheless, Sergeant Baker checked for broken creepers, scuffmarks, damage to the rose trellis . . . anything which might indicate that the attacker had entered or left the house by scaling the back wall. There were none.

The one obvious clue the diligent sergeant had noted raised little interest later – even though it posed tantalising questions. *The unlocked door.*

Who had unlocked the back door amid the horror of that night – and why?

Back in the hall, Sergeant Baker noticed something extremely odd. The 'object' he had seen earlier near the basement doorway was not a doll's leg at all. It was a length of lead piping 'bandaged' with sticky medical tape like Elastoplast. It was no longer white either. Since he had first set eyes on it, the object had inexplicably *changed colour*. Now it was blood-red.

Within less than an hour of the emergency call from the Plumbers Arms, the question which was to echo down the years and perplex people and police forces all round the world was first being put into words: 'Where is Lord Lucan?'

2

That night 'The Dagger with Wings', an episode in the 'Father Brown' crime detection series, drew to its thrilling climax on television at 10.00 p.m. A short distance from Lower Belgrave Street, in her bedroom overlooking Chester Square, Mrs Madeleine Florman, a friend of the Lucans, pressed the remote control switch at her bedside and watched the picture fade from the screen. Then she lay back and dozed off. She had had an exhausting day.

Shortly after 10.00 p.m., she was awoken with a start by someone ringing her front doorbell. The ringing was insistent, almost as if someone was leaning on the bellpush. Assuming it was a local youth who plagued families in the square by ringing their doorbells sometimes as late as 2.00 a.m., she ignored the sound and went back to sleep. The caller went away.

Soon afterwards, sometime before 10.30 p.m., the cream telephone at her bedside began to ring. In the semi-darkness she answered: 'Hallo?'

A distinctive male voice said: 'Madeleine —?'

'Yes?'

'I know you —'

From then on, she said later, the man's words were jumbled, unintelligible, incoherent. But his voice was familiar. She was sure it was John Lucan.

'His first four words were quite definite,' she recalled, 'but then it didn't make any sense at all. It was a complete mix-up of words.'

She put down the receiver and went back to sleep.

The next morning she suddenly thought: 'What was all that about?' Then she heard news of the murder. Later she remembered how, years before, she had been so shocked herself after being involved in a very bad car accident that she couldn't get her own words into place.

'So the man on the phone must have been trying to speak in a state of enormous shock,' she said.

She concluded that it was John who had rung her doorbell, then telephoned when he couldn't get an answer. And that his words were incoherent because he'd just fled shocked and in panic from the murder house.

'I know John couldn't possibly have done the murder, being the sort of person he was,' she said. 'He was a terribly kind man and he would never do anything to hurt anybody where his children were – he protected them as much as he could. But something had happened in the house where the children were and that must have been absolutely frightful for him. He was always terribly, terribly worried about the children. I think that after he found that ghastly situation at the house, he thought: "Well, somebody's got to get the children out, and it must be someone they know very well." He knew they would trust me absolutely, and living so close this would have been his first port of call. I wish I *had* answered the door. The children would have come with me immediately.'

When John managed to reach his mother for help that night, he was still partly incoherent.

Kaitilin (Kait), the Dowager Countess of Lucan, arrived back at her flat near Lords cricket ground in the St John's Wood area of London oblivious of the nightmare that was about to engulf her. Like her late husband Pat, the 6th Earl, Kait was a socialist, and at seventy-four she was still secretary of the St Marylebone constituency Labour Party. That evening she had been out at a meeting. The phone rang as she entered her flat on the eighth floor. It was John, sounding very shocked.

'There has been a terrible catastrophe at number 46,' he said. 'Veronica is hurt and I want you to collect the children as quickly as possible. Ring Bill Shand Kydd and he will help.'

John claimed later that he also asked his mother to ring the police, but Kait could not recall that.

'He was in a terrible state and I could hardly understand

what he said,' she said. 'He sounded as if he had had a tremendous shock, as if he'd really been knocked for six, in a way I had never known him before.'

Normally John was noted for being very cool under pressure. But that was the last thing he sounded now as he tried to tell his mother what had happened. Disjointedly, part-incoherently, the words stumbled out.

He said that he had been outside number 46 . . . that he had seen a fight in the basement . . . that he had gone into the house and interrupted the fight. He muttered about the 'blood' and 'mess'. He said that Veronica had been 'shouting and screaming'. He said that he had tried to 'clean Veronica up'.

In the confusion of the conversation, it was somehow established that the nanny, Sandra Rivett, had been hurt.

'Badly?' Kait asked.

'Yes, I think so,' John said.

Though Kait forgot this months later at the inquest, he told her: 'Oh mother, there was something terrible in the basement. I couldn't bring myself to look.'

Kait tried to find out more.

'But he just told me to get the children out as soon as possible,' she recalled.

'Who's going to let me in?' she asked him.

'I don't know,' John said. 'I suppose Frances.'

'Where are you going?' she asked.

'I don't know,' he repeated and rang off.

Trying, but failing, to reach Bill Shand Kydd by phone, Kait 'belted down' to Belgravia as fast as she could in her Hillman estate car. Pulling up quickly at 46 Lower Belgrave Street, she took in the sight before her.

'The house seemed to be ablaze with lights,' she recalled. 'The police were everywhere. There were police cars outside and policemen on the doorstep and policemen inside. It seemed to me that half the police force in London must be assembled there.'

Detective Chief Superintendent Roy Ranson, who was to become head of the murder squad, said later: 'I think what happens in these jobs, there's such a flap everybody's there. We found we had to turf so many police officers out of that address. It was: "Come and see the body!" and they all want to be the first on the scene.'

'I'm the children's grandmother,' Kait declared and walked straight in, turning left off the hall through the elegant double doors into the long, narrow dining room.

On the red silk-lined walls were hung gold-framed portraits of the 3rd Earl of Lucan and his brother-in-law, the 7th Earl of Cardigan – two stiff, bewhiskered and still-controversial military figures from the Charge of the Light Brigade in the Crimea in 1854. In days gone by, these nineteenth-century noblemen had gazed down from the walls at the Lucans' black-tie dinner parties: the high society guests resplendent in their finery and jewels, cut-glass accents filling the air, the long polished table gleaming with Georgian family silver. Now the room was full of police officers.

'I've come to collect the children at my son's request,' Kait told them. 'I understand there's been a fight?'

They confirmed that and told her Veronica had been taken to hospital.

Kait recalled: 'And then I said, "What about the nanny?" They made indeterminate noises and I asked, "Is she dead?" because it was quite obvious from their manner that she was. They gave me the straight answer, "Yes." It was the first indication I had had that night that she was dead. There was a policewoman very busy offering me cups of tea, but that's not my form of tipple. They said had I had a shock and I said no.'

The Dowager Countess would never have admitted to being thrown off-balance, even to herself.

But what would certainly have shocked her, had she known, was that the police were already looking for John. Detective Sergeant Graham Forsyth, from Gerald Road CID office, had been told by a colleague at number 46 that the Lucans also owned a mews cottage round the corner at 5 Eaton Row, a cottage Veronica had called 'The Lemon-Drop House' after the colour in which it had been painted. Living there at the time was the Lucans' friend,

Greville Howard, a cousin of the Earl of Suffolk and Berkshire. Sergeant Forsyth and other officers had gone round there and broken in, trying to find John, but the place was empty. Greville and a friend, Sarah Smith-Ryland, had been to the theatre and at that moment were either at or on their way to John's favourite gambling haunt, the elegant and exclusive Clermont Club in Berkeley Square, where they expected to join him for dinner. John did not turn up and they began without him.

Soon after 11.00 p.m., Sergeant Forsyth returned to number 46 from his search of the mews cottage, where he had posted a police guard, and began to interview Kait, who had been kept in the dining room. In answer to his questions, she told him that the Lucans were separated, that the children had been made wards of court, that John's car was a blue Mercedes, and that he lived at a flat nearby at 72a Elizabeth Street. She also told him about John's phone call. Then she was allowed to go upstairs and collect the children and take them to St John's Wood, accompanied by P.C. Beddick.

At about 11.50 p.m., Sergeant Forsyth and other officers went to 72a Elizabeth Street, where they found John's car.

'I saw a blue Mercedes car parked outside the address on the other side of the road,' Forsyth said later in court. 'It was the only one there. I put my hand over the bonnet of the car to feel the engine and it was cold, quite cold.'

Later it was discovered that the car's battery was flat.

Sergeant Forsyth went on: 'I was unable to get entry to 72a but I went in later. I broke the rear window. It's quite a large flat. There were a number of bedrooms, all quite tidy. In what I took to be Lord Lucan's bedroom, the bed had been made and there were some items of clothing on the bed . . .'

When the head of the murder squad, Detective Chief Superintendent Roy Ranson, visited the flat some while later, John's bedroom struck him as 'so curious'.

'It looked as though it was waiting for its owner to return from the bathroom,' he recalled years afterwards in

39

the *Daily Star*. 'There was a suit and shirt on the bed and an open book on Greek shipping millionaires that he had bought the day before. On a bedside table were his wallet, car keys, change, chequebook, driving licence, a handkerchief and his glasses – all the things a man normally carries in his pocket. His passport was in a drawer. Only Lucan was missing. We found his address books filled with names most people read about in newspapers.'

By the time Ranson was brought in on the murder, John was no longer in London but 42 miles away at Uckfield in Sussex.

Turning off Church Street at about 11.30 p.m., he had driven past a wrought iron gate and on up the gravel drive to Grants Hill House, the home of his old friends Ian and Susan Maxwell-Scott.

He found the rambling Victorian house, which was a former rectory, completely in darkness.

3

Ian Maxwell-Scott, a cousin of the Duke of Norfolk, had studied law at university but had become a gambler and then a director of the Clermont Club, where John played daily as a professional gambler. His dark-haired wife, Susan, a noted debutante of her day, had qualified as a barrister but had never practised at law.

On the night of the murder, she was alone at Grants Hill House but for two of her six children, who were asleep upstairs, and Fungus her new dog, a large and boisterous German pointer. At about 10.00 p.m., she said later, Ian had telephoned to say he had had several drinks and had therefore decided not to drive home and was staying in London for the night. She went to bed and was woken at about 11.30 p.m., when the doorbell rang. Then came a shorter, 'apologetic-sounding' second ring. She got up, went to the bathroom which overlooked the drive, and opened the window to see who it was.

To her surprise, she saw John standing by the front door, gazing up towards her at the lighted window.

'Susie, I'm sorry to disturb you so late,' he called.

'Hang on, John,' she said. 'I'll come down and let you in.'

She assumed immediately that something had happened to Ian. 'Shows how selfish one always is,' she commented later. Perhaps Ian had decided to drive home after all and there had been an accident and John had come to tell her ... It would have been totally in character for John to drive all the way from London to break bad news in person, in order to offer comfort, rather than to telephone. The anxious thoughts raced through her head as she put on a dressing gown, went downstairs and let John in, cutting short his apologies.

His first words were: 'Is Ian around?'

She felt the relief flood through her.

'No, I'm afraid he's in London,' she said.

They went into the drawing room, where she poured him a whisky and water. She made a cup of coffee for herself.

'I didn't want a drink myself,' she said later. 'It felt like the middle of the night to me, having been asleep.'

John took the glass and sat down in a square gold antique wicker armchair, his back to the French windows and the lawn beyond.

Several things surprised Mrs Maxwell-Scott. For a start, he had never turned up unannounced or so late before. Secondly, he was still wearing casual afternoon clothes: a pair of grey flannels, a pale blue polo-necked shirt made of nylon or silk, and a dark brown sleeveless pullover. Normally he'd have changed into a smart dark suit hours before, ready for the evening's gambling at the Clermont. Thirdly, he looked shocked and slightly untidy. His hair was dishevelled. Normally he was rather spruce, not a hair out of place. And there was something on the back of his flannels by the right thigh – a large wet patch, where it looked as if he had sponged something off with water and the material, being thick, had not yet dried. As she said herself later, she 'didn't have to be clairvoyant' to know that something had happened.

'What's wrong, John?' she asked.

'I've been through a nightmarish experience,' he said, standing up and taking a slug of his whisky. 'It's so incredible I don't think you or anybody else could possibly believe it. But I'll tell you . . .'

He told her the same story he had told his mother on the phone, but in greater detail and at much greater length.

Mrs Maxwell-Scott recalled: 'John told me he had been walking past the house in Lower Belgrave Street where Veronica and the children lived. He said he was on his way back to his flat to change for dinner.

'He said it was an "unbelievable coincidence" that he should have been there at that time. I said: "Well, don't you often walk past the house?" and he then told me that

42

he made a point of going past every evening or more than once a day. He would peep in and, if he thought Veronica was out, quite often go in and see the children. He was worried about them and he liked to check up that they were okay. So it wasn't coincidence at all that he should have been outside the house that night.

'Through the window, he said, he saw what appeared to be someone struggling with Veronica in the basement. So he let himself in at the front door, because he always had a key, and ran down the stairs.

'He got a little bit emotional telling me the story at this point, having been very calm before. The sight he had seen was so frightful that he put his hand up to cover his eyes at the memory of it.

'He said something like: "I can't tell you how awful it was. The room was ghastly. There was blood everywhere. Veronica was covered in blood. I even slipped and fell into a pool of blood as I went into the room. The man ran off."

'I asked John whether he saw the man clearly enough to recognise him again because it was obviously very important, and he said no – he had just got the impression that the man was large. I got the impression that John saw the man's back as he disappeared . . .'

After describing further details, Mrs Maxwell-Scott continued: 'John told me he then calmed Veronica down a bit and when she was calmer he took her upstairs. Frances was still up and was watching television in the room. He was worried about her because Veronica was covered in blood and he said it was a terrible sight for Frances to see, so he sent her up to bed.

'He got Veronica to lie down and when he thought she was calm enough for him to leave her, he went into the bathroom to soak some towels in water.

'He told me that his intention was to clean up the blood on Veronica and then, when he could see how much damage was done, whether her injuries were superficial or deep, he was going to ring the doctor and he was then going to ring the police. But while he was in the bathroom, Veronica rushed downstairs and out of the

43

house. John said he heard the door slam and Veronica in the street shouting: "Murder! Murder!"

'And that's when, in my opinion, though John didn't say so, he panicked. He told me he decided he'd better get out because of the position he was in: no sign of the murderer, a body in the basement probably, blood all over the place, and blood on him too. He said: "Blood on me, blood all over the place . . ."'

'He told me that he telephoned his mother and asked her to look after the children and to notify the police. He didn't say where he telephoned from. It could have been from the house before he left, but I got the impression it was afterwards. He also tried to telephone Bill Shand Kydd but there was no answer and he presumed the Shand Kydds were out.

'Partly because of my knowledge of John and of how his mind was working, I knew that his main worry the whole of that evening in fact was the children . . . And I got the impression, though he didn't say this, that after he'd left the house in a panic, he probably hadn't rushed more than 5 yards when he thought: "My God, the children! Alone in the house . . . blood . . . body . . ." you know. I mean just think of it! They'd come downstairs at some stage looking for nanny and find her in a sack in a pool of blood. I mean even if one wasn't as loving a father as Lucky, one wouldn't want that, would one?

'I have a vague idea he said something about the mother of a friend of Frances, that he'd rung her doorbell but there'd been no answer. I'm confused about that. I might have read about that later. But he could easily have thought: "She'll look after the children" and banged on her door. No answer. And then telephoned his mother to collect the children. I hadn't met the Dowager Countess. Obviously she was elderly and some elderly women would get too flustered but John said he could absolutely trust her to cope. Having rung her, that was the children taken care of. Then he rang Shand Kydd for advice, you know: "For God's sake, Bill, what do I do now?" No answer. So then presumably he thought: "There's no

Shand Kydd. Go and see Ian." He must have, because as far as we know he didn't go and see anyone else. He came down here. It was Ian he came to see, not me. He had expected to find Ian here because Ian had told him the day before that he planned to return here on Thursday afternoon.'

Mrs Maxwell-Scott paused to light another cigarette. The smoke curled up towards the ceiling in the drawing room. She spoke sitting in the same gold wicker armchair John had sat in that night, Fungus the German pointer playing around her feet. That night Fungus had bounded in as they talked and John, who loved dogs, had stroked him affectionately and said: 'Hello, you're new. I haven't met you before.'

'To me,' Mrs Maxwell-Scott remarked, 'it is an enormous point in John's favour that the person he turns to, Shand Kydd, admittedly an old friend of his, is the husband of Veronica's sister. If John had just tried to murder Veronica, it's rather odd that he'd turn to her sister's husband, isn't it? It never entered my head that night that John could be guilty, and it never has since. I know he is innocent. But from John's point of view, it was the children he was worried about. That night he said to me that he didn't want his children to see him in the dock.'

At about 12.15 a.m., after telling his story, John rang his mother to check that she had the children. Mrs Maxwell-Scott stayed with him and heard his side of the conversation.

At St John's Wood shortly before, Frances, George and Camilla had been shepherded up in the lift, undressed and put to bed in Kait's flat. George occupied the sofa in a partitioned-off section of the sitting room. The two little girls shared Kait's double bed. In the other bedroom John's childhood nanny, Miss Flora Coles, who still lived with Kait, slept peacefully undisturbed through the anxious comings and goings of the night. The day before had been her ninety-first birthday.

The flat seemed to be full of people. Kait was to spend the whole night sitting upright in an armchair next to the telephone in the sitting room. There was nowhere for her to lie down and rest, even if she had felt able to.

Around midnight, she alerted John's younger sister to the tragedy. Lady Sarah, known as Sally, was 70 miles away, in the village of Guilsborough, Northamptonshire, where her husband, the Reverend William Gibbs, a shy 6-feet, 4-inch Church of England clergyman, was vicar of St Etheldreda's church. Sally offered to drive to London immediately, but Kait put her off till the morning.

Shortly after midnight, John rang from Uckfield. Kait thought he sounded 'much steadier than he had earlier, more on all fours, much calmer and much more rational, though still shocked.'

'Where are you?' she asked. 'Are you all right.'

'Have you got the children?' he asked.

'Yes,' she assured him. 'They're all safe here. They're in bed now and I hope asleep.'

Kait recalled: 'I think he asked me if I'd been in touch with Bill, but I'm not quite sure of that. It was very much on my mind that I hadn't been.'

Did he in fact ask, as Susan Maxwell-Scott claimed, having heard John's side of the conversation: 'Did you phone the police?'

Kait only remembered saying to him: 'Well look, the police are here with me. Would you like to speak to them?'

He hesitated. It became one of her lasting regrets that she did not press him then and there to agree.

'No, I think not now,' he said. 'Tell them I'll speak to them in the morning and I'll ring you too.'

He rang off.

Kait put the phone down. The call had lasted no longer than 90 seconds. While they spoke, P.C. Beddick had sat within arm's reach of the telephone, listening.

'Looking back,' Kait said, 'I'm amazed that the youngster didn't snatch the phone from me.'

Susan Maxwell-Scott recalled that, during the phone call, John had also asked his mother: 'Has Veronica turned up?' She said: 'He told me afterwards that his mother said Veronica had been found and taken to hospital. He seemed much calmer after that. He had appeared to be in a state of shock when he arrived but perfectly in control of himself. He was always a man of great self-control. After he had told me what had happened, after he had spoken to his mother and been reassured that his children were all right – and, indeed, that Veronica was all right – he said: "I feel much better now." He tried to ring Shand Kydd again but there was no reply, so he asked me for some writing paper so that he could write to him.'

Had John's next move already taken shape in his mind, or did the idea occur to him as he wrote? He had predicted himself that no one would believe him. He finished the letter and wrote a second one.

'I suppose I should have asked him why he wanted to write to Bill, but I didn't think about it, stupidly,' Mrs Maxwell-Scott said. 'I took it that we both accepted the fact that obviously he must go to the police. There was no suggestion in what John told me that night that he had done anything other than try to *help* Veronica.

'And it never seemed to me to be in any doubt that the police would sort it out, and that nobody would arrest John. I never got any idea that he was not thinking of going to the police.'

Having completed and sealed the two letters, both addressed to Bill Shand Kydd at his London house in Cambridge Square, Bayswater, John asked if she would post them for him in the morning. Then he changed his mind.

'No, you'd better not,' he said. 'The Uckfield postmark might involve you and I don't want you to be involved in any of this.'

'Oh no, John, don't be silly,' she replied, taking them back.

'He was a remarkably considerate person,' Mrs Maxwell-Scott said. 'I mean he didn't say: "No, then

47

people will know I've been here.'' He said no, he didn't want me involved. Apart from the letters and the postmark, let's face it, there's no proof he ever came here. The police couldn't find any trace of blood here or anything like that. The whole thing could have been an invention on my part.'

Though John had told her he'd got blood on him at number 46, she said she saw no sign of it. Nor did she notice blood on the letters he wrote. Yet curiously, when Bill received John's letters, which Mrs Maxwell-Scott's 7-year-old daughter Catherine posted the next morning, there were light blood smears on them which he pointed out to the police. If John had sponged blood off his clothes before reaching Uckfield – which perhaps accounted for the large wet patch on the back of his flannels – was it possible some traces had remained unnoticed and been smeared inadvertently onto the letters?

It was well past midnight. For a time he and Susan Maxwell-Scott talked of the old days. Then she asked whether he would like to 'wash and tidy up', have a meal, stay overnight. John refused each offer.

'I tried to persuade him to stay and said we'd go to the Uckfield police together the next morning,' she said. 'He almost wavered. If Ian had been here, he would probably have convinced John to remain. If I'd had any idea of what was to happen, or if John had seemed more distressed and in need of Ian, I'd have rung my husband. But John seemed very self-contained and not to need anybody really.'

Just before he left, he said he thought he might have difficulty sleeping and asked if she had any sleeping pills.

She had none but managed to find an old bottle containing four 2mg Valium tranquillisers, a low dose. John took them with a glass of water. He had drunk a couple of glasses of whisky. Shock, alcohol and pills: it was an ominous combination.

She remembered him saying: 'I must get back and straighten things out.'

'I assumed ''back'' meant to London and that he would see the police there in the morning,' she said.

At their parting, he kissed her on the cheek and said: 'Goodbye, Susie. Thank you.'

'He left at about 1.15 a.m.,' she said. 'He seemed quite calm. He said he would let me know how things turned out.'

She watched him get into a car parked in the drive. She could see it was not his Mercedes, but could describe the car only as an ordinary-looking dark-coloured family saloon.

John started the engine, drove off down the drive – and vanished into thin air.

Thirteen years later, police throughout the world were still hunting him, dead or alive.

BOOK TWO

The Lucans

4

Wherever he was, Lord Lucan was separated from his children, possibly forever. And for such a devoted father, who had wanted them to have a settled childhood, unlike his own, that was perhaps the most cruel fate of all.

Either side of John's birth in London on 18 December 1934 – appropriately under Sagittarius, the astrological sign of the gambler – there were two unfortunate occurrences. That October, seven months pregnant, Kait was involved in a car accident in which her husband Pat was injured. And immediately after John was born, doctors found a blood clot on her lung. She was forced to remain confined to bed at the nursing home in Bentinck Street while her baby son was taken home alone to the family's house in Cheyne Walk, on the Thames Embankment in Chelsea.

The family nanny, Miss Flora Coles – known to her friends as 'Floss' and to the children in later years as 'Red Hot Coles' – was busy looking after the first child, Jane. So John was taken under the wing of Lucy Sellers, the nurserymaid, whose usual task was to act as the nanny's skivvy, washing nappies and preparing nursery tea.

'I grew very attached to him,' she recalled, 'having taken him for his first airing at two weeks while his mother was still in the nursing home.'

She remembered him growing into 'a delightful little baby and toddler, a little backward with his words . . . and he had to wear glasses when he was very young.'

When he was about fifteen or eighteen months old, however, Kait found her son 'an awkward child'.

'He cried a lot, he was constantly waking up and carrying on and he had headaches,' she said. 'We never knew why. We let people look at him of course and they all said it was nothing and would pass. And sure enough it disappeared after infancy. It was a completely infantile thing.'

After the third child, Sarah (Sally), was born, the family moved to a larger house at number 22 Eaton Square. A short time later, at the age of three, John was sent with his sister Jane to a pre-prep school for babies in Tite Street. This meant being apart not only from his parents and Nanny Coles but also from Lucy, his beloved nurserymaid, who then left. John rebelled volubly.

'Luckily,' Kait said, 'they were very good and sensible at Tite Street and said: "Well, his Mum can stay here with him for as long as he wants her." And of course after a few weeks he stopped wanting it. But none of the other children ever wanted one to stay for a single, solitary second.'

When the war came in 1939, Jane and John were evacuated with the baby school to a spot near the Welsh border – another separation. And in April 1940, fearing an invasion, Pat and Kait sent all four of their children to safety in Canada. The children embarked from Glasgow and must have looked a sad little group as their parents waved them off from the dock. Jane was aged seven, John was five, Sally was three and baby Hugh was barely a year old. Nanny Coles, remembered by some as 'a gloomy Right-winger', crossed the Atlantic with them.

'A nanny is a sort of mother-substitute and was much more so then than now,' Sally said. 'The feeling was that if Nanny was there with us, everything was all right.'

For several weeks Miss Coles and the children were looked after by unknown well-wishers in Toronto. Then they crossed the border into the United States. Pat and Kait wanted the family kept together if possible, which seemed a tall order in the circumstances.

But as luck would have it, Pat's elder sister, Lady Barbara Bevan, was already in America with her own three children. And she knew someone who was willing and had the resources to take on the four little Binghams for as long as the war might last.

The resources of the indomitable Mrs Marcia Brady

54

Tucker were almost beyond limit. Mrs Tucker, who died in her nineties shortly after the murder leaving John $15,000 in her will, was a grand old American multi-millionairess. She was short, held herself very erect, walked with tiny steps like Queen Mary and ruled her empire in an extremely autocratic manner.

For many years the Binghams mistakenly believed that she was the daughter of the nineteenth-century American folklore character 'Diamond Jim' Brady, whose chequered life and times were featured in two Hollywood films. 'Diamond Jim' was a flashy, flamboyant speculator who made a fortune from the railroads. He gained his nickname by decking himself out in diamond tie-pins, cufflinks and such worth an estimated $2 million. According to legend he owned a different set of diamond jewellery for every day of the month. The mere thought of a family connection between her and such a man brought a shudder to Mrs Tucker. 'Diamond Jim', Jane learned years later when she finally dared broach the subject, was as nothing compared to *her* Bradys.

Mrs Tucker, or 'Aunt Marcia' as she became known, owned the last private house, as opposed to apartment, on Park Avenue in New York; a place near Palm Beach in Florida known by the name of the area, Hobe Sound; a vast ocean-going yacht fit for royalty called *Migrant*, in which the Tuckers had sailed to and from the Greek Islands and which they handed over to America for use during the war; and a palatial summer mansion called Penwood, which was situated about forty miles outside New York City in the little town of Mount Kisco, Westchester. She became the Bingham children's 'fairy godmother' and Penwood became not merely their refuge but an introduction to an elegant life of unimaginable style and luxury. They lived there 'like kings', inspiring in John a lifelong desire for only the very best.

The children lived in a separate house on the estate with a staff of their own: an American governess, a butler and a cook. The 'Big House' itself, to which Mrs Tucker and her entourage moved each summer when the heat in

New York City became oppressive, was a smaller version of the English stately home. From a courtyard lined with carefully tended fuchsias, beyond which literally acres of rolling lawns were watered daily by an army of gardeners, the building spread itself in a great E-shape with the centre missing. Inside the dark, cool beautiful hallway, suits of armour stood in alcoves beneath hanging baskets of more brilliantly-coloured fuchsias. Around the house were ultra-luxurious furnishings; chandeliers, hanging tapestries, tapestry chairs. The library was panelled. The dining room was large enough to seat twenty for dinner. And a verandah where drinks were served led into an enormous dark baronial-style main drawing room where a Gainsborough and several mounted buffalo and deer heads peered down their noses from the walls.

The maids wore two uniforms each day: crisp white outfits during the heat of the sun and dark blue silk with lace aprons at night. The regiment of servants at Penwood was ruled by an almighty head butler named Herbert. When Mrs Tucker was robbed by armed bandits in later years, it was said that, because she had suffered the indignity of being roped and bound to Herbert, the poor man had felt obliged to resign. Though the story was untrue, the flavour was accurate. Between employer and servant at Penwood there lay a great divide. Mrs Tucker's orders would be dictated to her private secretary, written down and then delivered to the staff by proxy. Her orders were always obeyed, inside the house and out. No cat, for example, was allowed to set foot on the thousands of acres of land around Penwood because Mrs Tucker was a keen bird-watcher.

'Aunt Marcia' and her husband Carll, who owned a fortune in his own right, occupied one wing of the 'Big House'. In the other, there were countless guest bedrooms and bathrooms, each with a different colour scheme. The sheets and towels were monogrammed with Mrs Tucker's initials, MBT, or else bore the *Migrant* emblem from the yacht. The Tuckers had a chauffeur-driven Rolls Royce and for the use of their guests they provided a whole string of motor cars, including an open-topped Mercedes. Cigarettes of every known brand were available; and for the sporty there were three tennis courts, one indoor, two outdoor, plus two swimming pools. Being so rich, Mrs Tucker had one swimming pool in the sunshine and another in the shade. They owned a collection of old carriages, which ended up in a museum, and a couple of horsedrawn sleighs. At the stables there were a dozen or so horses and ponies to ride. And when sport in the heat became wearing, there were the vast grounds of Penwood to explore. These featured orchards and farmland, woods and a rose garden, with cool summer porches dotted everywhere.

'It was all very very nice and lots of it,' Jane recalled with typical British upper-class understatement. 'It stamped itself on us.'

Sally said: 'I suppose those years gave John a taste for the very rich life at the impressionable ages of five to ten which he never lost.'

Yet for all the material benefits of those five years in America, John was not happy. Even there he had more separations to endure. In the place of Nanny Coles – who had been returned protesting to England, Mrs Tucker preferring American ways – came a succession of nursery employees with different, all-American methods. At the local Harvey prep school where he was enrolled, John not only spoke with a different accent but also looked an outsider in his funny little round steel-rimmed spectacles from England. And during the school holidays he was sent miserably away from the rest of the family to summer camp in the Adirondacks. Even at Penwood, Jane recalled, John had no one to relate to as a parent, though baby Hugh found a 'mother-figure' in the form of a nursery nurse called Delia. Mama and Daddy seemed very distant. There were, of course, letters from home, but they were 'political letters about current affairs and how the war was going' according to John's aunt, Dorothea Bingham.

'Their parents always tried to treat them in an adult way which they thought was more seemly and up-to-date,' she said.

It was little surprise that John grew up to be so independent, so determined to rely on himself. Years later when someone asked what he believed in, he replied: 'I believe in myself.'

Alone among the Bingham children, John longed to return to England. Because he was normally so reserved, even at the age of ten, Sally never forgot the day he ran out onto the lawns at Penwood shouting with unbridled joy: 'We're going home! We're going home!'

The children sailed back to Britain in the temporary care of a governess called Miss Harrison in February 1945.

'Pat and I thought that they would feel bad if they hadn't seen anything of the war in their own country,' Kait said. 'It was perfectly apparent then that there wasn't going to be an invasion.'

Back home, Sally, then aged eight, played among the bombed shells of buildings and rubble, ironically finding blitzed London 'a paradise for children'. The old house at Cheyne Walk had had a direct hit. At 22 Eaton Square all the windows had been blown out. Everything had changed – and though it wasn't by any means a case of from riches to rags, the contrast with life at Penwood was total. For the children the homecoming was rather a shock.

In place of plenty came economy and rationing.

'In America we had everything and thought nothing of eating wartime luxuries like bananas and cream,' Sally said. 'But in postwar London, we existed on Marmite and dried milk.'

In place of the Tuckers' gleaming fleet of limousines and chauffeur-driven Rolls Royce – according to John's Uncle John, Sussex farmer John Edward Bingham – Pat had a 'shabby old car with a leaky roof'.

In place of the Tuckers' yacht, Pat owned a canal narrow boat called *Hesperus* on which the children took holidays along inland waterways like the Oxford and Grand Union canals.

In contrast to the grandeur of Mrs Tucker, Kait, the

staunch socialist despite her aristocratic background, never bothered to live up to her title. She would rather have been a plain 'Mrs' anyway. And she had a complete disregard for feminine props like make-up, scent, jewellery and fashion. More often than not, at home, according to Uncle John, she'd 'come slopping in, wearing worn-out sandals and awful baggy trousers' – though she could look 'frightfully smart' and after Queen Elizabeth II's coronation went off to Buckingham Palace 'in all the trappings looking really magnificent'.

In place of the outrageous luxury at Penwood, 'there wasn't a big Lucan estate any more'. Though 22 Eaton Square was a fine address, according to another relative the drawing room was 'virtually unfurnished' and featured a rope dangling from the ceiling 'which they used to practise climbing up during the war for exercise'.

Unlike Mrs Tucker, Kait had no vast staff of servants to keep the place spick and span and the family wasn't noted for its tidiness. After the 5th Earl died, by which time they had moved to another address, some of his 'old family stuff, a lot of crates and probably swords and scabbards' lay around Lucan-fashion for a time 'in heaps on the floor'.

'John came back from the very rich life he'd had with Mrs Tucker to this "slum" and I think he rebelled against it,' his Uncle John said. 'What he wanted and had when he was old enough – big cars, bright lights, gambling, the high life – were the things his parents didn't like.'

From being different in America the children returned to find themselves different in their own country: English children with an American education and American accents.

'We were neither one thing nor the other,' Sally recalled. 'It wasn't easy. For a long time after we came home we were all very keen to be as English as we possibly could.'

The fact that they'd been abroad at all left them open to rather unfair criticism.

'We stayed here to see it out!' declared the nanny to

their cousins, the Alexanders, the family of Field Marshal Earl Alexander of Tunis.

Sally said: 'I realised later that a lot of people disapproved of children being sent abroad. It was considered almost a betrayal, running away – but we had no choice.'

Even in spiritual terms the return to England meant confusion and another mental leap back and forth.

'Our parents were agnostics and brought us up as agnostics,' Sally said, 'but Mrs Tucker brought us up as Christians. Back home it was agnosticism as before but at school we were expected to be Christians! It was rather chop and change and it was very difficult for us. Our parents did not tell us what to believe but there was an atmosphere about it at home which children are very sensitive to. Suddenly religion was something that was laughed at – not openly, but you sensed this. We very quickly realised that God was alive and well and living in America, so to speak, but not at home. It was quite a volte-face for us to take in. People are either Christians or they aren't and my parents weren't.'

The irony was that in later life Jane wed an American Roman Catholic and Sally married a Church of England clergyman. And that the Lucan family motto, translated from the Latin, was 'Christ Is My Hope'.

'John and I had a good few laughs about that,' Kait said.

Though the Lucans were not openly affectionate, they were strong on laughter.

John remained an agnostic as an adult. But once he was a parent he made sure that his own children went to Sunday school with their nanny each week. And when he took them to stay at Guilsborough vicarage with Sally and her husband, William, the country vicar, he accompanied them to church.

Sally said: 'He wanted his children to have a normal, unbroken childhood, a traditional Church of England upbringing like their friends – brought up with no funny ideas like we were.'

Though at prep school John was remembered as a

'rather mischievous' boy, the disruptions of his childhood had left their mark.

Kait said: 'John began to have bad nightmares from which he would awake greatly distressed, sometimes screaming. We took him to see a psychotherapist and the man said he thought John's nightmares were a side result of us having been in the Blitz and that this was one of the rare cases where the child would have been better staying behind with his parents. Once more we were advised that time would do the trick and once more apparently it did. As far as I know the nightmares disappeared and never came back.'

5

It was at Eton, Britain's most famous public school, that John, as the young Lord Bingham, finally found his feet. He also found a circle of rich friends and gained an enduring love of music from a tutor called The Baron.

In Kait's view, however: 'Though he never had any trouble with Trials [examinations], John didn't stretch himself and his career at Eton was far from creditable.'

At about sixteen, he discovered the passion that was to dominate his life – gambling. He ran a book to supplement his pocket money, opened a 'secret' bank account for his winnings and, according to his mother, was 'always being bawled out by the school for going to the races'.

Nevertheless, he ended up as Captain of Roe's House over about forty-seven other boys before leaving to join the Army and do his National Service.

In October 1953, after emerging from officer training school as a 2nd lieutenant, John was posted to Krefeld in West Germany to join the 2nd Battalion of his father's old regiment, the Coldstream Guards.

'As a soldier he was very accomplished, good with people and always a character,' a contemporary recalled. 'Even in those days his slit-trench appeared to be more amenable and comfortable than anyone else's. He was popular, he treated people well and he had leadership. If he'd said: "Over the top!", people would have gone over the top.'

At Krefeld – unlike London, where fellow officers could enjoy the myriad delights of the debutante circuit during the social season – spare-time entertainment was 'at a low key'.

The officers played tennis in the summer and went shooting in the winter. For the most part in the evenings, however, they played cards – especially poker. John was in his element.

'He was a master at the art of bluff and became the best poker-player in the battalion,' said his contemporary. 'We played virtually every night. I remember once, being "marched" in is the wrong word, but the adjutant saw about three of us and said that the poker stakes were getting too high and a limit of £5 per hand was imposed, which seems pathetic when viewed against what John played for subsequently. Sometimes we'd drive down the autobahn to the casino at Bad Neuenahr and £20 up or down of an evening meant a lot to us all in those days. John was a very private man but he was always immensely good company on any party, game for anything.'

In 1955, after completing his two years' National Service, John joined William Brandts, the merchant bank, in London. For 'a born gambler' the world of the Stock Exchange was an obvious choice of career. Kait remembered the day he came home from his interview and she asked if he'd landed the job.

'What do you think, Mummy?' he replied, ever-confident.

'I've heard him say that he never could or would fail an exam,' Kait said. 'What he meant was that he would put in enough work to make sure he passed. Or, alternatively, if the exam was beyond him, he wouldn't take it.'

His self-esteem was very important to him.

'He was greatly determined to be good at whatever he did,' Jane said.

In later years a friend who recalled John's success as a financial adviser, in silver dealings, as a gambler and as a sportsman would cite a particular talent and add, somewhat surprised: 'He was damn good at *that* too!' The reason was simple. If he wasn't good at something – skiing for example: 'He was Daddy-Longlegs on skis' – he didn't bother to do it. What he did do he was determined to do well and with *style*.

'He was a toff,' one friend said, 'and he wanted to live like a young lord, like his great-grandfather.'

'He wasn't snobbish about birth,' Kait said, 'but he was about other things, which is a different kind of snobbery. In a sport like golf, for example, John would only play if he could play rather well and probably win, if he had the very best clubs, if he played where the best players played and if he could do it in the most grand and expensive way possible. It was the same with travel. My idea of travel was to go to Turkey eighth-class if there was one and really meet the local people and have fun, whereas John wouldn't go unless he could go by the Orient Express as far as Constantinople and then hire a rather grand car. If he couldn't travel first-class, he wouldn't go. It wasn't that he minded being uncomfortable but he wanted to do things in style.'

A former Coldstream officer who accompanied John and a party of other friends on one of his early winter sports holidays to Switzerland recalled: 'Typical of his wish to be debonair, I remember when we discussed which hotel to go to he specifically wanted a hotel where we would have to change for dinner. He wanted to be in a first-class, top hotel. Mind you it was much more usual to wear dinner jackets in those days, but John wanted luxury. He wanted to do everything with style.'

Back in London, as a young man-about-town, John spent his spare time playing for one of William Brandts' bridge teams, racing his greyhound Sambo's Hangover – a name which delighted his Right-wing friends – and gambling at the private Mayfair parties held by John Aspinall, doyen of the smart London gaming set since the 1950s. A friend remembered a gambling weekend at Deauville casino.

'Three of us flew out from London and stayed at Trouville, which is the bang-next-door town to Deauville, separated just by a river. It was an example of John's style that he organised a private aeroplane to fly us there. Surprisingly, it cost very little money but only John bothered to pick up the telephone and ask. I'd made friends in America with a very rich financier and his wife who had racehorses out in Deauville and had taken a house there, and we all went round to meet them. I think they rather enjoyed John being a peer and a typical English gentleman and so on. I remember the three of us falling asleep on the beach after a very good lunch with them.

'That weekend was the first time I felt that John had entered into a different league as a gambler. Halfway through the first evening at the casino, by which I mean about 1.00 a.m., I had lost my £25 or £50 or whatever it was and John had lost £200 or £300. We had another evening still to go and, being anxious for him, I said: "Look, for God's sake, enough's enough!"

'But he then disappeared and came back two hours later, by which time he had recouped it all and won another £200 on top! We were playing roulette I think at that stage though he later went on to baccarat and chemin de fer. One then felt that it was no longer fun money to John. His attitude towards gambling had become much more serious. Although he was a very bottled-down person, he had a laugh which I can still hear now, a laugh which always I think indicated that even if he'd lost money there was a chance of winning it back and: "We'll show the bastards – they're not going to keep *my* money!" And I mean, by the law of averages, he should have lost another £100 or £200 instead of winning, but you know luck was on his side.'

John's Uncle John never forgot the shock of visiting Le Touquet and finding his nephew perched on a high stool, totally immersed in the action on the green baize table before him.

The extraordinary importance John placed on luck was shown in a letter he wrote to his uncle in 1956 when he was twenty-one. Uncle John had worked at a merchant bank himself for about six years as a youth before 'kicking the City dust' from his heels and embarking on adventurous world travels. Knowing that his nephew had recently joined Brandts, he wrote what he later described as 'a very pompous letter' full of advice. The reply seemed so 'sophisticated' at the time that Uncle John kept it.

Part of John's letter read:

Your warning of straying from the straight and narrow path has been duly heeded. The only thing that does worry me is where that path leads. While I appreciate that the people to whom you refer have by their industry and intellect reached the top of their professions [Uncle John had cited several City businessmen as examples to follow], they at least had a carrot to help them. I wonder whether the final furlong of that straight and narrow path is paved with gold now. In 1930 the future was extremely rosy, for who could have predicted that in less than twenty years they would be living in a Welfare State and paying tax at 18/6 in the £ to provide that welfare; that great riches would come to be regarded as something to be ashamed of, and profits and dividends immoral. For the last hundred years we have been living on our colonies, our coal and our brains. In ten years time we shall have no colonies and there appears little prospect of persuading the miners to give us any coal. Without a million unemployed our workers are bolshie, and with a million unemployed we will have Nye Bevan in power and if we reach that stage I don't want to be Chairman of ICI or Governor of the Bank of England. So on the long term I'm 'bearish' for England although our grouse moors and Stately Homes should keep Old Consols above the level of Greek sixes.

There is no Financial reward for hard work today as our system of taxation is designed to prevent people from accumulating large or small capital sums. Anyone in England who lives on a decent scale is either evading taxation or spending his capital. I agree with your suggestion that 'chasing girls round the West end of London' is neither profitable or likely to lead very far (unless it's a sausage skin heiress) but it can be enormous fun. 'Tottering to one's desk' at 9.30 probably means 'smooching' in some night club till 6.30 and I am not rich enough to do that. But sponging dinner and breakfast off the Mamas four nights a week [during the London debutante season] is quite harmless and certainly not too exhausting to interfere with one's daily toil. If I had wanted to be a play-boy and could have afforded it I should have stayed on in the army which is the only place one can be a play-boy without being labeled one. I have come into the city to attempt to make my 'pile'; I don't know whether I shall succeed because it is not just a question of staring at ledgers; in my opinion the formula for success is as follows:

a) 60% Luck
b) 20% Industry
c) 20% Gambling ability.

Mr Niarchos does not agree with me: he believes that his success is only 40% luck and 60% hard work. Obviously there are other requirements such as an ability to get on well with people, honesty, trustworthiness and all the usual virtues, but taking these for granted, all I now ask is ten times my ration of good luck! It is impossible to qualify for this unless full use is made of (c) on the 'nothing venture, nothing win' theory. Nothing has been ventured in this family since our great-grandfather [the 4th Earl] ran up a grocer's bill of £4,000! Messrs Coutts [trustees of the Lucan money] knew perfectly well that neither Granddaddy or Daddy had any interest in money . . .

This letter probably sounds as if I do nothing but dream of shekels and how to make them: I certainly keep an eye on my bank balance or overdraft, but I do dream of other things! Too many people say that 'money isn't everything' – 'can't buy happiness' and all the usual patter. This is either sour grapes or stupidity. Avarice is the spur of industry whether it is avarice for the sake of oneself or one's children or any 'cause' it is avarice nevertheless; this is probably an ultra-cynical attitude to other peoples good works; I will allow that there are a few exceptions. I am perfectly happy now (that is to say I am not unhappy) but I know that with £2m in the bank I should be happier still (who wouldn't?). It wouldn't be a case of Buying Happiness, but motor-cars, yachts, expensive holidays and security for the future would give myself and a lot of other people a lot of pleasure. These are some of my carrots and I'm certainly not ashamed of them.

But banging this typewriter is not the shortest route to Cannes, so I must stop now and do some work.

I hope Aunt Dodo's [Dorothea's] neck is fully recovered and that all my cousins (who I never see) are flourishing.

In black ink he signed the letter: 'Yours, John (or Arthur)' and added the parting shot: 'P.S. If you ever "have a go" nowadays, a speculative interest in K.G. (Holdings) 1/– sh. @ 6/9 is strongly recommended!'

Since John was 'a man of few words' who usually kept his thoughts and feelings well hidden, it was a surprise to find him spelling out his philosophy so openly and at such length. It seems apt, however, that such a dark horse should be known by so many names. Though his first name was actually Richard, his family and earliest friends always called him John. In the Coldstream Guards, for some now-forgotten reason, he was known as Arthur. And in the gambling world, he answered to the names Lucky, Johnny and Luke.

In 1960 John encountered a man who was to play a key role in his life as confidant, 'father-figure' and gambling mentor. Stephen Raphael, who was about twenty years John's senior, was a rich stockbroker and top backgammon player who once shared a flat in London with Errol Flynn. It was Raphael who taught John how to be shrewd enough as a gambler to survive. He also introduced him to his friends and, with his blonde actress wife Eve – who later became a godmother to John's eldest child, Frances – took him on winter holidays to the Bahamas.

'When I first met him he was very, very shy and didn't talk a lot,' Stephen Raphael recalled. 'He was so typically a man's man. In Nassau he used to play golf, water-ski, play some backgammon and some poker and be with my wife and myself. At that time he never seemed to be that madly interested in girls. He had one or two girls but they were sort of secondary.'

According to one of John's girlfriends, he was 'perfectly normal sexually' – but gambling came first.

John had always said he would not get married until he was in his mid-fifties, if at all.

'It was a standing joke: "Oh, John will never marry",' said his friend Caroline Hill, whom he used to take to the 400 Club, haunt of the Princess Margaret set at the time. 'He always enjoyed his free life and sort of teased, you know: "Tied to a wife and family, that's not for me!"'

Many girls enjoyed nights on the town with the dashing, handsome and generous Lord Bingham. Years later one ex-debutante still glowed at the memory of a magical evening she spent with him at the casino in Monte Carlo during a holiday in the South of France.

'It was the most glorious, perfect evening to be given,' she said. 'I can remember a candlelit balcony where we sat down to have dinner and John said: "Now, we are having caviar and champagne." It went with the setting. John knew how to do things well if he wanted to and it was fun, and he had a tremendous sense of humour – a dry sense of humour about people and situations. After all, the casino in Monte Carlo is not one's normal sort of habitat and to find yourself there having caviar and champagne was rather gorgeous really. That was how he wanted it.'

Had she known, casinos from Monte Carlo to Mayfair *were* soon to be John's natural habitat. Though he was 'very fond' of that particular ex-deb – and she loved him, and at that age might have married him, had he asked – his passion for gambling ran deeper.

Christina Shand Kydd said long after: 'I always felt that John was very much attracted by what I call the twin set, string of pearls, regimental badge type girl, the very *very* straight country lady. But I think he also realised that that sort of girl would never have lived a gambler's life.'

6

In the classic way, John's life changed abruptly when he suddenly won thousands of pounds at chemin de fer. As a result, following the footsteps of Uncle John, who had made his own early departure from Lazards years before, John 'retired' from Brandts at the age of about twenty-seven.

An American friend, Charles Sweeny, first husband of Margaret, Duchess of Argyll, said: 'I heard that Brandts were going to make him a director. But in two nights he won £26,000 at gambling and said to me: "Here I am working for so much a year less tax and I can win £26,000 in two nights! I'm going to quit and gamble." And I said: "Don't be ridiculous. Keep your job and gamble if you want to." But he said: "Oh no no, it's just a waste of time. I'm going to quit."'

Veronica said long afterwards what a 'brave' decision that was. But Stephen Raphael disapproved.

'I held that against him,' he said. 'He told me he'd have to work for years at Brandts to make the kind of money he could make gambling. I said to him: "Yes, but you can lose it just as quickly."'

They were prophetic words.

As usual, John's parents did not find out until after the event that he had decided to become a full-time professional gambler. They didn't pressure him to change his mind – 'Fortunately,' he remarked to them once about something else, 'you're not the kind who interfere' – but they were distressed and appalled.

'I thought and think gambling is a most disreputable way of earning a living,' Kait said. 'Chiefly because it's wanting to get something for nothing, and that's not in my view what anybody ought to do. But John was very keen on it.'

He celebrated his new freedom with a long holiday in America, where he played golf, went powerboat racing, and toured the West Coast in his Aston Martin, crossing the Mojave desert to see the Grand Canyon. He also stayed in New York with his elder sister Jane, who had qualified as a doctor. And for some of the time he based himself with 'Aunt Marcia' Tucker, whose links with the family had been maintained since the war years.

On his return, the top London gaming clubs became his new 'offices', and he also found a new home. He moved out of his parents' flat at Hanover House in St John's Wood and into Flat 50 at 22 Park Crescent, a tiny bachelor apartment tucked behind the grand Regency columns of a semi-circular Nash terrace close to Regents Park.

By this time both of John's sisters and several of his friends were married, and despite his earlier protestations, he was a family man at heart. Suddenly John wanted to get married. Being the private man he was, hardly anyone knew. And even if they had, it's doubtful they'd have guessed the object of his affections. Years later, old friends fell back in astonishment with cries of: 'Zinnia? No! They were just friends!' But according to two men in whom John confided, the woman he wanted to marry was indeed Lady Zinnia, the willowy blonde daughter of the 4th and last Earl of Londesborough. They would have made a very handsome couple.

'Zinnia was divine. *Divine!*' one woman said. 'Slim and tall and gorgeous-looking with lovely long streaky-blonde hair down to here. Her father was the earl of somewhere or other and she knew everybody and she'd been married . . . one? two? or was it three times by then? I can't remember. She always went her own way and she was mad about horses, always rushing down and riding and breeding horses and Lord knows what. She was absolutely heavenly and *exactly* the sort of person that people expected John to marry.'

Apart from her pedigree and sex appeal, Lady Zinnia was said to have inherited around £350,000 under the terms of her father's will. The combination was irresistible, as the number of her admirers proved. Her friendship with John dated back to the mid-1950s when, after attending finishing school in Paris, she 'came out' into London society as the debutante Lady Zinnia Denison. She had joined John and other friends on winter holidays in St Moritz in the past, and early in 1963, after her second marriage foundered in Kenya, he once again invited her to join him and friends in St Moritz at the famous Palace Hotel.

Lady Zinnia – now the wife of advertising agency chairman Jamie Judd, whom she married following the death of her fourth husband, John Pollock – recalled:

'I remember distinctly John's kindness. He knew I was about to get a divorce and he really was a super friend. He said: "Come and join us ski-ing for a fortnight. I'll meet you at the airport." And he motored for miles at 1.00 or 2.00 a.m., to come and fetch me. In that way he was just simply an exceptionally good friend. I could discuss all sorts of things with him.

'Usually I was in trouble or about to get divorced or do something stupid, and he was a very level-headed person who gave me his advice. He was one of the few people I could have rung up in trouble. I'd been to him with all my problems and I'd taken his advice many times. It was always very sensible and very logical and very fair really. He was a lovely person and a lovely friend.'

What if anything John said about marriage is not clear. Zinnia, who had had more proposals than most, didn't recollect.

'I'm just trying to remember if John *did* propose. I honestly don't think so,' she said. 'I knew he was very fond of me but I never thought about him in those terms really. I knew him almost too well. I was always so involved, probably rather selfishly, with other people or other things that I maybe never realised.

'I remember that holiday very well. We knew quite a lot of people there. John stayed on after I left. There are a lot of games always in St Moritz in the evening and he was there for a couple of months playing backgammon and bridge. I suppose if you were married to John, you married him accepting the fact that he was a gambler because I don't think in any way he'd have given it up. For sure that was his game and that was his life. Always was.'

Shaking his head at the memory, Charles Sweeny said: 'I told John: "Why don't you go to New York? There are lots of lovely girls there and they're loaded." But it was Zinnia he wanted to marry. He was very keen on her. He said: "She won't marry me" and he was very upset.'

As Stephen Raphael understood the situation: 'John fell madly in love with Zinnia although they never had a romance as such or an affair. He told me he asked her to marry him when he was in St Moritz and that she said: "I'm very fond of you, John, and I like you very much as a person, but I don't feel for you in that way and I could never marry you." He came back from St Moritz ready to marry the first girl he met.'

Though they came from such different backgrounds, John and Veronica had several things in common. As children they had both had to face separation from one or both parents, in Veronica's case permanently. They had both experienced the discomforts of being different from other children as foreigners living for a time abroad. And they had both had problems. Veronica's began at about the age of eight.

Veronica regarded her childhood as unhappy. Her father, Major Charles Moorhouse Duncan, died in a car crash in the summer of 1939 when she was only two. Her mother Thelma, widowed at twenty-one, was heavily pregnant. Shortly afterwards, on 3 August, Veronica's sister Christina was born. When war was declared that September, they moved to Bournemouth where they lived at a house called Midwood. When Veronica was about ten, the family emigrated for a while to South Africa and the two sisters were enrolled at a boarding school in Port Elizabeth. But being newcomers with foreign accents, they came in for the worst of schoolgirl ragging and taunts. Some Sundays they returned from church to find their young persecutors had been busy – leaving their drawers emptied, their bedding stripped. Veronica was hypersensitive and after only one term she and Christina were withdrawn from the school and sent to another one in Grahamstown.

Back in England, they eventually moved to the Wheatsheaf Hotel, a sixteenth-century country pub on the A30 at North Waltham near Basingstoke in Hampshire. Though the family wasn't rich, they did better than many others in those days. They owned a car, at one stage a second-hand silver Bentley. The girls went to a fee-paying school, St Swithuns in Winchester. They went to dances. And they had their own ponies and rode with the local hunt, which met outside the Wheatsheaf. It was hardly 'grinding poverty', the term Veronica used in a later Press interview, but her attitude towards her early years was largely negative.

Thelma had remarried and her second husband, Jim Margrie, was the tenant of the pub. Veronica did not get on with her stepfather. In addition, the jealousies and squabbles common to most families were accentuated in the passionate 'love–hate' relationship between the two Duncan girls. There were times, of course, when they shared confidences, laughed uproariously, and had moments of 'tremendous sweetness and closeness'. But on occasions there were bitter rows.

The contrast between the two girls was quite marked. Veronica was a blonde, Christina a brunette. As a child Veronica was the prettier daughter, 'Mummy's golden girl' according to her sister. Christina remembered bursting into tears once when described as 'the ugly duckling of the family'. On the other hand, she had greater confidence. She was socially more at ease. And at five-feet-seven when fully grown, she was also five inches taller than Veronica, who had a curious complex about her petite height.

Significantly, even as adults both sisters claimed the other was their mother's favourite child.

'Veronica said she always came second, that her mother made more of Christina,' someone recalled.

But Christina disagreed. She said: 'The first time it was brought up that Veronica took "second place" I found myself really without thinking saying: "But that's nonsense." If my mother loved anybody more and gave either of us more attention, I'm quite certain it was Veronica. And I would think for the very obvious reason that Veronica needed her so much more. She was terribly pretty and had lovely yellow hair but the fact was that I was a happy, healthy, laughing type of girl with lots of friends buzzing around and Veronica wasn't. She was also the first child and the child who was born while my father was alive. I arrived after Daddy had died. And though maybe my birth was lovely for my mother in the sense that I was part of her dead husband, it must also have been a very unhappy moment for her. To give birth to a child three months after your husband has died and you're only twenty-one – there's a lot of pain attached to that.'

At sixteen or seventeen, Veronica had blossomed from a spotty schoolgirl into 'the prettiest thing in the area'. Hoping to make a career for herself as a commercial artist, after leaving St Swithuns she moved back to Bournemouth to attend art college. Then she moved to London and rented a £3-a-week bedsitter – by coincidence at the top of a house in Gloucester Place, where the 5th Earl and Countess of Lucan had had their residence at number 10. To earn a living she took a brief modelling course – 'although I was hopelessly too short really' – and then got a job showing coats and suits as a house model.

In Christina's opinion: 'Veronica had tremendous resilience to go through with it because she was living alone in that horrid bedsitter. I remember I stayed one night with her once. We shared a bed. It was all pretty ghastly and depressing.'

Veronica's earnings were such, she recalled, that she was lucky if she managed to save a pound a week. So after eighteen months she quit the modelling world and learned secretarial skills instead. Later she took jobs as an office 'temp', became involved with a group of people who were behind a musical called *Little Mary Sunshine*, and went into business printing scripts.

Christina, meanwhile, had also become a beauty. After leaving St Swithuns, she commuted daily from the Wheatsheaf to secretarial college in London, where she eventually found a flat in Melbury Road, off Kensington High Street. She shared the accommodation with Veronica, two schoolfriends named Carol and Roberta, and another girl, Rachael Blacklock. It was through Rachael that Christina met the rich, attractive and amusing Bill Shand Kydd.

Rachael had eventually left Melbury Road to become the flatmate of a girl who happened to have money – and had entered a different world. In St Moritz she had met Hans Heyman, a Cresta-riding friend of Bill's, and had since become his wife. Rachael believed that Bill and Christina would be well suited, and had tried to bring them together. But she did not succeed until an invitation arrived to a dance in Cumberland. Veronica, who had also been invited, knew one of the organisers and asked if Christina could go too. Rachael and Hans offered to drive Veronica up to Cumberland in their car, and asked Bill to give Christina a lift in his. He agreed.

'In fact,' Christina recalled smiling, 'Bill had his girlfriend with him and I was very much the lemon of the three. We all drove up together, much to the other girl's fury.'

Back in London after the dance, Bill took Christina out with a group of friends. A month or so after their second date, they were engaged to be married. Bill gave Christina an exquisite flower-shaped diamond engagement ring worth £1,300 from Cartier. Their wedding took place at Holy Trinity Church, Brompton in London on 17 January 1963. Bill was twenty-five, his bride twenty-three.

Christina was followed down the aisle by a pageboy, three little bridesmaids in white dresses with red cummerbunds, and three adult bridesmaids dressed in red. The chief bridesmaid was Veronica.

The Shand Kydds at first shared a luxury flat in Davies Street, near Claridges, with Bill's widowed mother, Freda. Then they moved into a grand Nash terraced house in

Chester Terrace with spectacular views over Regents Park. They had the services of a butler, a housekeeper and a chauffeur. They had a fleet of cars. Christina had food and clothing accounts at top London stores like Harrods and Peter Jones, and a hairdressing account at the Knightsbridge salon Carita in Sloane Street. They spent weekends at Horton Hall, the Shand Kydds' family home in Bedfordshire. The house had six bedrooms and stood on a site dating back to 1030, when the moat around it was dug. The Shand Kydds' land behind stretched for 600 acres. In the garden there was a heated swimming pool, and about a mile away stood Grove Farm, which Bill and Freda ran together as a partnership. The Victorian farmhouse and surroundings at Grove were to be converted by Bill and Christina into their own weekend retreat and racing stud, where at one point the Whaddon Chase hunters were stabled. Even down to the smallest detail, Christina's life was transformed.

Though Bill expected her to keep a record of household expenditure, as his mother had done for his father, he was generous with his money. Yet one of Christina's first purchases as his wife was a simple bottle of pine essence. Since the age of about nine, when she had visited a house where there was 'wonderful green stuff you could put in the bath', this had been her symbol of luxury. Now she could afford gallons of it.

Within the space of two years, all the girls who had originally shared the flat at Melbury Road had got married except for Veronica. Rachael had wed Hans Heyman. Carol had become the wife of a man in Ceylon. Roberta had married in America. And now Christina was Mrs William Shand Kydd and appeared to have everything. She had married into riches, she had a social position, and her future was assured.

7

The contrast between the luxury which had enveloped Christina and Veronica's existence at Melbury Road was stark. Recognising the latter's financial situation, Freda Shand Kydd kindly decided to help. So from now on, until after she was married herself, Veronica was paid a regular weekly sum of money through a deed of covenant by Freda. 'It was five or ten pounds a week, I can't remember which,' Freda said. Veronica left Melbury Road and moved into a bedsitter with its own kitchen and bathroom in a more fashionable part of London. She socialised with the Shand Kydds, spent weekends at Horton and met an ever-wider circle of their friends. Though no one knew it then, she too was on the threshold of a fantastic new life.

Though she frequently criticised her mother, Veronica was 'very proud' of her father – who, like Pat Lucan, had been awarded the Military Cross. By another coincidence, Major Duncan had once been married to the daughter of an Irish peer. His first wife, Violet Louisa, was the daughter of the 6th Baron Castlemaine, which seemed 'frightfully grand' to his subsequent family. Indeed, as her husband, the major's name had been published alongside hers in the British 'snobs' Bible' *Debrett's Peerage* – otherwise nicknamed 'the stud book'. Though Major Duncan may not have cared a fig for social prestige, he had acquired it simply by marrying into the peerage, as Veronica herself was to do. Years later, when she had the lot, Veronica told Sally that her ambitions in life had been to gain money and to get into 'the stud book' herself.

In about March 1963, just back from his holiday in St Moritz with Lady Zinnia, John visited the Shand Kydds at Horton Hall and was introduced to Veronica. They met at a cocktail party after a golf match. Apparently the only words they exchanged were the inevitable 'How do you do?' 'I suppose we glanced at one another across the room afterwards,' Veronica said later.

That spring, John immersed himself in his latest passion – powerboat racing. He had a new powerboat built at vast expense and named it *White Migrant* after Mrs Tucker's yacht.

In the summer he had the boat with him on holiday in the South of France. The Shand Kydds were also there and suggested he join them for a weekend at Horton as soon as they all returned to England.

'Which bird would you like invited along?' Bill asked.

Somehow Veronica's name came up.

'God, you don't want *her*!' Bill said.

'Oh shut up, Bill!' Christina retorted.

'I think I've met her,' John said. 'She's short with blonde hair, isn't she?'

The die was cast.

Veronica recalled later that she was 'duly trotted up' to Horton and added: 'John drove me back to London after the weekend and we were out together every night after that.'

John's involvement with Veronica remained unknown to most of his friends. His passion for his powerboat, however, did not. By the eve of the *Daily Express* offshore powerboat race at Cowes that August, many of them were bored to tears with the subject.

'John was a supremely confident individual,' said a business friend who'd known him since their schooldays together at Eton. 'He'd met a boat builder who convinced him that he could build him a specially designed boat which would win the race. John watched it being built for months and months and he got very worked up about it. It was called *White Migrant* and it cost him £10,000 and he said, of course, it was the most magnificent powerboat there'd ever been. We had this huge build-up from him about this wretched powerboat. Well, on the big day I went off to Lords to watch the cricket. I remember hearing on the wireless that *White Migrant* was in the lead with John at the wheel. This was out of about sixty boats and the race was to run for about seven hours. At lunchtime I bought an evening paper and it said *White Migrant* was still in front. I left Lords at the end of play and saw on the placards: "POWERBOAT SINKS". Well, I mean, there was actually no point in looking at the paper! It had to be him! But John led that race until his boat broke up and sank – and he was absolutely furious, though not because he didn't win. He *knew* he was going to win, you see, so he'd hired this helicopter and a cameraman to get film of him winning.

'And do you know what this helicopter pilot did? He flew off with *White Migrant* in the lead to refuel and when he came back of course the thing had sunk, so we never even saw film of *White Migrant* going down! John's reaction wasn't really fury with the helicopter pilot. He would probably have said something dry and telling, like: "Why did you have to refuel? I would have thought a pilot of your quality would have had a large enough tank." While making a point, he always understated. He would never want to make anyone feel uncomfortable. But it was a very plucky effort of John's that, it was a marvellous exhibition, and he loved it, he absolutely loved it. He was great fun and he had a terrific dry wit. He said to us about this boat: "As the helicopter pilot knew I was one of the great drivers of all time and had a fantastic boat, there was no point in following me any longer. Just refuel, you know, and come back for the finish. But unfortunately there was a slight hitch and the boat went down." And there was John treading water with his insurance papers held up high over his head! He was picked up by another boat that was just watching. A week later I was rung up. "By the way," he said, "you probably read about my exploits last weekend – not an *entire* success but I think we can file this one away to experience." That was the sort of conversation. "What you ought to do is to come round and see the film." So I said: "Well, that's tremendous. Is the film of the whole race?" "Well," he said, "it *slightly* highlights *White Migrant*." And I saw this half-hour film which was beautifully filmed and John looking round as the boat went *sweeping* past the favourite! I mean it was absolutely classic stuff, wonderful stuff. He was very proud of that sort of exploit and it wasn't by any means his last.'

It was curious how often that pattern occurred for him: almost there, then disaster.

John's courtship of Veronica was brief and honest. He even gave her books on gambling so that she could study his occupation for herself.

'He was playing a lot of poker before they became engaged and he had taken her out quite a bit and he explained to her that he had no intention ever of changing his way of life,' Christina said. 'He very definitely and rather fairly, because I think he *was* a fair man, said: "If you feel this is a life that you cannot accept, because there are millions of women who couldn't, don't accept my proposal." You know: "Don't think you can change me because that's it." And she knew it totally and she accepted it quite happily. She knew exactly what she was going into.'

Veronica accepted John's proposal of marriage and the next day he whisked her round to Cartier for a ring.

Kait remembered the day he turned up at Hanover House and announced: 'I've come to tell you I'm getting married.'

'Who to?' his mother asked, never having been told anything about his girlfriends.

'Veronica Duncan.'

Kait was not familiar with the name.

'What's she like?'

'Well, she's pretty,' John said, 'at least, I think she is. She's an ash-blonde, she's very short and yes, you'll be pleased – she hasn't got any money!'

Kait laughed at that memory.

'Because he so very much valued the things that money could buy, our anxieties had been that he might perhaps have found a rich American heiress,' she said. 'We weren't so much surprised by him marrying Veronica as relieved.'

Sally said: 'My parents were delighted about Veronica. John obviously wasn't marrying her for money or sex, the silly things that wouldn't last. And being the least snobbish people, it didn't matter to them whether he married a princess or a pauper as long as he was happy.'

A woman John had known for years said: 'I remember when he rang up to say he'd got engaged. I said all the right sort of things: "Oh how marvellous, how exciting! Who is she? When can I meet her?" and John said: "Well, I'd love you to meet her but you won't like her – she's not your type." I thought: "That's funny." It was strange because when you get engaged to somebody usually everything is marvellous, isn't it? He knew, I suppose, that she *wasn't* my type. When I did meet her she was very quiet and it was very difficult to get her to talk. I didn't particularly like or dislike her, though one was honestly wanting to like her because she was marrying John. But she was the kind of person you could probably meet five days a week and you'd never get to know any better.'

The official announcement of their engagement appeared in *The Times* and *The Daily Telegraph* on 14 October 1963. Friends who hadn't yet been told read the news with stunned disbelief.

That morning Caroline Hill was telephoned by another of John's women friends who said: 'Have you seen the newspapers? Isn't it *grisly*?'

'Yes,' she replied, agreeing: 'No more lovely dinners at the 400!'

'We were delighted for John if that's what he wanted but jolly sad for ourselves because it was such fun spending an evening with him,' Caroline said later. 'The news came as a complete surprise (a) because he was getting married at all, and (b) because he was marrying someone out of his own background, it's fair to say really. He knew the right sort of people and the fact that he wasn't marrying someone with a long pedigree was amazing. And also I think most of us hadn't realised that he was walking out with anybody at all, you see.'

'They were crazy about each other and seemed very happy at first but no one could understand why John had picked Veronica,' another friend said. 'She seemed such a little *mouse*.'

The whole family gathered to greet Veronica at a cocktail party given by John's grandmother Violet, widow of the 5th Earl, at her luxury flat at Orchard Court in Portman Square.

On John's stag night, he and a group of old friends and relatives dined at the Boulestin restaurant in Southampton Street. Among them were Bill Shand Kydd, artist Dominick Elwes, stockbroker John Wilbraham, the Reverend William Gibbs and John's cousin Shane Alexander, later the 2nd Earl Alexander of Tunis. Afterwards some of them went on to the Stork Club, where a hostess was photographed snuggling up to John with the clergyman on her other side.

Jane felt 'it fitted' that John felt 'a certain amount of sympathy for Veronica', who described her own personality as 'normally . . . docile and meek'.

Then and later, most people's initial reactions to Veronica were of sympathy, and John *was* exceptionally thoughtful and kind.

When John Wilbraham's father was very ill in hospital, for example, John not only visited him there several times but took Wilbraham's mother out to dinner as well to cheer her up.

'A lot of young men wouldn't have been bothered,' John Wilbraham said. 'There was clearly no advantage in it for him. But it meant a lot to my family at a difficult time, and such a kind act was typical of him.'

Sally said: 'John was very protective, always the first to be there if someone was in hospital. We thought with Veronica it must have been a case of the bird with the broken wing.'

8

On 28 November 1963, at Holy Trinity Church, Brompton, where ten months before she had been chief bridesmaid at Christina's wedding to Bill, Veronica walked down the aisle to become John's wife, Lady Bingham. She was twenty-six, John was twenty-eight. The wedding guests included Princess Alice, Countess of Athlone, who was then eighty. Uncle John, looking at the people on Veronica's side of the church, realised he 'didn't recognise a single face'. 'I thought that was rather sad,' he said.

Veronica was a picture in a beautiful white wild silk gown, the train cut in one with the apricot-tinted skirt. Her four bridesmaids wore long white dresses trimmed in emerald green and emerald green satin coronets, an allusion perhaps to the Irish peerage. She was given away by her stepfather. With John at her side, towering a foot above her, Veronica looked even more petite and fragile. She weighed only about 6 or 7 stones and made 'an almost ethereal bride', one person said. It seemed as if a mere gust of wind catching her long tulle veil could have swept her billowing into the clouds. She carried a sweet-scented bouquet of gardenias, lilies-of-the-valley and freesias, and her veil was held in place by one of the dazzling Lucan family diamond tiaras.

It was a momentous day. Veronica had married her 'dream figure', she had joined the aristocracy and her name would now appear alongside John's in *Debrett*.

Yet years later, looking at her wedding photographs, she was quoted as saying: 'All I remember is how heavy that tiara was. It left me with a headache and a crick in my neck.'

At the reception at the Carlton Tower, members of the family lined up to greet the hundreds of guests who flowed in, many of them anxious to catch their first glimpse of John's bride. Caroline Hill thought she looked 'terribly pretty'. A late arrival, circulating amid the crush of people drinking champagne and eating caviar and smoked salmon canapes from the buffet, was the delectable Lady Zinnia.

The newly-weds spent their honeymoon in Istanbul, travelling there on the legendary Orient Express. Agatha Christie might have thought it a fitting start for a couple whose lives were to be rent apart by murder.

Their best man, John Wilbraham, said: 'I remember thinking right from their wedding day that I wouldn't have put high odds on that marriage working. I thought it was going to be an uphill struggle.'

Two months later, Pat Lucan – who had been a member of the Labour Government under Prime Minister Clement Attlee, and later Labour chief whip in the House of Lords – died suddenly, aged sixty-five. He and Kait, whose children had never once heard them have a row, had recently celebrated their thirty-fourth wedding anniversary.

John now succeeded to the earldom – becoming the 7th Earl of Lucan, Baron Bingham of Castlebar, Baron Bingham of Melcombe Bingham and a baronet of Nova Scotia. Veronica also moved up the ladder. Two months before she had been plain Miss Duncan. Her marriage had made her Lady Bingham. Now she was the Countess of Lucan.

Soon Veronica was pregnant, but that fact was yet to be discovered when, in February 1964, John flew to Miami with Bill. They had arrangements to make for the Miami to Nassau powerboat race taking place that April, and they also had ringside seats for the world heavyweight title fight between Sonny Liston and the young up-and-coming Muhammad Ali, then called Cassius Clay. Rather than stay alone at John's tiny flat, Veronica moved down the road to stay with Christina and her three-month-old baby daughter, Lucinda, at Chester Terrace.

The relationship between the two sisters seemed sunny at that stage and as in days of old they shared a bed, Bill and Christina's double. According to Christina, Veronica 'did not like' to sleep on her own.

But trouble was not long coming, and by the time Bill and John returned from their five-day jaunt to America – Clay having whipped Liston for the championship – they found themselves on either side of another battle.

That April, however, staying at the Racquet Club in Miami for the powerboat race, Veronica and Christina came face to face for the first time since the row and were, as usual, reconciled.

That autumn, as the birth of Veronica's first child approached, she moved into the London Clinic. In the middle of her labour, according to a story she told later, a nurse slapped her on the stomach and said: 'Come on, grin and bear it. Your mother did it for you.'

'I wish she hadn't,' Veronica replied.

At which the nurse gave 'a demoniacal laugh' and was instantly silenced by Veronica declaring: 'I shan't tip *you*!'

A mother who was at the clinic at the same time said: 'I thought it showed real wit to say something like that in mid-labour. Veronica was very humorous telling that story. She might have been tiny but she was very wiry and strong. The nurses said she had fantastic guts because she was this petite little creature and she had a very big baby.'

The baby, a girl – Lady Frances Bingham – was born on 24 October.

'It was the unkindest blow of fate that George didn't arrive first because Veronica was frantic for the heir,' Christina said. 'But John was awfully sweet about it. He said: "I can't understand why Veronica was so upset. It simply didn't matter. I have nothing to leave a son anyway." There was the name but little else left of what his family had ever had.'

A letter which arrived that November pressing John for £1,400 to finish paying off £8,530 he'd lost gambling at the Clermont Club shortly after the honeymoon was a foretaste of the future. Yet another glimpse of what lay ahead came that December. By then the Lucans had moved from Park Crescent to the house at 46 Lower Belgrave Street. On 5 December *The Times* reported that detectives were investigating the theft of £2,000 worth of jewellery from the bedroom on the second floor. The jewels were apparently family heirlooms which Kait had handed down to Veronica after the wedding. The police found no sign of a forced entry to the house – just as they found no sign of a forced entry when Sandra Rivett was murdered near the safe ten years later.

Could there have been a door-key in existence which was never traced? Curiously, neither of the two senior officers on the murder squad seemed aware of the earlier crime at the scene where Sandra was killed – by an intruder John claimed was probably 'a burglar'.

Veronica set about transforming the Lucans' first proper home into 'a miniature castle in Belgravia'. Up went the ancestral portraits and out came the Georgian family silver. On the first floor, the L-shaped drawing room was given a yellow and green colour scheme, and to furnish it several little antique French gilt chairs and a sofa with lemon silk covers were bought for thousands of pounds from Malletts in New Bond Street. John rather hoped that another major furnishing item might turn up free.

'He had great expectations of Mrs Tucker,' said a friend, grinning. 'When she asked what he'd like for a wedding present, he had in mind a set of dining room chairs. But what she had in mind was something quite different that was infinitely smaller. So John was always making jokes about the dining room chairs that never arrived.'

Like many outrageously rich people, Mrs Tucker was no spendthrift, and Uncle John never forgot the time she bought an old car from him and 'quibbled' about an odd hundred pounds. Nevertheless, the Lucans were ever-grateful for her kindness to the family over a span of thirty years.

Seeking a new nanny for Frances, Veronica applied to

the Beauchamp Bureau in Beauchamp Place and late in February 1965 Miss Lilian Jenkins arrived at number 46 for an interview. Miss Jenkins, who came from Gwent and still had a strong Welsh accent, had a short, matronly figure and brown hair. She was then aged about fifty-five, but because she had her hair tinted regularly and had a cheerful, relaxed disposition she seemed younger. As John would have admitted, the Lucans could scarcely have found anyone better. Miss Jenkins adored children, she revered God, the Queen and the Establishment, and she delighted in nature's gifts like warm, summer sunshine and the sight and smell of flowers. In short she was a thoroughly nice, decent woman and a 24-carat-gold British nanny of the old school. She had worked previously for a member of the Dewars whisky family in Tunbridge Wells; she had looked after the five children of banker James Guinness, including Prince Charles' later girlfriend Sabrina; and most recently she had been nanny to Sholto, the son of Princess Margaret's author-friend Robin Douglas-Home and his wife Sandra Paul, the model. The only reason she was looking for a new job was because the couple were splitting up.

'Ah!' said Veronica, piecing together details she had heard earlier from the agency, 'now I know who's getting divorced!'

Frances at four months and later was a pretty little girl with fair hair and an appealing smile. Miss Jenkins was hooked the moment she peered into her organdie-frilled Harrods cot.

'What a lovely baby you've got,' she said.

It was later agreed that Miss Jenkins would move in as the new resident nanny towards the end of March. She would have a room above the nursery at the top of the house, she would be paid £8 a week and her day off, in accordance with the nannies' tradition in London, would be Thursday. Robin Douglas-Home still wanted Nanny to look after Sholto part-time, every third weekend, and Veronica agreed.

At Lower Belgrave Street, Nanny Jenkins swiftly

established her routine. She would rise at about 7.00 a.m., get Frances up, attend to her feeds in the nursery and after lunch take her for walks in her pram. Often they went to St James's Park to feed the ducks and to Buckingham Palace to watch the Changing of the Guard and to listen to the marches played by the Guards bands. Sometimes other nannies and their charges would come for tea in the nursery on the third floor and sometimes Nanny and Frances would pay return visits to other people's houses for tea. On Thursdays Miss Jenkins would meet her friends – usually other nannies – go shopping, have her hair done or visit one of her sisters who lived in Sevenoaks, Kent. And every third weekend, while a relief nanny replaced her at number 46, she would get the train to Pulborough in Sussex where Robin Douglas-Home would pick her up in his car and drive her to his country house, Meadow Brook. There she would look after Sholto while he attended to weekend guests like David Frost.

The Lucans also established a regular pattern of life. Veronica, now a lady of leisure, invariably stayed in bed until midday when she would come downstairs to cook lunch for herself and Nanny.

To Miss Jenkins, number 46 seemed a 'very quiet' house. She saw very little of Lady Lucan at first. More often than not, after lunch Veronica went back to her bedroom. Often, when she was around the house, Veronica wore a fur bonnet and sometimes a tweed overcoat as well. She told Miss Jenkins it was to give her 'confidence'.

John was a creature of habit and by 9.00 a.m., he would be up and dressed and down in the breakfast room in the basement. He would make coffee, sometimes taking a cup up to Veronica in bed, and then spend his mornings dealing with letters, reading the newspapers and playing the upright piano. He preferred classical music, particularly Bach, but he also taught himself to play Scott Joplin rags – a fact he kept from most of his male friends who, according to Dominick Elwes, would have found it 'soppy'. Often he went for a run in the park to keep fit and in the early days, when he had his Doberman pinscher Otto, he would take him for walks and try to train him to obey commands. Apart from savaging other dogs, Otto was a benign great beast and John loved him.

'He'd have to have a Doberman, he couldn't possibly have had a spaniel,' said one friend smiling. 'John always had to be different.'

During the week he invariably lunched out, usually at the Clermont gaming club founded by John Aspinall in Berkeley Square, and he would make his way there at midday dressed casually in flannels and often a soft white polo-necked sweater.

The Clermont occupied an elegant eighteenth-century house with a marble staircase and painted ceilings which had been designed around 1742 by the architect William Kent. It had been modelled in part on a Venetian palace and built for a royal mistress, Lady Isabella Finch. The white-wigged ghost of Lady Isabella's major-domo was reputed to haunt the premises, though less often than Lucan who became 'one of the fixtures'. John knew the staff by name and was regarded by them as a club 'favourite' with his unfailing courtesy and good manners.

Below the Clermont was the fashionable nightclub Annabel's, reputedly host to five kings on one night and 'perhaps the most exclusive nightclub in the Western world'. Owned by John Aspinall's Old Etonian friend Mark Birley, the club was named after his wife (later the wife of Sir James Goldsmith) Lady Annabel Vane-Tempest-Stewart, granddaughter of the legendary political hostess Lady Londonderry. When John and his friends weren't upstairs gambling, they'd often be downstairs drinking or dancing at Annabel's.

Among the men John lunched with regularly over the years in the restaurant at the Clermont were Dominick Elwes, John Aspinall, Stephen Raphael, racing correspondent Charles Benson, Ian Maxwell-Scott, and Dan Meinertzhagen, the son of a merchant banker. Others who might join them included multi-millionaire tycoon Jimmy (later Sir James) Goldsmith, Greville Howard, the Earl of

Suffolk and Berkshire, Prince Charles' friend and extra equerry Nicholas Soames, who was the grandson of Sir Winston Churchill, backgammon champion Philip Martyn and the racing driver Graham Hill. While Aspinall owned the club, John and many of his gambling friends were on the 'free list' which meant they enjoyed some of the best fare in London for nothing.

At lunchtime John would down his first vodka of the day. Like James Bond, his tastes were specific. He preferred the Russian vodka, Stolichnaya, advertised as 'The Vodka of the Tsars', which he liked served neat in a martini glass. For lunch he would usually order soup or smoked salmon with a main course of fillet steak rare or grilled lamb chops, cold en gelée in summer, with a white wine, Sancerre. He chose cheese to follow if there was a good Brie or Camembert and he would finish the meal with a glass of vintage port, Croft '60, a chilled Framboise, or a Mirabelle – which is a French liqueur with the flavour of plum. He seldom smoked cigars but his favourite brand of cigarette was Peter Stuyvesant, conveniently for a later fugitive 'the international passport to smoking pleasure'.

Dominick Elwes and Charles Benson were the jokers and when they were on form the men at the lunch table rocked with laughter. As 'court jester' to rich people who gave him their patronage, Dominick returned good measure. He had a brilliant wit and a talent as a raconteur and mimic which Kenneth Tynan later compared to Peter Ustinov's. Underneath, like so many funny men, there was a darker side, a 'manic-depressive' personality which required in-patient psychiatric treatment and sometimes turned his thoughts to suicide. But in those days Dominick managed to keep the demon at bay and successfully rode his highs and lows. The all-male lunches were characterised by banter and insults, each man being ribbed in turn. John criticised Charles Benson in a jocular vein for not wearing a hat at the racetrack which 'a gentleman ought to'. Lucan himself was teased about the untrendy image he liked to project.

His Clermont friends nicknamed him 'The Old Fossil' and declared that his ambition was 'to be eighty and an old club bore'.

After lunch, he would play backgammon at the club, perhaps watch a race on television and then return home to have a bath and change into a dark suit before going back to the Clermont. At about 9.00 p.m., in her finery and jewels, Veronica would join him there for dinner. Then they would mount the marble staircase to the gaming tables upstairs, where she would sit for hours drinking champagne on a banquette nicknamed 'the widows' bench' while John gambled.

During the Lucans' engagement celebration at the Mirabelle restaurant in Curzon Street, Stephen Raphael had asked her: 'Don't you mind marrying a man who doesn't go to work, who gambles for a living?'

'I don't care,' she had said. 'He can do what he likes.'

Early in the marriage another friend made a similar remark. 'Amazing decision of yours to marry John,' he said to Veronica in front of them both. 'I mean he goes out and gambles every afternoon. That must be an awful bore really.'

'I think you must understand that this is a profession,' John answered for her. 'I go out and *work* every afternoon. We all have a job of work in life, they all happen to be different, and this is mine. And I work as hard at that as you do at your job. After all,' he added, lightening the conversation, 'in another job I wouldn't be able to take Otto for a walk.'

Charles Sweeny said long after: 'Gambling is a vice like smoking and drinking. But it wasn't a fun thing with him – it was a business. Luke was a good gambler.'

Now that Veronica no longer had to work for a living, she painted a little, tried golf for a while, and went fox hunting with the Shand Kydds, who were avid supporters of the Whaddon Chase Hunt. John bought her a bay hunter, which they named Travelling Light, and later a more docile animal called Bombproof.

The Lucans also owned racehorses, including one

called Le Merveilleux II. A woman friend recalled: 'It was Veronica who would say: "John's bought two mares in France" or "John gave me an emerald and diamond brooch." He would just say: "I'm going to race this weekend" and you would then discover he was going to Deauville and you would only find out later that they were *his* horses they were going to watch. That was typical of John.'

It was at Deauville in 1966 that Vittorio de Sica spotted John in the casino and wanted to launch him as a movie star opposite Shirley MacLaine in his forthcoming production *Woman Times Seven*. 'I suppose he was looking around for a typically square Englishman,' John told a reporter, somewhat bemused.

The original idea was that he should play a young British diplomat at the United Nations, vying for the heroine's favours with an Italian delegate – who was to have been played by Vittorio Gassman. In their big scene, after watching Miss MacLaine do yoga on her bedroom floor, the rivals were to come to blows – very un-Lucan-like. John was known to get angry with golf caddies and inattentive waiters at times but he'd never been known to throw a punch at anyone.

Nevertheless, as Miss MacLaine told the Press: 'Mr de Sica can make anybody act and he thinks Lord Lucan is great.'

Billing on the film credits would have run: '. . . and introducing LORD LUCAN'. His friends must have loved it.

Rating his chances of becoming a star at about fifty to one, John flew to Paris for a screen test that September – and failed.

'He was very philosophical about not getting the part,' a film company official said later. 'He laughed about it, and it was *just* the kind of laughter and expression de Sica was looking for! The trouble was that before the cameras he just froze up.'

In the early days of their marriage, the Lucans entertained at home.

John's childhood friend Juliet Hill, who was married to Caroline Hill's brother Robin, recalled: 'The one dinner party we had at their house was fantastic with what seemed like sixty-two chefs and cooks and everything. It was all done in tremendous style. They had a butler and a footman in livery and four courses at least with lots of different wines. I would think we were ten at the table and there was silver everywhere. Veronica was a good hostess. Her dress was so beautiful I should think it was from Bellville Sassoon, and she looked smashing.'

Another couple arriving for dinner one night remembered glancing down through the basement window on their way to the front door, and seeing the hired chef busy preparing the meal in the kitchen. 'One was amused that John had obviously got the best chef available, one good enough to wear a tall white hat,' they said. 'That was just like him. The rest of us would just get a little person, whoever we could, to help out in the back.'

But though people went home impressed, few could remember Veronica being relaxed or chatty. Curiously, however, she came into her own when men were not around. One evening when John and a Coldstream friend went off together to a regimental dinner, Veronica and the other wife went out to a restaurant in Chelsea.

'Veronica and I dined *à deux* at La Popote,' the other woman said. 'It was the only time I got her by herself and she was intelligent, vivacious and amusing. When I got home I told my husband: "My gosh, we've got Veronica wrong. She's fun!" In fact, she was such fun that I made a mental note to go out with her again. But the next time I saw her was at some other dinner party with John and she was the same as she'd always been before — monosyllabic.'

After the murder, reporters conjured up dazzling visions of 'society dinner parties with titled friends in Belgravia'. But Veronica painted a different picture. Years on, older and perhaps wiser, she was quoted as saying: 'Having a title is a millstone round your neck. You're constantly living up to an image of what people expect you to be, and not what you really are. You are sitting there at a dinner party trying to prevent the coronet slipping from your head.'

9

If the truth were known, even Cinderella might have lived to rue the day she married her prince and didn't settle for a semi in the suburbs with Buttons. Marrying into a different social class is likely to cause problems for anyone. A degree of snobbery, for example, was common in John's circle, although there were limits. An Old Etonian friend remembered a time when John and others stayed on the French Riviera as guests of an American woman who was a notorious snob. Pushed beyond endurance, they rigged up a hidden tape recorder and then egged her on with comments like: 'And did you see the Prince of Wales?' to count how many names she could drop over dinner.

'John was an aristocrat of course and arrogant,' the friend said. 'He'd say to me: "We Binghams and Lucans have been around a long time, you know." I'd say: "Well actually, my family has too, although we're still plebs." And John would reply: "As long as you realise you're still plebs, that's the important thing." He'd talk like that but it was tongue-in-cheek.'

Another friend, John Wilbraham, said they used to 'laugh' about John's title. 'I remember when we were abroad, we'd always get a slightly better table if he booked it than for instance if I did,' he said, 'and he found that useful. But anyone who knew him well knew that he was the most unpompous person.'

For Veronica, however, the Lucan family's unpretentious ways seemed perhaps curious.

'Veronica didn't seem to expect aristocrats to be ordinary,' Sally and William said, 'to wash up and make beds like everyone else.'

According to John's brother, Hugh, Kait came in for 'severe criticism' from Veronica. One thing that rankled was the comfortable 'mess' John's mother lived in, surrounded with books.

'We were very different,' Kait said. 'We didn't think as Veronica did or enjoy the same things she did. If she had any illusions about joining the aristocracy she may have thought the title alone would be enough to have us dwelling in grand circumstances with chandeliers and so on. John certainly wouldn't have given her that impression. He would have been much more likely to have led her to expect that we lived in a garret on bread and water. Perhaps he said nothing and left it to her to imagine.'

Pat's mother Violet, the widow of the 5th Earl, was, however, another matter. She had originated from country stock and had risen up the social scale herself.

As Kait put it: 'My father-in-law's father [the 4th Earl of Lucan] was a villainous old man who did little but run up debts, not nearly as respectable in the proper sense as my mother-in-law's side of the family, but the Lucans were a different set. My mother-in-law came from the country, the sort of country-gentleman touch, and it's a different piece of the English framework. They were well-to-do people but they weren't *London* people. On the other hand, she had had this young English lady upbringing of a governess-bred kind which I had had.'

Violet's governess, according to John's Uncle John, was 'an extraordinary bossy old German called Miss Schmalz who had an enormous bosom, a wig and one of those magnifying pince-nez things and whose only claim to fame was that she was a friend of Brahms.'

Having been brought up remotely in the countryside as an only child under the domination of Miss Schmalz, he said, Violet was 'not a good mixer'.

'She led a very sheltered life, with a personal maid until she was ninety,' he said, 'and she tried nobly to keep up with the times but was shocked and appalled by mini-skirts and such. She was hypercritical, a natural pessimist and fastidious rather than snobbish – but she did like the sort of *select* titled people rather than some jumped-up knight.'

Though John's grandmother was loved and respected by

her family, meeting her must have seemed quite an ordeal for a newcomer. Uncle John's wife Dorothea, who described herself as 'the daughter of a penniless parson', remembered her own anxiety when she first visited Violet after their marriage. To her surprise, Violet pressed a diamond bracelet into her hand and didn't confess until much later that she had 'searched all the red books' – *Debrett, Burke's Peerage, Who's Who* – in vain for her pedigree. Dorothea's family wasn't listed. So social prestige wasn't everything to Violet.

'What she *didn't* like,' Dorothea said, 'was anything which was vulgar.'

When her son Pat had joined the Labour Party, Violet had regarded the matter as tantamount to a scandal. 'Unlike the rest of the family,' she had remarked stiffly at the time, 'he has always leaned a little to the Left.'

But John had put the Lucan line back on its true blue course, both in the aristocratic style in which he chose to live and also in terms of his political allegiance. Until she discovered he was a professional gambler, Violet regarded him as her favourite grandchild. He used to shower her with 'armfuls of lilies' and take Veronica to have tea with her at Orchard Court.

'Then they went rather less often,' Kait said. 'I think it just didn't go with a swing.'

According to Kait, Violet was 'much more grand than Pat in the way she lived, and very sophisticated'. Her clothes were impeccable, though long outmoded. She was aware of nuances of polite behaviour and etiquette which most of the rest of the world had largely forgotten or never known. And she was hypersensitive to any breach of the code of genteel conduct to which she subscribed. Violet didn't like Veronica because she wore 'too much' jewellery and 'chain smoked' at Orchard Court. Kait, who thought these were 'rather inadequate' reasons, remarked: 'I'm not sensitive to such things, but I know that my mother-in-law was. She did set the greatest possible store by what she thought were genteel manners, and anybody who slipped on any minor thing would jar her frightfully.'

Ironically, Veronica herself was hypersensitive to anything which she felt was less than her due as a countess, and acutely aware of social precedence.

A few weeks after the Lucans' third wedding anniversary, Veronica became pregnant again. Nanny Jenkins had never found her an easy mistress to please but now at number 46 the going got harder. George, the future 8th Earl of Lucan, was born at the London Clinic in the early hours of 21 September 1967. *The Times* carried the announcement of the birth and an immediate cable was despatched to the Shand Kydds, who were abroad, proclaiming the joyous news that the heir had arrived.

'Lady Lucan was elated about George,' Nanny Jenkins recalled. 'She rang me up when he was about a day old and said: "Come and see him", and she was all dolled up like a duchess when I arrived. Her room was like a film star's, almost ceiling to floor with gorgeous flowers and pot plants.'

Greville Howard, a friend of both the Lucans, had visited Veronica in hospital after the birth of George. By April 1968, Greville had met the girl who was to become his first wife – banker's daughter Zoe Walker, a pert seventeen-year-old blonde debutante and model who received the accolade of being chosen by the French couturier Lanvin to show his collection that July. In September they and other friends joined the Lucans for a two-week cruise in the Mediterranean on a 138-foot chartered yacht. The same month Greville and Zoe became engaged, and in December they married.

Months before then the Lucans had found themselves sailing into uncharted seas and approaching the point on the old maps which used to be marked: 'Beyond here there be dragons.'

10

By May 1968, John had become concerned at what he thought to be Veronica's disturbed state of mind. He wanted her to see a psychiatrist from The Priory private psychiatric clinic at Roehampton. Around that time, the Lucans drove down to Sussex. John was playing golf at Littlestone, and they stayed with his Uncle John and Aunt Dorothea at their isolated farm set in rolling countryside near Rye.

'John said Veronica was ill and he didn't want to take her to a hotel,' Dorothea said, 'so we invited them here.'

She liked Veronica but noticed how nervy she was, particularly when John was around – her hands shaking, her knife and fork jerking up and down at the table. Uncle John, an amusing, talkative man, remembered how difficult it was to make conversation with Veronica at a dinner party they held for the Lucans during their stay.

John's aunt recalled: 'I just thought she'd had too many children too quickly. I remember the day we were having the dinner party. John sent her back early from the golf course to get some rest beforehand. She took a taxi, but the woman driver lost the way in the country lanes and when John got back Veronica still hadn't arrived. He was terribly upset and worried about her and went straight out to look for her and bring her back.'

'He was touchingly anxious about her,' Uncle John said. 'He was devoted to her.'

Years later Veronica talked to the Press of the first time she arrived at The Priory, John having told her, she said, that they were merely 'going for a drive'. Medical staff were waiting but she refused to be admitted. She agreed, however, that she would have psychiatric treatment if she could be based at home.

'Only,' she was quoted as saying, 'because I wanted

[John] to see that I would co-operate. You see he told me that it was the sign of a mentally ill person when they refuse to recognise that they are ill and won't have treatment.'

Constantly worrying, as the years went by John took an obsessional interest in what he believed was Veronica's poor state of health. To begin with he didn't even know the difference between psychiatry and psychology, fields confused by many laymen. But he learned as he went along, collecting a small library of books and pamphlets over the years with titles which included: *A Short Textbook of Psychiatry, Psychiatry and Anti-Psychiatry, Stelazine in Psychiatry, Lithium in the treatment of mood disorders* and *The practical management of lithium treatment.*

'I think it started off with a genuine interest in me,' Veronica was quoted as saying. 'He studied me as he studied gambling and he was quite obsessive about anything in which he was interested. He didn't have an awful lot to occupy his mind and he read a lot of books so he became a sort of amateur psychiatrist.'

At Easter 1969 the Lucans visited Venice, Florence and Rome during a three-week trip to Italy and West Germany. According to Veronica, it was the only non-gambling holiday they ever had. The gambling had really got to her. Year in, year out in London, she spent most of her days in her bedroom and most of her evenings sitting drinking at the Clermont Club while John gambled, becoming ever more unhappy.

'I think she found it glamorous at first but then the glamour wore off,' William said.

Stephen Raphael said: 'At first she'd said she didn't mind John gambling, yet her chief complaint throughout the marriage was that he gambled.'

'It's no life for a young girl, let's face it,' said one gambler's wife. 'I hated that Clermont routine and I very seldom went there.'

'Unless you were incredibly beautiful or incredibly

101

witty or very rich as a woman, you didn't get an awful lot of attention at the Clermont,' said Michael Hicks Beach, a friend of John's from the club. 'People were nice to you, and as Veronica was the Countess of Lucan people were probably nicer to her than they would have been otherwise. But all the women there had to put up with the fact that it was an excessively male-orientated world. The men might be so busy gambling that they didn't stop to chat to them, or they'd ring up and say: "Look darling, we're dining here not at home, please come round." And when you came to dine the conversation could be very boring because it was about who threw six-four and how the other one promptly threw six-two again and this sort of thing. Now that can be terribly tedious, though in fact it's no more tedious than any other businessman talking about how he just missed a £25,000 order on Leyland cars or whatever it happens to be. But there's no doubt at all that at the Clermont women did take second place and Veronica may not have liked that. In fact I know damn well she didn't.'

Chief Superintendent Ranson was among those long after who sympathised over Veronica's years as a gambler's wife.

'We haven't heard [Lucan's] story, except what we've got on [his secret tape recordings] and through his friends,' he told me, 'but when you hear her story about the breakdown of the marriage . . . You know, would *you* go night after night after night to the Clermont Club and have dinner with your husband and then [he'd] say: "Oh well, I'm going to play roulette or backgammon" or something and leave you sitting there like a lemon three or four hours? You'd do it once or twice or three times but come three years you'd say: "I've had enough of this", wouldn't you?'

Veronica didn't, though in later days she complained.

'She used to sit in a corner of the Clermont drinking champagne until 3.00 or 4.00 a.m., and nobody half the time talking to her,' one woman recalled. 'And I'd say to her: "Why do you sit there?" "Well, I'm waiting to go home with him." And I'd say: "But you're nuts. You're crying because you have no life, you don't know anyone your own age, you hate his gambling. Don't sit around there if it makes you miserable." She said: "It's the other women." I said: "He's never *looked* at another woman!" "Ah, but they look at him. Sooner or later . . ." And I said: "Look, he's too interested in his gambling." It's no easy life for a woman to be married to a gambler but one has to realise you can't change them. Gambling is a thing that's born with you, quite amazing. But basically gamblers are not great womanisers – most of their drive goes into gambling.'

Stephen Raphael said: 'Veronica used to follow John round when he was gambling because she was worried he'd get off with other girls. He was a handsome man but he wasn't interested in other women. If there'd been ten naked girls prancing around him he'd have taken no notice. All he cared about when he was out gambling was the game.'

Veronica made it clear later that people's sympathy for her as a gambler's wife was misplaced. She had enjoyed being at the Clermont because 'all human life was there' and she felt she shared 'a camaraderie' with the gamblers John knew. What worried her in fact was the thought that one day she might *not* be a part of John's club life.

'I used to think: "What happens when my looks start to go and he doesn't even want me to go to the club with him? What will I do then?"' she was quoted as saying. 'It might seem an enviable life to have a nanny to look after your children and someone to clean your house but then you think: "What is there left for me to do?"'

Aristocratic inactivity had driven even the indomitable Lady Astor into a decline years before until she found a lifeline in politics. Yet the example Kait set seemed lost on her daughter-in-law. Even when she reached her seventies, Kait was still busy with political activities, learning Russian for GCE exams, taking walking holidays abroad alone, collecting stuff for jumble sales and baking and icing Christmas cakes by the score for local charity bazaars. But Kait's advice to Veronica to develop her own interests fell largely on deaf ears.

One of the few things Veronica did at the house was to cook lunch.

Nanny Jenkins said: 'During the week she would cook fish fingers and frozen vegetables or something similar for lunch, or we'd have slices of ham warmed up between two plates. Lord Lucan wouldn't be in for lunch except at the weekends when the children were older, unless he was playing golf.

'His favourite meal on Saturdays was bangers and mash. On Sundays to begin with Lady Lucan would cook frozen beef slices in those tin foil things, but I think as the children grew older Lord Lucan suggested having lamb because after a while it was roast lamb and frozen peas on Sundays mostly. Lord Lucan would get the joint ready and put it in the oven and I'd switch it on. And very often after lunch what we hadn't eaten just got thrown in the ashcan. Lady Lucan wouldn't sort of do it up. And I remember Lord Lucan saying: "Most people make a shepherds pie out of what's left over for Monday." So in the evening he'd cut the meat up and get it ready for her to do that. He was wonderful really. Sometimes Lord Lucan would put the dishes in the dishwashing machine or else they were left for the daily. And he used to bring his socks and pullovers and that up himself and he'd put them into the washing machine and say to me: "Nanny, would you mind hanging the washing up for me when it's finished?" and I did. All the rest, even her smalls, went to the laundry and he used to take it.

'Ever since I went to the house,' Nanny said, 'Lady Lucan spent much of her time in bed. She practically lived in her bedroom, in a sort of twilight with the blinds drawn all day. She hardly ever went out in daytime. She lived a very odd life. It was when she was pregnant with George that she started getting more difficult, and it carried on all after that and just gradually seemed to get worse.

'She was very tense all the time. She hardly ever smiled. She'd never remark on the weather or say: "What a lovely day," and I never once heard her laugh – not once in all the years I was there.'

On 30 June 1970, at St Mary's hospital, Paddington, the Lucans' third child, Lady Camilla, was born. Someone who inquired about Veronica was told that she was 'very ill' and that only the closest relatives were allowed to visit her.

Almost a year later, at the end of April 1971, the Shand Kydds' three-year-old son, Caspar, who was a few weeks older than George, was rushed to hospital. The doctors diagnosed leukaemia. Veronica heard the news on 3 May, her thirty-fourth birthday, and was devastated.

Kait recalled: 'I remember John telling me that V was upset because she felt "guilty" for having normally healthy children when Christina was suffering this dreadul anxiety.'

'Lady Lucan was very funny for about twelve weeks after she found out about Caspar's leukaemia,' Nanny Jenkins said.

On 14 July 1971 Shane Alexander – now married to the Honourable Davina Woodhouse, a lady-in-waiting to Princess Margaret – married his first wife, Hilary van Geest, the banana heiress. Jane had flown in from New York for the wedding, and afterwards stayed with Sally and William at Guilsborough vicarage. Late one evening while they were there, and John was away golfing, Veronica rang the vicarage in a distraught state from Lower Belgrave Street.

Sally recalled: 'Veronica sounded desperate and said the world was against her. We all tried to soothe her and put Jane on the phone, Jane being a doctor.'

William said: 'She asked if Sally could go and join her immediately.'

Sally packed an overnight bag while the others tried to calm Veronica down on the phone. 'Be careful,' William said, kissing his wife goodbye. Sally drove 70 miles down the M1 in darkness, having no idea what to expect when she reached number 46.

'I found Veronica at home shaking and wide-eyed, pacing up and down the floor and wringing her hands . . . ,' Sally recalled. 'I was very frightened of being in the house with her that night. She said she wasn't going to sleep. I lay down on her bed but couldn't sleep.

'I sweated with fear the whole time I was there, expecting the tension to become an explosion. Veronica stayed in the drawing room and I could hear her footsteps pacing up and down as I tried to get some sleep. At 5.00 a.m., she bundled me out of the house saying she didn't want me there any longer.'

Nanny Jenkins had previously thought of quitting and now, once again, she told John that she would have to leave.

'Lady Lucan used to say: "*Now* we'll see how much you love Camilla!", playing me up,' Miss Jenkins recalled. 'If I thought enough of Camilla, I'd stay.'

As before, John asked Nanny: 'Try to stay for the childen's sake,' and, as before, Nanny agreed.

John urged Veronica to become a voluntary in-patient at a private psychiatric clinic. That summer, arrangements were made, her suitcase was packed and John took her to a nursing home in Hampstead. But when she got there, according to Press interviews she gave later, she noticed 'alarming-looking electric equipment' beyond a door marked Treatment Room, remembered she had heard that, 'once you had [ECT], you were never the same again', and changed her mind. She made an excuse, 'got away', caught a taxi and then walked round Regents Park before going home on her own.

11

In July 1972, the Lucans took their two eldest children to
Monte Carlo for a three-week holiday at the Hotel
Metropole. But only a week after they had left London,
Veronica flew home prematurely to consult the latest of
her psychiatrists.

Charles Sweeny, who was with them in Monte Carlo,
remembered John turning down his suggestion to 'get a
little Monegasque girl' to look after the children. 'Oh no
no – I'm on holiday *with* my children,' said John, who
looked after Frances and George, and gave them their
lessons himself.

Back in England, Nanny Jenkins was on holiday with
Camilla at Westgate-on-Sea, and the house at Lower
Belgrave Street was empty. So Veronica went to stay at
the Shand Kydds' house in Cambridge Square, to which
they had moved from Chester Terrace. Christina went
with her to see the current psychiatrist, Dr Ann Dally.

Though there were long periods when Christina was
'*persona non grata*' with Veronica, the two sisters had
been seeing more of each other than usual at around that
time. For about two years the Shand Kydds were separated
to the extent that, although they spent their weekends
together with the children at Grove, during the week in
London Bill lived at a separate address. Veronica took to
visiting Christina regularly.

'She came back into my life in a big way when she
discovered I was living at Cambridge Square alone,'
Christina said. 'By that time her relationship with John
had obviously broken down considerably and she'd go on
endlessly about how she hated him and all the rest of it.
Sometimes it was a fear that he was going to leave her.
She had this tremendous fear of that.

'And I used to say: "But why do you think he should

want to leave you? I mean you always say there's nothing wrong with you, so why should he want to go?" And she used to say: "Well, he says I'm mad. He says I'm mad." And I'd say: "Well, you haven't been very well." And she'd say: "Oh, he's made me like that. He's made me like that because he's always trying to shut me in places."'

Christina disagreed with Veronica's belief that John was at the root of her problems. She felt that John was desperate to help Veronica.

As Christmas approached, Sally went to London to do some shopping and arranged to have lunch with Veronica. Instead of coffee and a sandwich at number 46, which Sally thought would save expense, Veronica decided they should eat in style at La Popote in Chelsea. She seemed to be on one of her 'highs', talkative and restless.

'It was a terrible lunch for me,' Sally recalled. 'Veronica kept changing tables. We would sit down at one and she would say no, it wasn't any good, and we spilt the flowers and moved to another table. We had a heart-to-heart talk during the meal, and Veronica went on about how she had wanted to get into "the stud book". I hadn't heard the expression before, but she meant that her name was now in *Debrett*.'

Though many staff had come and gone from number 46, Nanny Jenkins had now been there for seven years. But on Friday, 1 December 1972, while John was away, Veronica fired her at short notice. The reason behind the sacking has always been disputed but Nanny Jenkins claimed that it was a misunderstanding over a telephone call whilst Lady Lucan maintained, among other causes, that Nanny kept a bottle of sherry in her room.

Fortunately, although it was just before Christmas, Nanny was able to get a room at the Helena Club near Sloane Square, where nannies used to meet in those days. But by the next day, part of her thumb, where she had accidentally cut herself, had swollen up like an angry purple bilberry and she went to have it examined at St George's hospital.

By Sunday the blood poisoning had begun to spread up her arm and when she returned to the hospital to have the wound dressed she was admitted immediately for an operation.

'I heard someone say that it was lucky I hadn't lost my arm,' she said. 'That cheered me up a lot, I must say!'

Veronica must have taken the rest of Miss Jenkins' belongings to the Helena Club and discovered where she was because a day or two later she appeared at the hospital carrying a red umbrella.

'I think it was to give her confidence,' Nanny said.

By the time John returned home and discovered she had been fired, Miss Jenkins had already been in hospital for about two weeks. He hurried to St George's full of concern to see her.

'I only found out half an hour ago and I came straight here,' he said. 'How are you? Tell me what happened.'

Nanny did.

She remembered afterwards how squeamish he was about her thumb following her operation. Months later, when it had healed, he couldn't even bear the sight of the scar – and asked if she would mind covering it with a plaster.

'He was squeamish about anything medical or messy,' Bill and Christina said. 'He couldn't stand the sight of blood either. When dogs fought and there was blood everywhere, he made no pretence about it. He just said: "I simply can't stand it."'

Before John left the hospital that day he made sure Nanny had enough money to pay for her room at the Helena Club. His parting words were:

'If there is ever anything I can do to help you, let me know.'

In days to come, whenever she approached him, he never let her down.

In a reference he wrote for her later he stated that Miss Jenkins had been dismissed 'at ten minutes' notice without my knowledge and against my wishes', said that she had been 'at all times totally trustworthy, loyal, discreet, industrious and dependable' and gave her 'the highest possible recommendation'.

If nothing else, at least Nanny was at last free from the trials and tribulations of life at Lower Belgrave Street.

But John wasn't.

12

There's nothing quite like Christmas to set people at each other's throats. Suicide, marital breakdown, family crises: the season of 'goodwill to all men' is a boom period for them all. For the Gibbses, Christmas 1972 was a nightmare never to be forgotten. For the Lucans, it became the point of no return.

Sally and William had invited John and Veronica to join the festivities at the vicarage with them and their four children, Kait and Nanny Coles. With Frances, George and Camilla, that meant there would be an ominous thirteen.

Telephone messages to Guilsborough from Lower Belgrave Street as the holiday drew near were confusing. The Lucans were coming, then they were not coming, then they *were* coming.

Faced with organising rooms for everyone, and planning the Christmas meals, it wasn't until the last minute that Sally knew definitely whether to expect them or not.

In many ways, Guilsborough vicarage was a perfect setting for an old-fashioned family Christmas. A big log fire crackling in the drawing room, dogs sprawled on the carpet round the hearth. A huge Christmas tree garlanded with gifts standing in front of the French windows, the wintry grounds beyond. Carols round the grand piano, which Sally and John sometimes played together. Meals at the ancient refectory table in the dining room, or round the kitchen table – the elderly Nanny Coles huddling next to the huge old Aga cooking range, complaining about draughts in country houses. Children and pets everywhere, good wholesome cooking and plenty to drink, the church bells ringing from St Etheldreda's on the hill calling the faithful to Christmas services. Almost ideal.

But from the day the Lucans arrived on Friday, 22 December, a whole series of family disputes disrupted the festivities. On Boxing Day, earlier than planned, John drove Veronica and the children back to London to the relief of all concerned.

Within two weeks, in January 1973, the Lucans separated.

At first, John moved to the mews cottage in Eaton Row. Then, after a New Year holiday with friends in Acapulco, he rented the £140-a-week flat at 72a Elizabeth Street nearby, which was large enough for himself, the children, and a resident nanny. From this point on, his one consuming desire was to gain custody of Frances, George and Camilla.

The way he went about it is very telling when viewed against the later alleged events of the murder night.

John was determined to gain the children legally; he made certain they would not be exposed to the risk of witnessing any unpleasant scene at number 46; his planning was done with his usual meticulous attention to detail; and the operation was carried out with total success, nothing botched.

He instructed solicitors and a firm of private inquiry agents and Friday, 23 March 1973 was earmarked as the day for getting the children back under his own wing. At noon, on that day, a private detective went to 72a Elizabeth Street. John handed him photographs of Veronica and Camilla and went over the pre-arranged plan again. That afternoon, he explained, having made an ex-parte application to the High Court, he expected to be granted an order giving him interim care and control of Frances, George and Camilla. The detective's task was to keep track of Camilla's whereabouts (Frances and George would presumably be at school) and report back so that once the order had been made, John could take physical custody immediately. He planned quite deliberately to take charge of the children before they returned home to number 46 and Veronica.

'It was the only way to take possession of them so that there was no risk of an unpleasant physical violent scene at the house,' Bill said, 'and this was done with the full cognisance of the court. I mean John wasn't going to turn up at the house with a court order. There could have been a fight and it would have been in front of the children, which is something he would never have allowed.'

The detective and a colleague began watch on number 46, and at 1.50 p.m. their wait was rewarded when a fair-haired girl apparently in her late-twenties left the house with Camilla, who was strapped into a push-chair, and with George, who for some reason had been at home. The girl turned out to be a temporary nanny named Miss Stefanja Sawicka who had been recruited earlier that month from the agency Knightsbridge Nannies of Beauchamp Place. The private eyes shadowed her and the children until they eventually reached Green Park, where the nanny unstrapped Camilla and let her run free with George while she sat nearby reading.

A message was relayed to John that his two youngest children were both in Green Park. By that time, he had obtained the necessary court order from Mr Justice Arnold and was legally entitled to take custody. At 3.45 p.m., Miss Sawicka left the park with George and Camilla and walked through to Constitution Hill with the two private eyes and John in discreet pursuit. At 4.00 p.m., when the group reached Grosvenor Place, John approached the nanny and spoke to her briefly. He then dismissed the detectives and drove off with the girl and the two children in his car. Frances was collected from school later.

Veronica's description later of the way John took custody was that, armed with the court order, he had 'hired two "heavies" and snatched' the children from the nanny in the park.

For the next three months, before both the Lucans put their case at the full custody hearing in June, the children lived with their father at Elizabeth Street.

John helped them with school work; wrote to one of Frances's teachers about her difficulties with French, despite the fact that he'd been 'employing a French girl for forty-five minutes a day as many weekdays as possible' to give her extra tuition; went through red tape with the Home Office to try and extend the stay in Britain of a

Yugoslav girl named Jordanka Kotlarova, whom he had chosen to be the children's nanny; and contacted his old friend Caroline Hill, a piano teacher, to ask her to give Frances lessons.

'I hadn't seen him for ages and ages,' Caroline said. 'He got in touch out of the blue and said he wanted me to help Frances with her music since he was worried about her progress with the piano at school. I agreed and we began the lessons immediately during the Easter holidays.'

At Lower Belgrave Street, however, life was far from rosy and a battalion of some twenty hired nurses streamed in and out of number 46 on successive shifts to be with Veronica round the clock for practically three solid months.

Not that she spent the whole time at the house. On 13 April she went to stay briefly with the Shand Kydds at Grove. And on Monday, 16 April, she voluntarily went into The Priory psychiatric clinic at Roehampton for about a week. This may well have been so that her current psychiatrist, Dr John Flood, could make an up-to-date assessment on her for his medical report to be presented to the forthcoming custody hearing.

One newspaper to which Veronica later gave interviews implied that it was Dr Flood 'who was able to establish that she was not schizophrenic and did not need Moditen'. To another, she said she was 'grateful to the last doctor . . . [who] saw that it was unnecessary and I stopped taking the drug'.

Dr Flood did, however, feel that Veronica required some psychiatric support.

At Lower Belgrave Street, the local vicar had also provided support and it soon bore fruit. Veronica turned to religion. In May, when Christina phoned to invite her out to dinner, she was surprised to hear Veronica announce that she was getting confirmed, and would bring the vicar along with her.

John had kept 'Aunt Marcia' Brady Tucker in touch with

events and on 6 May he wrote to her outlining the situation. Part of his letter read:

Dear Aunt Marcia,
    I meant to write to you after your telephone call at Easter but there has been very little to add to what I told you then.
    As you know, I was awarded interim 'care and control' of the children on March 23rd pending a full hearing of the case. That full hearing will start on June 11th. The best result for me would be to be given permanent 'care and control' with 4 weeks access for her – that is to say she would have them for 2 weeks in the summer and a week at Christmas and Easter. The worst result would be the return of the children to her with virtually unlimited access to me.
    Both these extremes are unlikely for the following reasons: during the last month she has been under the care of a psychiatrist who has persuaded her to take a drug called Lithium. This drug . . . has had a beneficial effect on Veronica. The argument will therefore be that although the judge's decision to take the children away from her on March 23rd was correct, she is now a cured person and should have them back. Even if the judge did not go that far, he would have difficulty in refusing her a good deal of access.
    On my side I have the very strong evidence of my own family, George and Camilla's headmistresses, the ex-nanny and of course Veronica's psychiatric record going back to 1962 (before I met her). We will argue that the Lithium which she is taking is only alleviation . . .; what happens when she comes off the drug?
    We do have against us the natural inclination of most judges to award children to the mother, but I have the best Q.C. in the country working for me and what is more important, he is not a lawyer with a reputation for being too brilliant on behalf of his

client right or wrong; the judges all respect him. The fact also, that by the time the case comes up, the children will have been with me for the best part of three months, and that they are happy and contented, will weigh very much with me . . .

So much for my domestic problems but I think of nothing else.

Love,
J.

As additional evidence for the custody case, John used a hidden tape recorder to make secret tapes of his conversations and exchanges with Veronica.

He also asked Michael Hicks Beach – who had quit gambling in 1970 and become a literary agent – to help him compose his statement to the court.

Michael said: 'Although he felt he had a strong case against Veronica for the children, his worry was that his mode of life, being a professional gambler and a club man, would influence the judge against him. He called on me as an ex-professional gambler and also somebody with slightly more literary ability than he had, to, as it were, put his defence into words. He knew what he wanted to say but he didn't quite know how to say it. At that point, John was fairly confident, I think, that he was going to get the children. He was fanatic about them, and he genuinely felt that he should bring them up. When I went to John's flat, he showed me Veronica's medical reports. I seem to remember that she had had about six psychiatrists, and I think he had a report from every single one of them, apart from the new one. I read a couple of the reports, not all of them, and then John commented on the lot.'

The diagnoses of the various psychiatrists who had seen Veronica over the years differed – which is not unusual.

Michael said: 'I think John was hoping that the medical reports would influence the judge to say that Veronica was not a "fit" person to look after her children.'

But John was not prepared to go into battle without first having a heart-to-heart talk with Veronica's mother to explain the situation from his standpoint. He told Mrs Margrie how worried he was about Veronica – and how worried he was about the children.

Christina recalled: 'But he did not ask us to give evidence at the custody case on his behalf. He said: "I would never presume to ask either of you. To put a mother or a sister in that situation would be intolerable. Appear for Veronica. Appear for the Official Solicitor. Or don't appear at all. I could not ask you to appear for me. It would not be fair."'

Christina and Mrs Margrie were left entirely free, when they were approached by Veronica's side, to give evidence for her.

The case, heard in secret, came up before a different judge, sixty-seven-year-old Mr Justice Rees, on Monday, 11 June, and went on through that week and into the next. As the matter dragged on, the legal costs facing John, who paid for Veronica's costs as well, spiralled to an estimated £20,000 – and he felt forced to concede.

Under stringent conditions, the children were ordered to be returned to their mother, with access for their father every other weekend. Worse than the worst John had envisaged had happened. He strode out of the courtroom ahead of Veronica. She last saw him sitting on a bench, his head in his hands, beaten. 'It was horrible . . .' she said later.

John was desolate. He complained about the lawyers, he complained about the judge, he complained about some of the witnesses. For hours he sat brooding alone at Elizabeth Street and, when others saw him, he could talk of nothing but the case, Veronica, and the children, the children, the children . . .

'His expression changed completely for about a month,' Nanny Jenkins said. 'He didn't smile and he looked older. His faith in the law was quite shaken.'

'The court case was desperate for him,' Caroline Hill said. 'He couldn't believe, *none* of us could believe, that it would go against him.'

John Wilbraham said: 'I remember endless discussions with him about the custody case. He did very much give the impression that the cards were stacked against him, that no matter what you do as a man, the woman always has more power in claiming custody of the children.'

Bill recalled: 'The consensus of opinion was that if the case had continued, John would in all probability have lost it. And the consensus of opinion was equally that if he had lost it, it would have been chiefly on Christina's evidence. She gave evidence for her sister.'

As Christina remarked later: 'Blood is thicker than water.'

'I did not perjure myself in any way,' she said, 'but I proffered nothing that wasn't asked. I did say very clearly that I thought Veronica was capable of looking after the children *with* medical treatment.'

Others felt it was mainly the evidence of Dr Flood which had the strongest effect. After the case, John complained bitterly about Flood.

The children were returned to their mother at the beginning of July, just after Camilla's third birthday. According to Christina, they had hardly got back to number 46 when Veronica rang her, said she had the children and 'couldn't cope', and asked her to get round to the house quickly . . .

Christina said: 'I was absolutely appalled that any court could have just chucked the children back into the house like that, with no question of the fact that perhaps Veronica needed a holiday or a rest before she could cope. It just seemed to me to be absolutely monstrous. At that particular moment in time, there was absolutely no way that Veronica was fit to look after the children, no way in a million billion years.'

The best way round the problem at number 46 seemed to be to have the whole lot at Grove. Christina told Veronica: 'I can look after you and you can have plenty of rest and plenty of sleep and plenty of food and calm down. And the children will be all right because they're perfect ages for mine and very fond of each other, and your nanny will be there and my nanny too so they'll have company for each other as well.'

After an earlier argument, Bill had refused to have Veronica on his property. However, concerned about Frances, George and Camilla, he relented. The family visited on the weekend of 6 July, and on 23 July, after the school term ended, Bill's chauffeur, Dave Church, drove them all back to Grove to spend part of the summer holidays in the country with the Shand Kydds.

The day they arrived, the children's new nanny, a girl called Hazel, announced she was giving her notice immediately. She had had the job for exactly twenty-one days. For Christina it was almost the last straw. Her nanny, Diana, was paid to look after two children, not five 'rampaging round the house'.

'Veronica's three children were very sweet and lovely,' Christina said, 'but they'd led a pretty strange life and they weren't exactly what you might call easy to control. And they had definite scars. There were problems with George. Frances was terribly gay and roared with laughter but she was very wary and seemed to be forever on the watch. And little Camilla was very clinging. I literally couldn't spend a penny without Camilla coming in with me – she wouldn't leave me . . .'

Hazel was replaced on or about 24 July by an Irishwoman, Mrs Elizabeth Murphy, who put the wind up Christina soon after she arrived by asking to be brought a half bottle of whisky from the shops at Leighton Buzzard. Mrs Murphy was to become known for her drinking. In London she had a room at the Irish Club, quite close to number 46, where she took 'sundowners', drinks at twilight, which according to one claim 'left her incapacitated by 9.00 p.m.'

Christina, who never saw her drunk, felt her reputation was undeserved – though John might not have agreed.

Later on, he used Mrs Murphy's fondness for alcohol to try to prise information from her in his continuing search for fresh 'evidence' to take the custody case back to court.

13

Anxious about the children, John began to keep an eye on number 46.

Frances had continued to have piano lessons on Wednesday afternoons from Caroline Hill, and Caroline and John met regularly. She was among many others who knew he kept watch on the house.

'I would go out to dinner with John once every three weeks or so to discuss Frances's progress, and he would talk of the children for hours on end,' she said. 'And after dinner, without fail, we would drive past the house in Lower Belgrave Street. He never went in when he was with me – he just wanted to see that everything was all right. Eventually Veronica stopped Frances coming to me for piano lessons, and John was very upset about it because Frances was actually getting rather good. He was afraid that another pupil would take Frances's place, so he suggested he should take her lesson so that it would always be available for Frances if Veronica changed her mind. That is the sort of man he was.'

As John's snooping trips outside number 46 became common knowledge, so did his financial problems. With an estranged wife, three children, a resident nanny and three properties to support, plus the legal fees from the custody case to pay, he now *had* to win at the gaming tables.

But with his private life in turmoil, that became harder. His luck and skill began to desert him, and the problems increased when he started chasing his losses. He became deeply in debt – though he was such a soft touch that he still couldn't refuse to help friends in need, one of whom borrowed £5,000.

Meanwhile, the children once again had a new nanny. Mrs Elizabeth Murphy had stayed for about two weeks as a temporary before being replaced in August 1973 by two Spanish girls, apparently called Tina and Theresa. They had lasted for about fifteen weeks, and now a new temporary nanny called Christabel Martin had moved to Lower Belgrave Street.

Caroline Hill recalled: 'John was hoping very much that with the succession of nannies at the house, he could go back to court and regain the children. I think he thought that by Christmas time, he would have the children again. However, then he told me that James Comyn [his QC at the custody hearing, and later a judge] had said there really wasn't enough evidence to take back to court yet.'

By then, however, a new idea had been born, though who first suggested it to John is unclear. What Veronica really wanted, he maintained, was her title, status and money. Well, she would have it – and he would have the children. He hoped to persuade Mrs Tucker to help him buy Veronica off.

John flew to America to outline his proposition to 'Aunt Marcia' in New York; and on 24 November, back in London, he wrote a letter to her son, the Reverend Luther Tucker, who was then in Germany. Part of it read:

> I regret having to involve you and your family in my domestic problems, but I did everything I possibly could in court and although we did not have judgement given against us (we conceded after 2 weeks ruinous court action) we ran into a brick wall in the shape of the current psychiatrist; if I could have afforded to battle on, win or lose, there would have been an appeal and if we were still successful in keeping the children there would have been nothing to prevent her going to court once a year to ask for the children back.

John's proposed solution to the problem, as outlined in the letter, was that Veronica should be offered a maximum of a small flat in London, the jewellery and £100,000 capital to give up care and control of the children to him. How this amount was arrived at is unclear. Others remember the original sum being mentioned in connection with this scheme as a cool quarter of a million pounds.

While the plan was being considered by the Tuckers, the irritations continued. On 11 December, John wrote to his solicitors, keeping a copy for his files. The copy read:

> A note to mark your card in case you receive any complaints about 'access'. Today was Camilla's Nativity Play at the nursery school and Frances's Carol Service. Veronica informed me of neither but other parents told me. I arrived at 11.10 (for 11.15) for the Play and not seeing Veronica there I sat through it and after the performance Camilla came down from the stage to see me.
>
> If I had not gone, Camilla would have been, out of 50 children, one of two or three who did not have a parent present. Camilla's new nanny (Miss Christabel Martin) who I did not know by sight eventually came up to me and after a short time took Camilla home. In the afternoon I went to Frances's Carol Service at 2 P.M. Veronica arrived at about 2.15, stood next to me and started to tell me I was in breach of the Court Order. I told her to be quiet and at the end of the Service left without saying hullo to Frances.

In John's original letter to Luther Tucker, he had pointed out: 'The biggest snag to any "Buying-Off" operation is to make it irrevocable.' Time indeed proved that the plan was a non-starter, and the whole idea was dropped before the offer was even put to Veronica.

Veronica had been 'vitriolic' about John, but it was a measure of the passionate feelings she still had for her husband – and, despite everything, she wanted him back.

Hugh recalled: 'Veronica rang me up several times after the separation and she talked at enormous length and she'd throw everything in. She'd harangue me about John and about everyone else. I'd say: "Oh yes, really?" and wait, hoping that my ears would prick up if she said anything of interest . . . She wanted John to go back to her. But a reconciliation was out of the question . . . This was the thing. But Veronica had far too little in her life to write anything off, including John. He believed she had a consuming hatred for him which had been sustained ever since he had burned his boats by separating from her and making the children wards of court. He said things like she hated him and would do anything to destroy him. His attitude was that losing the children was a terrible thing and that he'd got to carry on the good fight in the courts to get them back.'

It had been agreed months before that Veronica and the children would spend Christmas 1973 at Grove with the Shand Kydds. Once again, Bill had removed his ban on his sister-in-law for the sake of Frances, George and Camilla. But, once again, there was trouble. This time it erupted in a telephone call between Christina and Veronica about the Christmas arrangements.

'This was about ten days, two weeks, before Christmas,' Christina recalled, 'and the next time I spoke to or saw Veronica was eleven months later in hospital after the murder. She never contacted me again and I never contacted her.'

John took the children to stay at Hobe Sound after Christmas, and on his return from Florida in January 1974, he asked Bill if he could take them to Grove occasionally for weekends. Bill suggested to Christina that there might be 'hell to pay' from Veronica – indeed, they later assumed it had cemented the Christmas breach – but for the sake of the children, they agreed. Grove became a regular haunt and so did Horton Hall nearby, where the children swam in Freda's pool in the summer.

On his access weekends, John also took them to stay in the country with Sally and William at Guilsborough, and with the Earl of Suffolk and Berkshire at his Jacobean ancestral home, Charlton Park in Wiltshire.

'John was tremendous with them,' Lord Suffolk said.

'He really did care about those children more than anything else in the world.'

But under the access arrangements, he was only allowed to see them every other weekend. He had to pick them up from number 46 at 5.30 p.m. on the Friday, and deliver them back there by 5.30 p.m. on the Sunday. It made their weekends together seem very brief, especially since so much time was spent travelling. If only Veronica would allow him to pick the children up earlier, or deliver them back later, he suggested, things would be easier.

'John was always so marvellous,' Freda recalled. 'He'd say: "Come on, children, we must go. I've got to get you back on the dot of time. Afraid you can't stay any longer." And it was always: "Oh Daddy, we don't want to go yet," you know. "Come along now, quickly. Get dressed," he'd say. "Mummy will be waiting." And he was always very good about that.'

During their weekends with the Shand Kydds at Grove, John was 'fantastic with the children', according to Christina.

'He used to play the most incredible games with them for hours,' she said. 'An awful lot of parents would have been bored stiff, but John never got bored with them. The children were permanently raiding him – and you know how you've got to be quite fond of an adult to actually dare raid their bedroom. They'd all go zooming in terribly early in the morning and leap on him – his children plus my children and whoever's children were staying. None of the children were ever alarmed by him. Although John was rather austere to look at, and had this cold, clipped voice, he radiated exactly the opposite to the children. They were always doing dreadful things to him, balancing bowls of flour on top of his door so that when he walked in, they fell on him – and putting things down his bed.

'He never did anything but laugh, whereas Bill would have got quite angry after a while. And they'd hide his clothes if they knew he was going out. The great thing always was the queue, everybody watching John on Saturday mornings to wait till he went to Leighton

Buzzard. The minute he got in the car every child that could would appear out of the woodwork and be in the car too because John was the softest touch of all time and if you could get into a town with him as a child you always came home with a long-playing record and a bag of sweets or something. And it wasn't "buying affection". I can remember when Caspar had a ghastly lumbar puncture and was having the most dreadful headaches after it and he was lying on the sofa watching television because he had to keep his head down. And when it was his bedtime John carried him upstairs for me and put him into bed and kissed him goodnight, and when he took his head away he had tears in his eyes. He was so upset that Caspar was suffering so much. It really bothered him. He couldn't bear the stories of what the hospital did to Caspar. He was always saying to me: "Things like that shouldn't be allowed. I'll find out who runs the place. I'll write to him. I'll have this changed." Although it wasn't anything that was *wrong* because it was the normal treatment for leukaemia. But John was terribly upset about it and wanted to write to the hospital. He felt it very deeply.'

He also felt very deeply about problems affecting his own children – for example, George's incontinence. In John's view, this problem was not the little boy's fault but was caused by 'emotional distress', and he believed his son needed 'help, sympathy and understanding' to overcome it. Delivering the children back to number 46 on Sunday, 17 February, after a weekend away together, John exchanged words on this subject with Mrs Elizabeth Murphy – who had returned as resident nanny, replacing the temporary, Christabel Martin.

As a result, blistering accusations were made and Veronica's new solicitors despatched a prompt letter on the Monday. The same day, John himself wrote an anguished letter to three people concerned with the little boy's welfare – the children's general practitioner, Dr Christopher Powell-Brett, the Official Solicitor, who was the children's legal guardian as wards of court, and George's headmistress. As had become his practice, John also drafted a suggested reply for his solicitor to send to Veronica's. The draft indicated the accusations which had apparently been levelled against John, and which he implicitly denied. Part of it read:

Our client would like answers to the following questions arising out of your letter:
1. In what way did he 'force his way into the house'?
1. What 'considerable distress' was caused to Mrs Murphy?
3. What did he 'shout' at her? . . .'

Since the disintegration of the 'buy off' plan, John had been left with three alternatives which had been outlined to Luther Tucker. He pinned his hopes on what became known as 'Phase 3'. If there were about six or seven changes of nanny at number 46, he might then be able to take the case back to court.

But the situation was taking its toll. John finished a 20 February letter to his solicitor with the words: 'I apologise for not doing anything about your other letters but I will deal with them in the next day or two. Phase 3 is getting me down!'

Three days later, private detectives paid by John kept watch on 46 Lower Belgrave Street. They kept vigil on certain days that February, March and April.

Kait recalled: 'He put these men on to say whether the children could be seen going out in the normal way to the park or what have you. And I think John was a bit disappointed. I think in fact the children went out, not perhaps as much as he would have liked, but you couldn't possibly have said that they were never out at all.'

In part of a letter to the private eyes on 4 March about their coming watch that weekend, John wrote:

. . . In fact on Saturday their most likely destination would be the health food bar at Harrods. However if the family were divided I am more interested in the hours spent inside and outside the house by the children.

If the whole party got in the car or a chauffeur driven car appeared (assuming Mrs Murphy was with them or had gone away) it might be an opportunity to install the telephone device. The number has not been changed as I had thought so the number I am interested in is 730 0534.

Was he planning that Veronica's phone should be bugged? He already recorded her telephone calls to him at 72a, sometimes made at night.

'I knew that Veronica was phoning him and abusing him,' one friend said. 'I heard quite a lot of it on the tapes.'

He also made secret tape recordings of her when he went to number 46.

Nanny Jenkins said: 'He told me he always had a tape on because Lady Lucan always used to accuse him of things, so he never went there without a tape recorder.'

At one stage, after an exchange of solicitors' letters about Veronica's spending, a story appeared in the gossip column of a national newspaper claiming that John had 'peremptorily cut off her Harrods account'. Not only was this a complete distortion of the truth, but it was also a foretaste of the kind of Press treatment John was to get later. Veronica's good fortune in gaining sympathetic publicity whatever the circumstances was, however, to stand her in very good stead.

Yet Veronica still wanted her husband back. Nanny Jenkins, who stayed at John's flat for three months between jobs, recalled: 'He told me she was always ringing him to go back. But he said no way – he'd never go back. He said: "It can never be." He also said that none of the staff stayed at Lower Belgrave Street very long, and that the custody matter would come to court again when there had been a few more changes.'

The vigils kept by the private detectives cost John hundreds of pounds in fees but there was little to show for their efforts. Apparently the 'telephone device' had not been installed at number 46. However, back on 23 February, Nanny Murphy had left the house with Frances, George and Camilla at 11.45 a.m. and been tailed to the Irish Club nearby, where she was observed sitting at the bar drinking. Alerted by the detectives, John had gone to the club himself and watched until the nanny and her charges emerged at 12.52 p.m. and returned home.

One of the conditions of the court order was that Veronica was obliged to employ a 'suitable' resident nanny chosen by her, approved by the Official Solicitor and paid for by John. But John's checks on the references supplied by Nanny Murphy worried him. Investigating further, he turned up allegations that she had been sacked by one previous employer for 'excessive drinking, heavy smoking, encouraging the child to drink', and, apparently, 'a tendency to walk nude in the house'. Another had fired her because she allegedly 'drank to excess' and 'had hallucinations'.

The Official Solicitor was told that it was 'only with reluctance' that the matter was being brought to his attention, but that Lord Lucan was 'genuinely concerned' about his three children and the possibility of 'something happening to them'.

John's draft letter on his own behalf stated: 'Our client is naturally concerned and alarmed that his children should be in the charge of a woman with this past. He feels most strongly that, whatever her other virtues, the risk that she might in a crisis be unfit to cope makes her continued employment undesirable.'

In the event, Nanny Murphy's ill health brought the matter to a close. By the end of April it became known that she had been admitted to hospital for serious surgery, and it seemed unlikely she would return to her duties at Lower Belgrave Street. Christabel Martin returned to number 46 as temporary nanny until a permanent replacement could be found.

On 28 April, John wrote to a Mr Ditch at the Official Solicitor's office. Part of the letter read:

> I told my wife on Friday that I was not prepared to pay a net salary of £35 a week for the next nanny. She told me it was impossible to get anyone for less and complained that I was 'sabotaging' her.
>
> In ordinary circumstances £16–£20 per week clear is the going rate. I recognise that the circumstances are not normal and that I must pay more, but there are limits. I do not have to remind you that £35 per week groosed [sic] up comes to about £2500 per annum and to this must be added the cost of housing and feeding the person. I don't know for instance how much your own department pay qualified female staff but I would guess that most would be more than happy with £3200 per annum with 8 weeks holiday on full pay.
>
> The point I wish to make is this: am I obliged to bribe someone to live in 46 Lower Belgrave Street so that my wife may comply with the Court Order? . . .
>
> I know that the choice of nanny rests between you and my wife but I would like to comment that a very high wage is just as likely to attract the wrong woman. I would like to put a limit of £25 clear per week for the next one. If you think that this proposal is unreasonable or unfair or that it is an attempt to 'sabotage' my wife's position, I will of course withdraw it . . .

By the summer of 1974, the children had a new nanny, Pierrette, described by one visitor to number 46 as 'a plump, busty French girl of about twenty-five'. In the continuing search for information, John apparently made contact with her and also made notes about mail which arrived at number 46. By now, neighbours and many of John's friends were well aware of the regular spying trips he made to the street where his children lived. Stephen Raphael and John Wilbraham were only two of those who drove or walked to or from his flat with him, specifically via Lower Belgrave Street, in order that John could try and check that Frances, George and Camilla were all right.

Juliet Hill recalled driving back from dinner with John one evening when he stopped the car in Lower Belgrave Street and got out to check on number 46. She said: 'He said: "Do you mind if I do? I'm sorry but I always have to do this every night if Veronica's there and the children are there." She had a variety of nannies, didn't she, and he just wanted to look and see what was going on. And I sat in the car while he went and had a look around.'

But though John spied on the house and taped Veronica's calls to 72a, in later days he tried to steer clear of her.

Hugh said: 'He didn't contact her personally at all. He wouldn't go into the house if he thought she was there normally.'

But his snooping trips had become more important because he could no longer afford to pay private eyes to keep watch.

Years later it was alleged in a Press interview not only that one of the nannies was 'a raving alcoholic' but that another one – unnamed – 'turned out to be a prostitute' and it was Veronica's car she used, 'cruising round for custom'.

Just as John fretted about the possibility of 'something happening' to the children, Veronica apparently had a premonition that 'something was going to happen' at number 46.

'The house had a very sad atmosphere,' one woman said, echoing a feeling voiced by several visitors. 'It was the sort of house you want to put some *life* into, especially downstairs. I'm a very psychic person and I wouldn't go down to that kitchen at night on my own. I'm not just saying that with hindsight. It was really spooky. These Irish friends of mine came over to the house one Sunday ... They were playing the piano downstairs where the murder happened later and the fellow playing the piano said: "I can't play any more. It's depressing here." There were vibrations. The last time I saw Veronica before the murder was at the end of August, and she was saying then that she thought something was going to happen. I had the same feeling. I was really scared. Veronica's house had an *evil* atmosphere.'

Evil – a strong word. Yet it was used over and over again by people involved in the Lucan case.

On 29 September, John drafted a note to George's headmistress which read:

> I enclose George's report. I am a little disappointed with his place in the class (ignoring the high position in French as he had a French nanny for the whole term). He has gone from 1st to 2nd to 8th in reading in three terms and his arithmetic from 84% to 72% and 45%.
>
> To keep you up to date on the domestic front, the French girl (Pierrette) left in August; they then had a temporary (Nadia) and now there is a girl (about 25 years old at a guess) called Sandra looking after them.

The new nanny was Sandra Rivett. Less than six weeks later she was dead, her arm hanging obscenely out of that sack like a shirt sleeve from a laundry basket.

14

Friends and relatives were completely divided in their opinions of how John seemed in those final weeks. Some felt that he was disillusioned and disheartened in his fight for the children and had turned to the bottle for solace.

'He was always a perfect gentleman even when drunk. His manners never changed,' said a member of the staff at the Clermont. 'But it was sad to see a nice man like that drinking so much.'

Charles Benson recalled: 'John was drinking heavily and, although he did not make a display of himself in public, he was getting privately drunk to the extent that his close friends were aware of it. His other behaviour deteriorated too. There was an important backgammon tournament at the Clermont in October and I was playing against an opponent who was a mutual friend. John came to watch, arrived drunk and kept passing comments. As it was, we were both friends of his and I was able to concentrate despite the interference and interruptions. But it would have led to anyone but John being asked to leave.'

Others thought he had finally begun to emerge from the long black tunnel.

Christina said: 'Throughout all that time after the separation John had been like a woman whose husband has left her, someone who *has* to talk because they are so desperately unhappy and then they feel better. John wanted to talk about his children and he wanted to talk about Veronica, but by this time he was running down. It had all been got out and he'd said it all a hundred times. And to me, I felt that he was coping better with his unhappiness.'

In mid-October, when he and the children spent a weekend at Grove, he 'seemed very relaxed' according to

Bill. That year it was John's turn to have the children for Christmas and he was looking forward to it with 'a great deal of pleasurable anticipation'. Bill also remembered him saying that Sandra Rivett seemed 'the most satisfactory nanny' at number 46 since the custody case.

Kait recalled: 'John told me he knew it was cutting off his own bough but he thought that in Sandra they'd found a winner this time. The children liked her and he liked her and he hoped she would stay.'

Frances's tenth birthday fell on 24 October. About twenty children were invited to number 46 and entertainer Norman Myers was hired to lay on party games and competitions before tea plus a Walt Disney film afterwards and to bring gilt chairs, tableware, hats, balloons, masks, squeakers, crackers and going-home gifts. The bill came to £96.09. Frances's schoolfriend Annabel Florman, one of the little guests, told her mother afterwards what a 'nice, jolly' person Sandra the new nanny was.

That day, 24 October, a conference had been arranged for John with his custody case counsel, James Comyn QC. What transpired is unknown. Note was undoubtedly taken of the fact that yet another nanny had been appointed to look after the children, but immediate action on the court front was unlikely.

The private eyes were gone now, and Veronica could easily spot John watching the house in his Mercedes. As she did, she said, on that very day. It was the last time she saw him before the fateful night of 7 November. Through the window, she told the inquest later, she spotted him sitting in the blue Mercedes outside number 46. He was wearing dark glasses and was about to drive away. As she told the coroner, the Mercedes was a car she 'knew well'.

At the Portland Club that week John asked his friend Michael Stoop if he could borrow his car. Stoop, who had two he hardly used, offered him the better one – his own Mercedes. John said he didn't want the Mercedes. He wanted the other car, the old Ford Corsair. He asked Stoop to keep the matter a secret and seemed 'sort of pent-up' when he asked.

'Mind you, he was pretty pent-up latterly anyway,' Michael Stoop said later.

No explanation was offered or sought – though Stephen Raphael and others assumed afterwards that he wanted the Corsair in order to spy less conspicuously on Veronica.

'He wanted the car specifically for that evening,' Michael Stoop said. 'It was of some inconvenience to me but he did want it very much *that* night. I was going home to change for a dinner which was being held that night at the Portland so I left the Ford outside the garage and left the keys in the car and said he could collect it when he wished.'

He was hazy about the date when this took place. He thought it could have been Wednesday, 23 October, but John normally visited the Portland Club to play bridge on Mondays and Thursdays, so it might have been Monday, 21 October or Thursday, 24 October.

But on Monday the 21st, John had driven his Mercedes to Charles Benson's birthday party at the Clermont, so he presumably hadn't wanted Stoop's car for that night. That suggested the relevant date would have been Thursday, 24 October – especially since Thursday was the night members usually gave dinners at the Portland. But would John have been keeping vigil outside number 46 in dark glasses in his own Mercedes that day if he *already* had another car? It seems unlikely. The simple explanation may be that he realised Veronica had spotted him on 24 October, drove off and then asked Stoop for the Ford Corsair the same day. After all, Veronica was hardly likely to expect to find John keeping watch from what Stoop himself described as 'a filthy old banger'.

But Chief Superintendent Ranson had a different theory. He thought Lucan wanted a 'totally non-descript car' in order to hide his wife's body in the boot after removing it from the basement of number 46. In other words, the police chief believed that by late October, John was planning to murder Veronica, and the Ford Corsair formed part of his plan.

Ranson's theory, however, took no account of one glaring fact. John, the master of bluff, the meticulous planner with the cold, calculating mind, did not *keep* the Ford Corsair a secret. He didn't hole it away in some distant garage. He parked it openly outside his flat in Elizabeth Street. On 31 October, a week before Sandra Rivett was killed, he even got a £1 excess parking ticket for leaving the Corsair too long on a meter a few steps from his own front door. And at least four people in those final days – Michael Stoop, Dan Meinertzhagen, Dominick Elwes and Billy Edgson, the linkman at the Clermont Club – knew that he had the Ford.

In addition to that, Caroline Hill saw John arrive at her house on the eve of the tragedy in a car which wasn't his Mercedes. It could have been the Corsair. And only about an hour before the murder, John drove Michael Hicks Beach home in an ordinary saloon car – which again could have been the Ford Corsair. Was it likely that Lucan intended the Ford as a hearse for a forthcoming murder when he parked the car openly within yards of his flat, when so many people could connect it with him? What kind of sense did that make?

The plain fact was that his own Mercedes was not only instantly recognisable to Veronica, but for some time it had also been plagued with battery trouble. It seemed the children had kept winding the electric windows up and down, which may have contributed to the problem. William had even had to tow the Mercedes with his own car at Guilsborough on one occasion to get it going. After the murder, when the police found the Mercedes parked outside John's address, the battery was flat. It was still flat when Bill Shand Kydd collected the car later after the police had removed it for forensic tests.

Stoop had told John he didn't care if he never got the Ford Corsair back. So had John simply hung onto it to keep watch on number 46 and as an alternative means of transport when the Mercedes was playing up?

In October, as it happened, John was hoping that by the first weekend in November he would be in California.

The Vietor Cup backgammon tournament for international-class players, which he had been unable to attend as defending champion the year before, was beckoning from La Jolla. Around 25 October, he and Stephen Raphael discussed going together. In the event, John couldn't raise the funds. But had they gone, they wouldn't even have been in London on 7 November, the night of the murder.

On Tuesday 29 October, John Wilbraham arrived from his home in Cheshire to stay at 72a Elizabeth Street for three days, during which he accompanied Lucan on one of his regular evening walks past number 46. He found Lucan still hoping to get the children back through the courts.

'Certainly we discussed how difficult it was,' he said, 'but John was hoping for some magic solution. I think he was getting undoubtedly more and more cynical about it – and with good cause. He took the view that all the dice were against him. I remember him showing me the gadget he had on the telephone to record Veronica's calls. He was fighting desperately to amass enough proof to regain the children, but no one seemed to be interested in the facts. And they *were* facts. But if someone had said to me then: "In a few days' time, this man is going to try and murder his wife in the most brutal way," I would have said: "Quite impossible." He just wasn't in that frame of mind.'

During John's access weekend from Friday, 1 November, which he spent with the children at Guilsborough, he helped William build a raised sandpit in the garden. William was struck by his strength.

'John was immensely strong physically,' he said. 'We were putting logs round the outside of the sandpit and there was this huge log I couldn't shift. He just picked it up and carried it on his shoulder like Tarzan. He was shaking with the exertion, but he did it.'

Whenever he saw them, John invariably pumped the children for information about life at number 46. That weekend at Guilsborough, Camilla told him that Sandra, the new nanny, had boyfriends, and went out with them on her days off.

John asked when her days off were and Frances said Thursdays. Since that was the traditional nannies' day off in London, and at number 46, that would hardly have come as a surprise. But what else did he know?

Did he know that Sandra's husband had left her in April, seven months before? Did he know that since then, according to Chief Superintendent Ranson, Roger Rivett had found a new girlfriend and Sandra had been 'having her affairs'? If John had kept his eyes skinned during his vigils in Lower Belgrave Street, he might have known of her cheery drinking sessions with the locals in the Plumbers Arms. But he may not have known about the men she had spurned. Did he know of a man called 'Ray'? The name was apparently an alias. According to what Frances told others later, 'Ray' had first met Sandra in a shop, drove a 'long black Mercedes, bigger than Daddy's', and came to the front door of number 46 to take her out. But then Sandra had said she wasn't going to go out with 'Ray' any more. According to Frances, he knew she had found another boyfriend – John Hankins, an Australian barman. Frances said Sandra had said she might marry John Hankins if he asked her. Did John know of the break-up between Sandra and 'Ray' only 'a few days before' she was battered to death? Whoever the killer was, after the murder Frances told a friend at school: 'My Daddy didn't do it.' Years later, when she was about to pass her law exams to become a solicitor, she still remained convinced of her father's innocence.

On Sunday, 3 November, John delivered the children back to number 46 after what turned out to be their final weekend with him. Kait thought that evening was the last time she and John had dinner together. She remembered him asking her to lend him a book called *The Intelligent Woman's Guide to Socialism*.

Michael Hicks Beach was equally convinced that he had dined alone with John that night at the Ladbroke Club in Hill Street.

'We had a quiet and amusing dinner together,' he recalled. 'He seemed in very good heart. He said that Veronica had had so many nannies and she would probably get more and after about three more he reckoned he could go back to the courts and get the children. He never gave up hope of getting them back. He may have been irritated by how long it was taking, but he thought that in the end he would get the children, and it wouldn't be too long before the end either.'

At his regular weekly piano lesson at Caroline Hill's small house in Chelsea on Wednesday morning, 6 November, John's manner and behaviour were completely normal. That fact weighed heavily with Caroline after the murder. If he had been planning to kill someone within the next thirty-six hours, surely even a man of John's self-control would have felt keyed-up and on edge? Yet there was no sign of that, not even when he played the piano.

Caroline said: 'You can't *fail* to notice if someone's nervous or tense at the piano – it's the most extrasensory thing and very emotional. I'd know immediately. But his playing was absolutely the same as always.'

Others who saw and spoke to him during the rest of that day and evening also found him at ease, perfectly normal.

On the morning of that fateful Thursday, 7 November 1974, photographer Andrina Colquhoun tried to get her plans organised. She had been invited to spend the weekend shooting in Kent and thought that John, who was a friend, might join her. She tried to contact him, finally driving past his flat 'at four-ish in the afternoon to see whether his Mercedes was parked outside, which it wasn't', then assumed he wasn't coming and left London without him.

At about four o'clock that afternoon, John was in Lower Belgrave Street calling on pharmacist Alfred Simons at John Harley the chemists, a few doors from the Plumbers Arms. He produced a capsule he'd brought in and said: 'Can you tell me what this is?' 'Just looking at it,' Mr

Simons told him, 'it's a Limbitrol capsule' — a comparatively mild tranquilliser.

Whether John had got it from number 46 he didn't say. But he had been in to see Mr Simons with similar queries 'four or five times over different periods' since about the time the Lucans had separated. Was he perhaps checking on which drugs Veronica was taking? One of the conditions under which the children had been returned to Veronica was that she should continue with her psychiatric treatment. But according to Hugh, John thought she was not.

Mr Simons recalled: 'Lord Lucan normally wanted to know what certain drugs were. He'd come through the shop to the back dispensary and in the main he used to ask me about various medicaments that he brought in and what they were and what they were for. And it seemed to me, chatting with him, that he had a damn good idea of the specific uses of these things, a fairly good knowledge for a non-pharmacist. He seemed to know a damn sight more than the ordinary layman would about them, as if he'd made a study of them. The drugs he asked about were tranquillising anti-depressants, things of that sort. I remember him asking me once about Camcolit [lithium carbonate] and he already knew what I told him. He never said where he got the drugs he brought in nor who was taking them. I wondered about it but never asked. He was always nice, always smiling, always charming and pleasant. That day when he came in he seemed perfectly normal, the same as he always did, under no stress whatsoever.'

Soon after his visit to the chemist's, John rang Michael Hicks Beach and invited him round for a drink after work. Michael arrived at 72a Elizabeth Street at about 6.30 p.m., and they discussed an article about gambling which John had apparently been asked to write, by someone else, for an Oxford magazine. John was wearing 'an old pair of flannels and a V-necked jersey over a polo-necked shirt', Michael said. While they were at the flat, John made a phone call. 'He called the restaurant and booked a table,'

139

Michael said. 'Obviously at this point I was taking very little interest. I do remember that he said they'd be dining fairly late. He told me he was having dinner with Greville.'

Greville Howard had rung John earlier in the day from his office in the City to say he had four tickets to see *Cole* at the Mermaid Theatre that night, and would he like to go? John replied: 'No, but would you like to have dinner afterwards?' They agreed to meet at the Clermont Club later, and John was due to book a table for five.

Around 7.00 p.m., a burglar alarm went off at a house in Lower Belgrave Street.

At about 7.45 p.m., John drove Michael Hicks Beach home to Chelsea from Elizabeth Street. 'As we left his flat, I think he probably picked up his dreadful old overcoat, sort of down to the knees and speckledy,' Michael said. They travelled in what Michael could describe only as a 'very ordinary, dark-coloured car'. It could have been Michael Stoop's Ford Corsair, though Hicks Beach could not identify it as such. The fact that it was not John's Mercedes did not strike him as unusual.

'That didn't surprise me in the slightest because John frequently had other people's cars,' Michael said. John dropped him outside his house at almost exactly 7.55 p.m. – just before *Top of the Pops*, which Michael's wife had been watching, finished on television.

'John didn't come in,' Michael recalled. 'But as I got out of the car, he asked if I was going to be in London at the weekend. I go away quite often at weekends and so did he. I said I was, and he said so was he, and he said: "Give me a ring. We might have lunch or dinner together."

'He usually played golf or something when he wasn't taking the children to the country so I didn't expect to see him at lunchtime on Saturday, but we quite often dined on Saturday or Sunday nights. I would have rung him the next day or Saturday to make a firm arrangement. So to sum up, I was with John for perhaps just over an hour that evening during which time he had two drinks, which for a man like him was absolutely nothing, and I had two drinks and I'd already had one beforehand, and neither of us was the slightest bit drunk. He was in very good form, quite relaxed, *very* relaxed in fact, not the least bit depressed – he didn't mention Veronica at all – and when he left me he'd made tentative arrangements to see me in the next three days.'

Did that sound like a man who was just about to commit murder?

Michael said: 'I imagined that he was probably going back to the flat to have a hot bath and change before going out to dinner with Greville.'

John drove away from Chelsea at almost 8.00 p.m., about thirty-five minutes before the earliest time Sandra Rivett could have been killed.

At 46 Lower Belgrave Street, Frances had also been watching *Top of the Pops* on the television in the nursery. Her mother, Camilla, George and Sandra were one floor below watching *The Six Million Dollar Man* on the television set in Veronica's bedroom.

At about 8.00 p.m., Sandra had a telephone call from her new boyfriend, John Hankins. She had changed her day off in order to see him on Wednesday, the previous day. She had also spoken on the phone recently to her mother, Mrs Eunice Hensby, who lived on a caravan site near Basingstoke. She had said she was very happy and was looking forward to going home for Christmas. Since John would be having the children that year, the prospect of Christmas for Veronica – alone in the house, estranged from Christina and almost bereft of friends – might well have seemed bleak.

Frances, like the two other children, had had her bath and changed into her pyjamas earlier in the evening. At about 8.05 p.m., after *Top of the Pops* finished, she said, she went down to Veronica's bedroom and joined the others watching television there.

At the Mermaid Theatre at Puddle Dock, the audience settled down to watch the 146th performance of *Cole*, an entertainment based on the words and music of Cole Porter and devised by Benny Green and Alan Strachan. The show began that night at 8.19 p.m.

At 8.30 p.m., when the television programme ended, Frances said, she went back up to the nursery and played a little more with her game. Sandra brought George and Camilla upstairs, she said, and put them to bed. *It was the last time Frances saw the nanny.*

At 'about 8.30 p.m.', according to Andrea Demetriou, the assistant restaurant manager at the Clermont Club, he had a telephone call booking a table for dinner.

'As far as I could make out it was Lord Lucan,' he said, 'because he was the only one who called me by my first name, Andrea. He said rather apologetically that they were going to the theatre and would it be too late for them to have a table for four at about eleven o'clock? So I said no. Lord Lucan had our greatest respect here. I said it wasn't too late and he said: "Okay, we'll be along about eleven o'clock, four of us." He was a very sincere person and he was apologetic because they were going to be late – just after 11.00 p.m. would normally be our last time. He was the kind of person who'd be apologetic about the least thing, you know. We have a couple of tables which we would like him to have and I suppose he was just making sure he would have one of his tables.'

The whole matter of the dinner table was confusing. Did John phone to book twice that evening – once before 7.45 p.m. from Elizabeth Street and again at about 8.30 p.m. – or was there some other explanation? And why did he only book 'for four', not five? Some people thought there might be a hidden significance in the booking 'for four'. But Ranson put it down to a simple 'lapse of memory'.

At about 8.40 p.m., according to Frances, she left the nursery and went back to Veronica's bedroom. *Sandra was not there.* Frances told the police later: 'I asked Mummy where Sandra was and she said she was downstairs making some tea.'

At about 8.45 p.m., according to Billy Edgson, the linkman at the Clermont, who parked members' cars for them, John drove up to the outside of the club in Berkeley Square and asked him: 'Anyone in the club?'

'No, none of the usual crowd, my lord,' Billy replied.

'Okay, I'll be back,' John said.

Billy recalled: 'He seemed his usual self. I'm pretty sure it was the Mercedes he was driving. I walked round to speak to him through the window. He was wearing casual clothes, the kind he wore when he went out golfing. He wasn't perturbed in any way. I thought he was probably going home to get changed.'

According to what Frances told relatives shortly after, once she had returned to Veronica's bedroom, she then spent about 'ten minutes' watching television with her mother before Veronica started wondering why Sandra hadn't returned with the tea. That would have taken the time up to about 8.50 p.m. (Veronica placed the events later.) To the police, who questioned her subsequently, Frances said: 'After a while Mummy said she wondered why Sandra was so long. I don't know what time this was but it was before the news came on the television at 9.00 p.m. I said I would go downstairs to see what was keeping Sandra but Mummy said no, she would go. I said I would go with her but she said no, it was okay, she would go. Mummy left the room to go downstairs and I stayed watching the television. She left the bedroom door open but there was no light in the hall because the light bulb is worn out and it doesn't work. Just after Mummy left the room I heard a scream. It sounded as though it came from a long way away. I thought maybe the cat had scratched Mummy and she had screamed. I wasn't frightened by the scream and I just stayed in the room watching television. I went to the door and called out: "Mummy?" but there was no answer so I just left it . . .'

Billy Edgson thought John had driven off after their conversation outside the Clermont at about 8.45 p.m., but it is possible he simply parked the car himself and walked back. Because at about 9.00 p.m., according to another employee at the Clermont that night, John was *still* in Berkeley Square.

He told me he saw Lord Lucan standing on the step outside the main door of the Club at 9.00 p.m. or a few minutes either side. He thought perhaps Lucan had stopped by to use the telephone in the lobby. As recently as spring 1987 – though he refused to be named in this book – the man repeated that he had seen Lord Lucan then and added: 'Actually it was at five past nine.'

15

Detective Chief Superintendent Roy Ranson was fast asleep in bed at his home when, some time around midnight, his colleague, Detective Chief Inspector Dave 'Buster' Gerring, rang to say he had 'a murder on his hands'. A nanny had been killed, another woman attacked – and her husband hat said he would be in touch with the police in the morming.

'You can leave it safely in my hands,' Gerring said.

Had he done so, Ranson might have missed what he later described as 'the decade's biggest manhunt and the most fascinating murder case of my career'. The whole story, he commented, was 'worthy of Agatha Christie'.

At about 1.00 a.m., Kait finally managed to get through on the telephone to the Shand Kydds at Cambridge Square.

She told Christina that there had been a 'terrible accident' at Lower Belgrave Street.

'The nanny has been badly hurt,' Kait said. 'Veronica is in hospital but she will be all right.'

There was a pause as the words sank in. Sensing the worst, Christina asked 'Will the *nanny* be all right?'

The answer came back: 'No.'

'Will she die?'

'She *is* dead,' Kait said.

Christina nearly dropped the telephone. 'How are the children?' she asked anxiously.

'They're fine,' Kait said. 'They're with me. But John will be ringing you and the police so I thought you ought to know.'

'Oh Lord!' Christina said.

Kait rang off.

Totally stunned, Christina put the receiver down, turned to Bill and said: 'Jesus Christ . . .!'

All through the early hours of that seemingly endless night, Kait sat in her armchair at St John's Wood, elbow to elbow with P.C. Beddick, and tried to make sense of the unreal jumble of events which had suddenly befallen her family. As the dawn light of the next morning filtered in through the picture windows onto the grim little group in her flat, the first shadowy anxieties that prefaced the long nightmare which lay ahead began to take shape in her mind. But even then, having heard John's version, real fear did not grip her. That was to come later . . . when the inconceivable fact sank home that the police suspected *him*.

Kait had slipped out to buy some food from the shops by the time Sally arrived at the flat. She found the children looking tired, rather white and a little over-excited, but they said nothing about the events of the previous night. They did not ask: 'How's Mummy?', 'How's Sandra?' or 'Where's Daddy?' All they had with them was the clothing Kait and a policewoman had packed for them hurriedly at number 46 the night before. It was agreed that Sally should take them to Guilsborough vicarage for the time being. After talking at length to the police, who were to remain at Kait's flat for some time, she shepherded the children into her car and set off back up the M1 towards Northamptonshire.

Soon after she left, the telephone rang. Kait reached swiftly for the receiver. At last! But her hopes were not realised. The caller was not John but the Lucans' GP, Dr Christopher Powell-Brett, who had already visited Veronica in hospital and heard her version of the events. He asked how the children were and Kait told him they had gone to Northamptonshire. For a second the strain told on her.

'Why the hell hasn't John rung us back or something?' she demanded.

Dr Powell-Brett hesitated for a moment before saying: 'Don't forget that he has been under fearful strain for seven or eight years.'

At Cambridge Square immediately after Kait's 1.00 a.m. call, the Shand Kydds telephoned the house in Lower Belgrave Street.

Bill said: 'I got that lovely fellow with the flat feet, old Forsyth, who was born to be a policeman.'

He mimicked Sergeant Forsyth as he recalled the conversation.

'"D'you know where Lord Lucan is, sir?" he said. "There is a scene of unparalleled violence down here and we are very anxious indeed to inverview him." He sounded just like something out of a rather bad Sherlock Holmes book. I told him I didn't know where John was. Obviously the police wanted to see him to tell him what had happened, and his children had been whisked off, but there was no question in my mind that John could have had anything to do with it. The next day they were banging on about it and it suddenly became clear that the police actually *were* suspecting John, which to me was a tremendous joke!'

By Friday afternoon, however, early editions of the London evening papers were blazoning pictures of the Lucans across the front pages. The banner headlines in the *Evening Standard* cried: 'Body in sack . . . Countess runs out screaming' and in bolder type: 'BELGRAVIA MURDER – EARL SOUGHT'. Suddenly the 'joke' was no longer amusing.

A pen-portrait of John was quickly drawn up as newsmen raided the cuttings files and delved into *Debrett*. A gruesome murder, a screaming countess and a missing earl – what a field day for Fleet Street!

But to those who knew the family, the news as it broke in the newspapers and on radio and television brought waves of shocked disbelief. John Lucan sought by the police in connection with a murder? How absurd!

Stunned and bewildered by the turn of events, Hugh made for St George's hospital, Hyde Park Corner, where Veronica had been taken by ambulance from the Plumbers Arms, to try and find out what had happened.

With him went Dominick Elwes, who had made international headlines himself years before by eloping across the globe with heiress Tessa Kennedy.

Charles Benson vividly remembered Dominick's later description of the meeting.

He said: 'Dominick told me that Veronica's first words to them were: "*Now* who's 'mad' then? *Now* who's the one with 'paranoia'?"'

Hugh recalled: 'She seemed frightened of us. When we arrived, she was cringing away at the far side of a rather large bed. Then she became somewhat hysterical and was vigorously haranguing us, complaining about everyone, including Mother. She went off at side tracks from time to time. I had not seen that side of her before.

'She appeared to have one black eye and her head had been partly shaved and was bandaged. I noticed an enormous amount of cigarette ends in two large ashtrays beside her. There was no dialogue – she did all the talking apart from a couple of questions we asked. In one of her more coherent moments we asked her what had happened and she said: "It's there in the newspapers." She told us Sandra went downstairs to make a drink. Then she went down to look for her. She said she could see nothing in the basement as the lights were off. She said she was hit from behind something, a curtain or a cloakroom door.'

Since there were two separate lavatories or 'cloakrooms' downstairs at number 46 – the one at the back of the hall and the other at the back of the breakfast room – and Veronica had mentioned 'the basement', Hugh assumed she meant the latter.

'As she talked,' he said, 'I remember forming an image of her moving across the breakfast room towards the boiler and being biffed from behind the curtains that covered the French windows or else from behind a door or cupboard in that part of the room. *I asked her if she had seen the person who had hit her and she said no.* Then there was a confused/confusing part of her tale leading to a scene in which she and John sat together on the steps talking . . .'

'Confused/confusing' or not, Veronica declared there and then that the man who had killed Sandra and attacked her was John.

Dominick broke down and wept.

'His tears were not for me,' she was quoted as saying later. 'He was deeply upset for my husband's sake.'

But Hugh was sceptical. From her hospital bed, Veronica reminded him that about a year before, she had said she thought John might 'kidnap' the children. That fear had proved to be unfounded. He had had ample opportunity to run off with them on his access weekends or when he had taken them abroad on holiday – yet he hadn't. Hugh was certain his brother wanted to regain custody through the courts, not by 'kidnap' – and still less by murder.

Others had doubts too, including Christina, who was convinced of John's innocence. But it was possible, she said, that Veronica might *believe* he was the killer.

Was it possible that the 'confused/confusing' part of her story covered the vital seconds when John ran in to the rescue and the real killer fled? In the circumstances of that night – the split-second timing, the horror, the shock – could Veronica have gazed up, dazed and confused, seen John there alone and assumed that he was the attacker?

'The story she told me at the hospital,' said Hugh, 'allowed the possibility that the murderer biffed her only because she got in the way, she passed out, John ran in and so on.'

Veronica had long given the impression that she believed John wanted her dead. When the violence erupted, wasn't he the first person she was likely to suspect – even if he had actually *saved* her life?

Chief Superintendent Ranson never forgot his first sight of Veronica lying 'half-conscious' in her bed at St George's hospital, her face and hair smothered in dried blood, an 'incredible necklace' around her neck, the jewels flashing in the hospital lights.

'She was mumbling to herself,' he recalled, 'but we couldn't make head nor tail of it.'

The morning after the murder, Ranson waited confidently at the investigation headquarters at Gerald Road police station 'quite convinced' that John would walk in with a lawyer and a prepared statement.

'It would have been so true to character,' he said long afterwards. 'I was quite sure the case would be virtually wrapped up in one day. But here we are, still looking . . .'

At lunchtime that Friday, a hurriedly summoned group of John's friends converged for lunch at the Lyall Street townhouse of John Aspinall, nicknamed 'Aspers', who had sold the Clermont Club in 1972 to the Playboy organisation. Since then he had concentrated his energies on wildlife conservation. At Howletts, his country house in Kent, he had a private zoo – where he was known to join gorillas in their cages and swim with Bengal tigers – and he also established a wildlife park at Port Lympne.

A reporter later described the lunch meeting as a gathering of the 'Just Men', a reference to the title of an old Edgar Wallace thriller. With the exception of Bill Shand Kydd, who made no secret of the fact that he 'didn't have a lot of time' for some of John's gambling friends, all of the men present were, or had been, regulars at the Clermont. Around the table with Aspinall and Shand Kydd sat Dominick Elwes, Ian Maxwell-Scott, Charles Benson, Greville Howard, Dan Meinertzhagen and Stephen Raphael.

Long before the media got wind of the murder, various friends had discovered something was amiss. Shand Kydd, of course, had rung the police at 46 Lower Belgrave Street immediately after Kait's 1.00 a.m. call. Stephen Raphael, independently, had been telephoned by a friend who lived locally to be told that police had been at the Lucans' mews cottage in Eaton Row and that something was up. Raphael, who loved John, 'literally turned green and cried like a baby', imagining that Lucan had killed himself because of his debts. Raphael rang Benson and Benson rang Gerald Road to try and find out what *had* happened. By Friday morning, they knew about the murder, that the police were looking for John, and that he wasn't around.

Bill recalled: 'I think it was Dominick who actually rang up and said: "Come and have lunch at Aspers. Let's all get round." There was a lot of discussion as to what would happen if John suddenly appeared – whether we'd hand him over, whether we'd help him out of the country, and an emotional thing from Elwes about "of course we'd help him flee". And I said: "Absolute rubbish!" I said there was no question of helping John out of the country or helping him to "escape": that was obviously totally ludicrous. I said that I certainly didn't believe John had done it. I told them what I wanted to do was to get hold of him and go down and sort it out with the police as soon as possible before he did something silly – like killing himself or pissing off. I was backed up by the others. They all came round eventually. But it was a totally inconsequential lunch. The "Just Men"? That's rubbish. It was all Lucky's old friends, and you know, what a sport he'd been and all that crap. It was a complete waste of time.'

Andrina Colquhoun got the first inkling of trouble when she woke up on Friday morning at the country estate in Kent where she had gone to spend the weekend shooting. Hearing the tail-end of the radio news, she learned that something had happened in the mews at Eaton Row. She hoped that a bomb hadn't gone off – Irish bombers were targeting London at the time – and if so, that Greville Howard, who was living at the mews cottage then, had not been hurt.

'I was out of the house all morning shooting,' she recalled, 'and we were having lunch somewhere when someone drove over from the house and said: "There have been urgent calls for you all day. You must phone this number immediately." I went back and rang London and eventually spoke to one of John's friends who said: "The most awful thing's happened. John's nanny's been murdered, Veronica's in hospital and John has disappeared. Is he down there with you?" To which I said: "No, he's not. I wasn't absolutely sure whether I was expecting him. He knows exactly where I'm going to be."

So he said: "I think you've got to come back to London straight away." I was absolutely shattered but it didn't occur to me at all that John could have done it. On the way up to London we saw billboards and the evening newspaper with huge pictures of John and headlines about "MURDER!" and "LORD LUCAN MISSING" and I then began to think: "Well, if he really is missing, there's more to this than meets the eye." I arrived in London at about 5.00 p.m. and spoke to Dan and Dominick.

'They were trying to work out in their minds what could possibly have happened. Nobody thought that John could have done it. But the theory that seemed to emerge at the time was that John might have hired someone who killed the wrong person. It's the only reason that any of us could think of as to why the nanny was murdered and not Veronica. But if John hired someone, what the hell was *he* doing at the house?'

What indeed? If Lucan *had* hired someone to murder Veronica at number 46 that night, he would surely have made certain that the children were not in the house at the time, and that he himself had a cast-iron alibi. Greville Howard had invited him to the theatre with friends. If he'd gone with them that evening, and then on to dinner with them at the Clermont, he would have been in the clear. So why had he refused? It didn't make sense. Indeed, Chief Superintendent Ranson himself poured scorn on any idea that Lucan had hired the killer.

Bill Shand Kydd drove to Bedfordshire after the 'Just Men' lunch to spend the weekend as usual at Grove, his country house near Leighton Buzzard. At 8.00 a.m. on Saturday morning, he was getting up when Ian Maxwell-Scott rang from Uckfield, told him John had visited Grants Hill House on Thursday night and asked: 'Have you had any letters?'

'No,' said Bill.

'Oh,' came the reply. 'John has written you two letters – to London.'

Bill checked on the telephone with the Shand Kydds'

nanny, who spent her weekends at Cambridge Square. She confirmed that two envelopes with Uckfield postmarks had dropped through the letterbox that morning. He rang Ian to tell him and then drove back to London.

'I read the letters,' Bill recalled, 'and took them straight down to the police station where I met all the boys, yer Ransons and yer Gerrings. I pointed the bloodstains on the letters out to the police.'

Though the murder headquarters had been set up at Gerald Road, Roy Ranson, as head of CID for the 'A' division of the Metropolitan Police, was actually based at Cannon Row, close to the Houses of Parliament.

Earlier in his long police career, which had earned him several commendations, he had worked in Brixton and Kings Cross and served with the Flying Squad. But his biggest coup to date had been the capture of Ian Ball, who had tried to kidnap Princess Anne in The Mall.

His second-in-command on the Lucan case, burly Detective Chief Inspector David 'Buster' Gerring, was the local man on the spot: head of CID at Gerald Road. Of the two, Gerring with his 'bouncer' build, his well-stocked drinks cabinet, his fearless asides, his bonhomie and his uninhibited and chauvinistic language − the word 'crumpet' figured large − was nearer the image of a detective as seen in *The Sweeney* on television. Whereas Ranson was the quiet, unemotional, contemplative 'Maigret' of the team, not a man who could be jollied along, Gerring was extroverted, expansive, 'one of the boys'. He had gained his nickname 'Buster' earlier in his career for his gang-busting activities in the suburbs of south London. Gerring was to find the Lucan affair 'a cat and mouse game' and his 'most challenging case'.

Bill was at Gerald Road for a couple of hours. The fact that Lucan had visited Uckfield on Thursday night and the police had only just found out about it left Ranson 'furious'.

Nevertheless, they had the two letters − and the first

153

confirmation of John's version of the events at number 46. The full text of the letters was not made public until the inquest. But the main letter to Bill mentioned the fight and the other man who had left the house, and implied John's innocence.

His story tallied with what he had told Kait in his first telephone call. When the police interviewed Susan Maxwell-Scott later, they heard exactly the same story again in more detail. If consistency in telling a story was considered to be a mark of the truth in Veronica's case – as it was – then the same applied in John's.

For Ranson, the main letter provided him with 'an insight into the relationship between Lucan and his wife, Veronica, and the deep and intense love he had for his children'.

The second letter, which John presumably wrote as an afterthought, mentioned creditors and a sale – of some of the Lucan family silver – which was coming up at Christie's on 27 November. John expected the proceeds of the auction to cover his overdrafts at three banks he named.

This letter, said Ranson, was his first indication 'that Lucan had money problems – and I was amazed'.

Whatever had happened at number 46, the main letter to Shand Kydd made one fact clear. When John left Susan Maxwell-Scott at Uckfield, he had had no intention of going straight back to London to see the police. Instead, in his own words, he was now, apparently, somewhere 'lying doggo' (low).

Leaving the letters with the police, Bill made for Stephen Raphael's house in Southwick Place.

'I wanted to find out what the hell he knew and to see if the police had been giving him a hard time,' he said. 'I wanted a drink by then anyway. And of course Dominick was there, flinging his head into his hands and doing a Hamlet all over the drawing room. I asked Raphael, who was John's broker, about the financial situation because people were suggesting that John had had £30,000 on him. I asked Steve if John had taken a lot of money out and he said no – John had nothing, no money on him at all.'

That was confirmed later by the police.

No money. No passport. No alibi. No motive. A motive to kill Veronica, the police might think, but not Sandra. Where was John and how could he hope to survive 'lying doggo' without funds? His appearance was distinctive at the best of times but now, with his photograph shown constantly in the newspapers and on television, he had one of the most easily recognisable faces in the country. How could be possibly vanish without trace?

And if he didn't kill Sandra Rivett, who did? At Uckfield, Susan Maxwell-Scott had suggested the obvious suspects when a woman is murdered – her husband or boyfriend. John had dismissed the idea, saying the intruder might have been a burglar the nanny disturbed. Or did the intruder not really exist?

Unbidden and totally unexpected, 'Mr X' was about to appear on the scene with an answer . . .

16

On Guy Fawkes' Night, two days before the murder, the
grounds of Guilsborough vicarage had rung with the
delighted cries of about 200 village children and their
parents enjoying the vicar's annual bonfire party. There
had been fireworks, a bonfire blazing on the disused
tennis court, baked potatoes and steaming hot soup
donated by a member of the Symington grocery family
who lived nearby. It was a happy family occasion, the
world on an even keel.

But now everything had gone haywire and for Frances,
George and Camilla, the vicarage had become a refuge
from the fierce glare of publicity. Sally and William Gibbs
banned newspapers from the house, kept the radio and
television news switched off, and did their best to ignore
the reporters and cameramen who gathered outside the
vicarage walls. The local police were in evidence too,
keeping vigil in case John appeared, though curiously they
never did make a thorough search of the rambling,
seven-bedroomed vicarage, part of which dated from
1773, nor of the seven acres of ground in which it stood.

It was Sally who squared up to the task of telling
Frances and George that Sandra was dead. Frances, who
tended to bottle up her emotions like her father, asked
simply: 'Who will look after us now?'

In an effort to get life for the children back to some form
of normality, it was decided that Frances and George
would temporarily attend the 180-pupil Guilsborough
Primary School with their cousins – Sally and William's
children – and Camilla would join the local playgroup
Sally ran.

On Monday, their first day at school and four days after
the murder, Sally was stopped in the village by a man who
approached her from a telephone kiosk. He had

apparently recognised her from a photograph in a newspaper.

'Are you Lady Sarah Gibbs?' he asked.

She said she was.

The man was Irish, aged thirty-ish, about 5 feet 8 inches tall and he looked athletic. He had a broken nose and dark greying hair. He told her he was a lorry driver, by chance making a delivery in the village. He said he had been checking her address and telephone number from a directory when he had seen her walk past.

'I know something about the murder,' he said.

Sally was astonished. 'I was so uplifted,' she said. 'I thought: "This is the breakthrough we've been waiting for." I believed him implicitly.'

According to 'Mr X', as the stranger was originally known, since he refused to reveal his name, address or telephone number, another man *had* left 46 Lower Belgrave Street on the night of the crime. Just as John's story implied.

Sally recalled: 'First he said with lots of winks and nods that he had seen the man. Then he said that it might have been him who had seen him or someone else.'

'Who are you?' she asked.

'Call me Joe Falcon,' he said. It was not his real name. He instructed that she was to say nothing to the police or the Press. Nor could she contact him. But he would be in touch with her again, he said, by phone.

'I do like to see justice done,' the man said. 'I don't like the police going after the soft option.'

It was a tantalising start but he refused to say more. Then, as abruptly as he had appeared, he was off, driving away through the village in his mud-stained lorry.

Sally quickly noted down the lorry company's name from the side of the vehicle as it disappeared from sight. Then, in high excitement, she dashed back to the vicarage to telephone John's lawyers. The response was predictable: 'Is he a nut case?' Sally didn't think so and neither, when he met him, did William.

The unscheduled meeting came early next morning

when the vicar and his wife, in their new role as self-appointed private investigators, drove to the lorry firm's offices which they had traced to Market Harborough, about 10 miles away. At about 7.00 a.m. they saw 'Mr X'/Joe Falcon, driving out in his lorry and flagged him down.

'He was surprised but quite amiable,' Sally recalled.

He said he was prepared to join them for a moment in their car. Indirectly, they offered him money for his information. Turning it down flat, Falcon declared: 'I'm not in this for money but for justice.'

He agreed to meet them the following evening. If William picked him up after work at the parish church in the centre of Market Harborough, he said, and drove him to Guilsborough vicarage, he would tell them all he knew.

By the next evening, the group at the vicarage had expanded to include John's solicitor and a private eye who had been hired by Bill Shand Kydd and Ian Maxwell-Scott to make independent inquiries into the murder. Falcon wore a fawn raincoat over a dark suit. There were two heavy gold rings, one of them set with a stone, on the fourth finger of his left hand. His broken nose suggested he was a boxer – a guess which later proved correct. 'Joe Falcon' was the name he had used in the boxing ring. He still refused to reveal his true identity, but otherwise needed no encouragement to talk.

'We had laid in bottles of beer for him but he said he didn't touch drink,' Sally said.

That night at Guilsborough vicarage, Falcon told a fascinating story.

Three days after the murder, at about 6.45 p.m. on Sunday, 10 November, he said, he had been at home with his wife. They were about to watch the annual Ceremony of Remembrance at the Cenotaph on television – an event the patriotic Lucan had often watched himself – when the telephone rang.

The caller, Falcon said, was an old friend, an Irishman living in London, who asked: 'Have you read about the murder in the newspapers?'

'What murder?' said Falcon.

'Lord Lucan,' came the reply.

According to Falcon, the friend then said that he had been passing 46 Lower Belgrave Street at about 9.50 p.m. on the night Sandra Rivett was killed when a man rushed out of the house, bumped into him, said something like: 'Get out of my way, you damned fool!' and ran off. The man was definitely not Lord Lucan, he said, and if he had known what had happened he would have 'thumped him'.

At the end of the telephone call, the friend changed the subject, asked after Falcon's family, and said he was going to France for two weeks on business. Why should the friend have rung Falcon with the story? That was unclear. But before he left the vicarage that night, Joe Falcon put his hand on the Bible and swore that he had told the truth.

Yet he was still not prepared to give his own name or address. The only contact the family would have with him, he said, was when he rang the vicarage.

In desperation a secret plan was hatched. Falcon had asked to be driven back to Market Harborough and dropped at the car park. It was their only chance. If he didn't ring again, if they couldn't trace him, all might be lost. The plot was simple. As William drove Falcon back, the private eye would follow at a discreet distance . . . and then tail him to his home. As the two men left the vicarage that night, William towering over the broken-nosed stranger, the plan swung into operation. They climbed into William's car and set off. Behind them the private eye followed quietly out through the kitchen door.

William drove Falcon down the winding country lanes in the darkness, waiting for the headlights of the second car to round the bends behind him. He saw nothing. The detective was certainly being discreet. William dropped his speed to a mere 10 miles an hour so that the private eye could catch up. But still there was no sign of the bloodhound in his rear-view mirror. At length William reached the car park in Market Harborough and was forced to watch impotently as 'Mr X' got out and disappeared alone and unshadowed into the night.

Back at Guilsborough the private detective returned to the vicarage 'disgusted'. For the first time on a job, he said, he had been unable to get his car started.

'It was rather a Laurel and Hardy episode the whole thing,' Sally recalled wryly.

No name. No address. No telephone number. An unsupported story which might be an invention. An Irishman in London who might or might not have rung Falcon. Who might or might not have bumped into Sandra Rivett's killer escaping from the house on the night of the murder. Why hadn't he gone to the police? It was fraught with uncertainties. Nevertheless Joe Falcon seemed a Godsend, a modern-day knight riding to the rescue in his mud-stained lorry. John had said there had been another man at number 46 – the man he had seen attacking Veronica, the man who made off when he ran in to the rescue. Now there was a chance it seemed, however slight, to prove that John's story was true.

The next day private detectives employed by John's friends were out on the trail of the mystery Irishman, if such a man existed. Falcon's lead took them to a dingy backwater in a cosmopolitan area of central London dotted with kebab houses and tandoori restaurants just off the Tottenham Court Road. The addresses Falcon had culled from his memory produced nothing. Questions were put to people who lived or worked in the vicinity, but progress was slow.

The search for the Irishman was hampered by other events which had brought violence to the city. By 1973 Irish bombers had stepped up their terror campaign to drive the British forces out of Northern Ireland, and guerilla activities had been extended to the mainland. In November 1974, London, the south of England and Birmingham were under siege from lightning bomb attacks. In the two months up to Christmas that year, 29 people were to be killed and more than 232 injured in explosions. At 10.17 p.m. on 7 November, the very night Sandra Rivett was battered to death, a bomb lobbed through the window of the packed Kings Arms pub in Francis Street, Woolwich, across the Thames in south-east London, killed two people and injured thirty-five others. It was no time to be an Irishman in London, nor to be seeking one. People did not want to be involved, and despite their efforts, the private eyes had no success.

While they continued to look for him and the murder squad searched for John, the family informed the police of Joe Falcon's appearance in the case. They too immediately suspected that he must be a 'nut', or out for money, but despite their scepticism they agreed to check him out.

True to his word, Falcon made contact again by telephone. He agreed to be interviewed and it was arranged for him to rendezvous with the police on Saturday, 23 November, at London's Victoria coach station, a stone's throw from Lower Belgrave Street. When the day came a posse of private detectives kept watch, determined not to lose track of him this time. The police waited for two hours. 'Mr X' did not show up.

The police were not amused. Falcon's address was soon traced through inquiries to the lorry company's office at Market Harborough and shortly afterwards members of the murder squad raced north up the M1 to roust Falcon from his bed at dawn for questioning. 'Mr X' stuck resolutely to his story. But though the police looked for the Irish friend, they were sceptical – Falcon was known as a 'do-gooder' in his area, someone who got himself involved in other people's affairs.

But why should being a 'do-gooder' make him suspect? Who else but a public-spirited citizen would involve himself and an old friend in a murder case? Especially when time and again history shows that 'have-a-go' heroes and similar stout souls often end up coming off worst, proving the truth of Noël Coward's comment: 'You can't expect to do anyone a favour without paying for it.' The newspapers often had stories about worthy individuals who did good deeds and ended up losing their jobs or a limb or their lives as a result. If the majority of people tend to look the other way or gather at the scene of some disaster simply to gawp it's not hard to understand why. Yet 'Mr X' had come forward. Was that because he was one of the dwindling band of Good Samaritans – or because he was a crank?

The devastating answer, or what at least appeared to be the answer at the time, came on 9 December. That day at Bow Street magistrates court in London, 'Mr X'/Joe Falcon – finally identified on the charge sheet as Michael Joseph Fitzpatrick, aged thirty-two, of Wartnaby Street, Market Harborough – pleaded guilty to wasting police time with a 'false report'. He was fined £25 with £10 costs.

The court heard that as a result of his story the police had spent seventy-seven hours finding his friend and that their search had extended as far as Ireland. Why it took them, and the private detectives, so long to locate the friend is a mystery – unless he had gone away to France or somewhere else. His current address and phone number were listed in the London telephone directory and had been for the previous six years. When the police finally questioned him, the 'silent witness' denied ever having telephoned Michael Fitzpatrick with the story and declared that he had not been in Lower Belgrave Street on the night of the murder. On 6 December, as a result of this, the police had seen Fitzpatrick again. This time, confronted with his friend's denial, he claimed he had made the story up and said: 'I am just a punchy fighter. I just do things out of my mind.'

John's family were desolate. What kind of man was this who had held out such high hopes and then crushed them?

Sergeant Forsyth from Gerald Road told the magistrates court that Michael Fitzpatrick had been born in Ireland and had become an amateur boxing champion before turning professional when he was seventeen. He had had about 700 fights. In 1971 he had retired from the ring and had since worked as a £32-a-week lorry driver. He was a man of previous good character, Sergeant Forsyth said, who gave exhibition boxing bouts to raise money for elderly people. His friends had described him as 'a bit of a character' who did a tremendous amount of charitable work. In 1973 he had joined a sponsored walk for Help the Aged and had run the whole 20 miles.

Why should a man like that go to such lengths to cause further distress to John's family? It didn't make sense. It was hardly in character.

In court Michael Fitzpatrick told the magistrate: 'I am very sorry. I will make sure it never happens again.'

The magistrate, Mr Kenneth Barraclough, asked him: 'Why did you start up this story?'

'I cannot remember really, sir,' the lorry driver replied. 'I am sorry I did it.'

'Apart from wasting the time of the police,' Mr Barraclough admonished him, 'you brought a lot of trouble and anguish to individual people.'

That, it seemed, was the ignominious end to 'Mr X's' involvement in the case. The police had washed their hands of him, a court had fined him, the newspapers had labelled him a hoaxer and his reputation as a 'do-gooder' had been tarnished if not destroyed.

But as far as Michael Fitzpatrick was concerned, the matter was by no means over.

On 30 December, three weeks after he had been fined, he claimed in a telephone call that his original story had been the truth. His friend had denied it, he said, because 'he did not want to get involved with the police'. His friend had even rung him after seeing reports of the Bow Street hearing, he said, to say that he was 'sorry for all the trouble'.

Long after, Michael Fitzpatrick's wife told me: 'I *know* my husband told the truth. But we don't want to be involved with the case any more.'

As if the disbelief from the police, the court fine and the bad publicity were not enough, she said they had been plagued afterwards by poisonous telephone calls from strangers.

'It just isn't worth it,' Mrs Fitzpatrick said. 'I didn't want my husband to do anything about it in the first place.'

William remarked: 'I thought Fitzpatrick was quite genuine from the start. When he then pleaded guilty to making a false report, I naturally had second thoughts. But later I assumed he'd pleaded guilty to get out of a difficult situation.'

In Market Harborough later, a local newspaperman pooh-poohed any suggestion that 'Joe Falcon' was just a punch-drunk old fighter who couldn't tell fact from fiction. So which of the two Irishmen told the truth? Was it the friend, who claimed he'd been working as a part-time barman at a pub near Leicester Square on that fatal evening? Or was it Fitzpatrick, the 'do-gooder' who'd said he wanted to 'see justice done'?

Ranson declared later that the police had taken Lucan's claim about 'interrupting an intruder' seriously and had 'started a house-to-house search'. But he told me that the murder squad had been looking for Lucan 'instantly'. From the start, in other words, they were convinced that Lucan was their man.

One fact was indisputable. Long before the police interviewed Fitzpatrick – or Frances, for that matter – warrants had already been issued for John's arrest. Veronica had proved an invaluable witness. According to one of Ranson's officers: 'Within two days we had all the evidence we needed to arrest Lucan, no problem at all. And since then all our efforts have been to find him.'

17

Veronica's vital first detailed statement to the police accusing John was made almost twenty-four hours after the murder. On Friday evening at 6.00 or 7.00 p.m., she told her story to Chief Superintendent Ranson, Chief Inspector Gerring and Sergeant Forsyth. The sergeant then began to go over it all again for the written statement.

Listening at her bedside in the hospital, where Veronica had rested for almost a whole day, Sergeant Forsyth might well have felt tired, overworked, and below par. He had the symptoms of a heavy cold, if not the cold itself. He had already been at work for more than thirty-three hours nonstop. And he was to notch up a tour of duty lasting over thirty-nine hours before he finally signed off for a break at Friday midnight.

He took down Veronica's version of the events over a couple of days, on and off. The reason for the delay, he explained later at the inquest into Sandra Rivett's death, was 'because of hospital routine and Lady Lucan becoming fatigued'.

Chief Superintendent Ranson was quoted as telling a reporter: 'Lady Lucan has given us a very full version of what happened.'

On Sunday morning, three days after the murder, newspaper readers learned that the police were looking for a Ford Corsair – the one John had borrowed from Michael Stoop a couple of weeks before. The dark blue Corsair, registration number KYN 135D, was found the same afternoon – abandoned at Newhaven. It was parked in Norman Road – where it had been since early Friday morning – close to the yacht marina and the embarkation point for cross-Channel ferries to Dieppe.

The hunt for John, or his body, was immediately

switched to the Sussex coast. Boarding houses, hotels and boats in the marina were combed. Cliffs, beaches and isolated coves were scoured and searches were made of gorse-covered scrubland and of an old Napoleonic fort riddled with passages. Frogmen investigated a spot near the mouth of the River Ouse. Weather was stormy. Throughout the murder night there had been a Force Eight gale blowing in the Channel. Was it possible nevertheless that John had taken out a small boat and made for France? Gone over the side in mid-Channel? Perhaps thrown himself from the cliffs? Or taken an overdose of drugs and crawled into the undergrowth on the Sussex Downs to die? Suicide was much in Ranson's mind.

But apart from the car, the searches at Newhaven produced no trace of John or a body. The police were not even sure he'd gone there.

'All we know,' said another police officer much later, 'is he went to Susan Maxwell-Scott's and we know the car finished up at Newhaven. But we don't know who took it down there. The car was parked at Newhaven anything between 5.00 and 8.00 a.m. – because a man looked out of his window at 5.00 a.m. and it wasn't there, and he looked out again at 8.00 a.m. and it was there. So it could have arrived at a minute past five or a minute to eight. What happened up to 5.00 a.m. is the $64,000 question. It's the question that has been worrying me all the time. You see, look: somebody thinks that he's got cause to murder somebody else – so much so that he plans a murder. He murders the wrong person and runs away, which is reasonable. He finishes up at Susan Maxwell-Scott's. He leaves there, she says, to go back to London. The car didn't arrive at Newhaven before 5.00 a.m., he left Uckfield I think about 1.30 a.m., so there's something like, what? – three and a half hours. It's 16 miles from Uckfield to Newhaven. What do you do in those three and a half hours?'

One thing John did do, apparently after leaving Susan Maxwell-Scott's, was to write a further letter – to Michael

Stoop, the owner of the borrowed Ford Corsair. It was waiting for Stoop along with other mail when he called in at one of his London clubs, the St James's, at about 4.30 p.m. on Monday.

The envelope was unstamped and the hall porter had to pay the postage. The letter sounded very final. John used the past tense and said that he had been 'destroyed'.

What did that imply? That he planned to kill himself – or to disappear forever?

'You see, look,' the detective said. 'It's all very well in the cold light of day to try and analyse, but you know if you're emotionally disturbed . . . The best way I can equate it is when you're taking examinations. Your mind just goes blank, doesn't it? You know, what must *his* mind have been like – because it was a cock-up, because he'd murdered the wrong person?' (Or hadn't, but knew he'd be blamed!) 'You see nobody knows what sort of mood he was in when he wrote those letters. Was he in the mood to commit suicide? Or was it a big bluff?'

Daily Mail reporters seemed to have come up with a lead that Monday morning when they claimed John had crossed the Channel to France. According to immigration people at Dieppe, they reported, he had landed just after 11.00 p.m. on Sunday evening. That meant he'd travelled on the British Rail ferry *Senlac* which had left Newhaven at 7.00 p.m. – about four hours after the Ford Corsair was discovered. An immigration official was quoted as telling the *Mail*: 'Lord Lucan was alone. We know it was him because we examined his passport. We had no reason to stop him and there has been no request from the English police about him.'

But Ranson discounted the story immediately. He told the Press: 'I have his passport in my possession and I was there checking personally all people leaving on that ferry.'

Nevertheless, in case he had fled abroad, on Tuesday the arrest warrants were issued. John was now officially a wanted man, on the run, a fugitive. Susan Maxwell-Scott was 'amazed and aghast' at the news. Bill Shand Kydd made a public appeal on *ITN News* for John to get hold of him or his own solicitor as soon as possible 'and we'll go together to the police station'.

A comment Caroline Hill was to make – that murder is 'not the sort of thing aristocrats do' – was borne out to an extent by history. No British peer had been wanted for murder in over 200 years.

'Right now,' said a detective giving a historical briefing, 'in 1765 Lord Byron – I dunno which Lord Byron it was, it might have been his Daddy mightn't it? – was tried by the House of Lords for murder. He was found guilty but he claimed benefit of clergy. I think it goes back to the time when peers of the realm of course appointed the local vicar and that sort of thing. Anyway he got off scot free. In 1760 a Lord Femers was tried for the murder of his steward and was found guilty. He was hanged at Tyburn where he argued with the executioner about his fee. Apparently in those days how much they paid determined how quickly they hanged. Prior to the Criminal Justice Act of 1948, if a peer was charged with murder he was entitled to be tried in the House of Lords by his fellow peers. Well, it's so ridiculous you'd laugh at it. And if found guilty they were entitled to be hanged with a silken rope, though what bloody difference it makes what sort of rope is round your neck I don't know. Now this is the first time that a warrant has ever been issued for the arrest of a peer of the realm. We discovered that subsequently. Peers of the realm are not arrested every other day, are they? The only reason we obtained warrants in the early stages was because we thought Lord Lucan had gone abroad and to expedite extradition proceedings.'

A 'red alert' was flashed to Interpol with a full description of John authorising police officers in 120 countries around the world to detain him on sight. 'He may be anywhere,' Ranson told the Press. 'I do not know whether he is abroad or in this country but he had friends in many foreign countries and there are also addresses in America. All these are being checked by local police.'

John's address books, crammed with the names of scores of friends and acquaintances, had supplied a ready source of leads. In America inquiries were made by the FBI. On the Continent detectives checked apartments in Paris and casinos and luxury villas on the French Riviera. A telegram which had arrived at Elizabeth Street on Monday offering John the use of a five-bedroomed house in Haiti was dismissed as a hoax. Speaking on *ITN News* John Aspinall said: 'I find it difficult to imagine him in Brazil or Haiti as a fugitive. I don't think he has the capacity to adapt. [But] he is a man of enormous virtue and honour. He could rely on many friends to help him with advice.'

Rumours that John was heading for Haiti with about £100,000 were described by Stephen Raphael as 'ludicrous'. He told a reporter: 'To have had more than a few pounds let alone thousands would show that his flight was premeditated. It's absolutely untrue.'

William Gibbs declared publicly: 'I know and the family knows that Lord Lucan is incapable of committing any crime. He is a man of honour. Those who know him must realise that he does not want the children to suffer the stigma of possibly having to face seeing their father in court connected with a murder.'

He did not expect John to reappear, he said, until the police had found the real murderer.

But as far as the police were concerned, the case had already been solved. If they hadn't actually caught their man, to their minds they had at least identified and named him.

Ranson's team, who quickly became nicknamed 'The Nob Squad', were not destined to become bosom buddies with the so-called Lucan set. They came from different backgrounds, they spoke different languages and their lifestyles were worlds apart. A certain class feeling developed at Gerald Road.

One detective, who termed the upper-class interviewees 'the Eton Mafia', remarked sourly: 'You know how the Mafiosa work, where they all stick together? Well, this lot stick together like shit to a

169

blanket. They're used to being aristocrats and everyone, but everyone, is looked upon by them as servants. And particularly so police officers, who are not there to arrest them of course. Oh no! They're there to look after the *interests* of the aristocracy!'

Ranson himself was less than enthralled. When he rang up to see people, he complained later, they were likely to say: 'Terribly sorry, old chap. I'm off to Austria, ski-ing. I can see you in three weeks.'

Billy Edgson, the linkman at the Clermont Club, who had spoken to John at about 8.45 p.m. on the night of the murder, said long after: 'The police said I had to go down to Gerald Road to make a statement as I said I'd seen him and I never went actually, to be honest, for a good five weeks afterwards. I didn't really want to get involved anyway with that. And I got a bit of a telling off from them.'

Joe Falcon, failing to keep his appointment with the police, had had to be tracked down.

And the relationship between the 'Nob Squad' and Madeleine Florman was a small saga in itself. Getting no reply to her telephone calls to John's flat after hearing about the murder, she dropped a note through his letterbox. The police must have been in the flat because within half an hour they rang Mrs Florman and asked if they could come to see her.

Mrs Florman recalled: 'A young detective came round and said: "Did anything happen on Thursday night which was unusual?" And I said: "Oh, only that the doorbell rang and rang and rang but I didn't answer it." I didn't tell him about the telephone call. I wasn't sure of myself because this sort of thing doesn't happen to you very often. I then wrote a note to John's mother and she rang me on Monday morning very early, about 8.30 a.m. I said: "Well, you know he did ring me that evening. It's very innocent and really I'm perhaps rather stupid." And she said: "Have you told the police?" and I said: "Well, I've told them about the doorbell ringing." And she said: "Well, you *must* tell them about the telephone call." So I went to the police and told them. They were very cross because they had to make out an entirely new statement.'

Later on, after returning from the police station, Mrs Florman noticed 'what looked like bloodstains' beyond the decorative stone lions on her doorstep – 'two bright red spots about the size of the end of a cigarette' close together on the ground below the doorbell. She thought they were 'just dirty marks', but mentioned them to Dominick Elwes when he turned up the following Friday. He had an appointment at Gerald Road afterwards and must have told the police because an hour later, Mrs Florman recalled, she had more visitors than she expected.

At about 7.30 p.m., Mrs Florman had changed for dinner and was waiting in her drawing room on the first floor for the arrival of her guests.

That evening she was entertaining ten people to dinner, including the Hollywood film star Tony Curtis, a neighbour in Chester Square, around whom the menu of chicken casserole and grapes in ice-cream, prepared by the Flormans' Chinese cook, had been planned. Five of the other guests were people Mrs Florman had never met, business friends of her Swedish husband Charles. By 7.30 p.m., when they were all due, Mr Florman had not yet arrived home. Right on time the doorbell rang, the cook opened the front door and a group of visitors stepped inside. The Chinese cook told them with a beaming smile: 'Do go upstairs.' Mrs Florman waited at the top to greet them.

'They came up the stairs pretty fast,' she recalled, 'and I sort of stood at the top and said: "Oh, how nice to see you. Won't you take off your coats?" I thought they were my husband's business guests. But it was Superintendent Ranson and Mr Gerring and a man with white hair and another one and a policewoman. And they said in very cross voices: "We would like to talk to you, Mrs Florman. We hear that you have bloodstains on your doorstep and why didn't you tell us about this before?" So I said: "I'm terribly sorry but I have people coming for dinner," which

I think seemed a rather fatuous sort of remark to make with something so serious. We went to the study on the ground floor and there was a man put on guard at the door and the police went on and on. I had never met the nanny but I was made to say like a schoolgirl that I was sorry about her death. My husband arrived home and came in and told me that all our guests were waiting. Then the forensic people came round to look at the carpet in the hall and to take photographs of the front door, and they kept the front door open while they were doing their forensic work and there was a draught blowing right through the dining room while the dinner party was going on. The guests stayed very late until 2.00 a.m. and at eleven o'clock the next morning I had to go to Gerald Road where I had to go over it over and over again.'

'There is a widespread feeling that the police are not getting all the help they should,' Marcus Lipton, Labour Member of Parliament for Lambeth Central, told the Press about a week after the murder. 'It looks as if some people are being a bit snooty.' He said he planned to raise the matter with the then Home Secretary, Roy Jenkins, and added: 'All citizens, whatever their station in life, must be made aware that if they have any knowledge which throws light on a serious crime, the facts should be disclosed to the police.'

Charles Benson responded with a letter to *The Times* asking Mr Lipton to 'identify those whom he believes to be failing in their public duty' or else to 'kindly withdraw his remarks'. Benson stated that John's friends had 'made themselves available' to the police from the start but that several of them had not been contacted for 'some days'.

At least one friend claimed it was 'weeks' before the police got round to talking to him. And a girl receptionist at the Clermont Club, where Lucan had been due to dine on the fateful night, said: 'By the time the police came two weeks later and asked me if Lord Lucan rang that day, I'd forgotten.'

Though people accepted that the 'Nob Squad' had a job to do, some were surprised by their first encounter with

The Law. Some bridled when policemen told them John had 'done' it, even in some cases how he'd 'done' it, for all the world as if he had already stood trial and been convicted. Wasn't a suspect under British law supposed to be innocent until proved guilty?

'I didn't believe for a second that John had committed murder,' Stephen Raphael said, 'but the police told me the evidence against him was overwhelming . . .'

The attitude to Veronica, by contrast, seemed very different. 'Everyone who knew Lucan and his wife spoke of the hatred between them,' Ranson said. 'But it seemed to me, looking in from the outside, that Lady Lucan had a very tough time.'

'I got the impression that the police all thought Veronica was wonderful,' Bill said.

Ranson talked later of the rumours 'circulated about Lady Lucan'. Indeed, tales were told in Mayfair, in Monte Carlo, and even down the Nile. Years later, Veronica remarked that she was 'accused of so much that was untrue at the time. The family wanted to make me out truly disturbed . . .' (John's family, in fact, said nothing about Veronica to the Press.) 'Others said I was a lesbian and inferred there had been something between Sandra and me.'

Bill Shand Kydd was among those most upset by the rumours. 'I always considered the scurrilous and scandalous stories that were whisked around to be counterproductive,' he said. 'Nothing's gained by making up stories to blacken her character.'

In fact one thing was gained: further sympathy for Veronica.

Christina said: 'The family stayed totally silent publicly so the other side of the story wasn't known. But I felt that people thought Veronica had been desperately hard-done-by . . . The thing that annoyed me most of all was this general consensus of opinion one seemed to gather from the Press and the police later that all of them felt John treated Veronica badly – when actually he had been terribly kind to her . . .'

Even the police apparently had some problems with Veronica. 'She's a difficult woman,' one of Ranson's senior colleagues remarked. 'Graham Forsyth was the only one of my men who could handle her.'

After Veronica left hospital, she was taken to Gerald Road police station where she made another statement. This, according to a newspaper report, 'clarified her earlier statements about the murder and the attack on herself'. If points in her story needed 'clarification', why hadn't they been questioned and cleared up *before* warrants were obtained for Lucan's arrest?

But Chief Superintendent Ranson maintained that 'she never wavered from her story, no matter how much we questioned her' and he was convinced that she was 'totally truthful'. There was 'no reason to doubt' her story, he declared, no reason at all.

Yet months later, he was to indicate that her version of the events still did not entirely add up . . .

On Wednesday, 13 November, the day after the arrest warrants were issued, the inquest into how Sandra Rivett met her death opened at Westminster coroner's court. Evidence of identification of Sandra's body was given by her estranged husband, Roger Rivett. Professor Keith Simpson, the famous Home Office pathologist, gave evidence that she had died from blunt head injuries. The inquest was then adjourned to 'await events'. But despite tip-offs which came from near and far, there was no sign of Lucan.

John's family, 'the opposition' as Ranson called them, considered the time and place for details of the case to be made public was at the inquest. Veronica did not. The first of her many 'exclusive' newspaper interviews appeared in January 1975, two months after the murder. And when she wasn't talking to reporters, the police apparently were.

As early as 12 November, only five days after Sandra Rivett was killed, one newspaper article gave alleged details of Veronica's 'five-hour statement' to the police, including a claim that: 'As a ruse, and to stave off any further attacks on her, Lady Lucan had pretended to persuade the killer that they could dispose of the body together.' Two days later, another newspaper gave an account of 'how Scotland Yard are now sure the events went', which echoed: 'Lady Lucan talked with the assailant for nearly an hour. In a bid to calm the man, she told him she would help dispose of the body of the nanny.' And running daily in the newspapers were stories about the police search.

Within a fortnight of the murder, the massive publicity given to the case had been so prejudicial that an article in the authoritative *New Law Journal* declared that even if he were found, Lord Lucan could never be given a fair trial in a British court.

Yet a month after the tragedy, a detective was quoted as saying: 'If he has not been found by March, we are prepared to make the inquest a virtual trial.'

In February 1975 a journalist wrote: '... The inquest will be more like a murder trial without the accused man being there ... Lady Lucan will be at the hearing to relive her ordeal. In the gloomy Victorian setting of the coroner's court, the incredible situation could arise in which a peer of the realm is accused of murder without any formal defence ...'

And so it did.

In the end the full inquest did not take place until June 1975, seven months after the murder. Justice delayed, it is said, is justice denied. Not that what eventually happened at the hearing could ever be described as just.

In the meantime, unaware of the whole story and deluged with prejudicial publicity, the public's belief that John was guilty could only be reinforced by the passage of time.

BOOK THREE

The Inquest

18

Following one adjournment after another, the four-day hearing into Sandra Rivett's death finally opened in a blaze of publicity on Monday, 16 June 1975. That very morning, the *Daily Express* splashed another of Veronica's exclusive interviews across the front page with the headlines: 'Lady Lucan in court drama today . . . I WILL NAME "KILLER".' The report stated that she was 'clearly nervous about reliving her nightmare at the inquest'. She was driven to and from the courthouse in a police car accompanied by plain clothes detectives, and led in by a back door to avoid the crowds.

To many people the case as a whole highlighted differences in society and the inquest became a bizarre attraction. Outside the redbrick courthouse in Horseferry Road, Westminster, crowds of onlookers jostled with Press photographers on the pavement. A woman in a wide-brimmed hat staged a lone demonstration, parading up and down appealing for help for battered wives. A poster pinned to her dress read: 'It affects us all, rich or poor.'

Passing buses slowed down for crews and passengers to get a better view of the crowds, and the witnesses arriving or leaving or crossing the road at lunchtime to the Barley Mow pub opposite. The week of the hearing coincided with Royal Ascot and even racegoers in top hats were observed stopping to catch a glimpse of the scene. On Thursday, having asked the coroner for the previous day off to do business, Bill Shand Kydd was piqued to find himself pictured in one newspaper in brown morning suit and topper with Christina in a picture hat at the races. 'That's where I was *doing* my business,' he said later. People involved in the case seemed worlds apart. By Wednesday the Barley Mow was reported to have sold out of beer. 'Business is good,' said an employee. One woman, explaining her presence in the crowd, remarked: 'It's not often you get the nobs washing dirty linen in public.'

But Her Majesty's Coroner for Inner West London, Dr Gavin Thurston, was not having dirty linen – or what he termed 'family tensions' – displayed in his courtroom, as soon became clear.

At the time of the inquest, Dr Thurston was sixty-four and he had made his mark in his profession. He was deputy coroner to the royal household, he had conducted previous inquests on headliners like Judy Garland, Jimi Hendrix and Beatles' manager Brian Epstein, and he rated a sizeable entry in *Who's Who*. However, after a couple of notable inquests, including that on the ex-boxer Freddie Mills, he had been criticised over evidence which 'went unheard'. Exactly the same criticism could be made about the hearing into the death of the Lucan children's nanny.

Months earlier, writing about the forthcoming inquest, a reporter had suggested that Dr Thurston would 'demand full direct answers, so that justice will be seen to be done by the eyes of the world'. But what actually happened during those four days in June was a travesty of justice. The world didn't hear 'full direct answers' to every question because some of the witnesses were muzzled. Sometimes Dr Thurston didn't even allow certain questions to be asked. As a full and fair inquiry, it was a farce. No one heard the full story, least of all members of the jury, who at that time still had the devastating power not merely to decide that the deceased had been murdered, but also to name the person they thought responsible.

The iniquity of this system had long been condemned as unjust. In Britain a person is supposed to be innocent until proved guilty at a trial in a proper court of law, which a coroner's court is not. Yet an inquest jury could brand someone as 'guilty' before the trial had even taken place.

The outcry which followed the result of the Sandra Rivett inquest finally forced a change in the rules to ensure that no such injustice could happen again. But by then it was too late for the ironically named 'Lucky' Lucan.

The inquest was a sensation from start to finish. Veronica accused John of being the attacker on the very first day. In turn, a barrister suggested she was lying.

The six men and three women of the jury took their places in the tiny, wood-panelled courtroom. The public seats and Press benches were packed to capacity. According to a court official there had not been 'such intense interest in an inquest' since that held into the death of Dr Stephen Ward, a central figure in the 1963 Christine Keeler scandal.

Huddled in a corner at the back of the courtroom sat Sandra Rivett's father, Mr Albert Hensby, and her aunt, Mrs Vera Ward, both of whom – like John's family – were to grow ever more unhappy with the proceedings. Throughout the inquest Sandra's mother, Mrs Eunice Hensby, stayed at her caravan home near Basingstoke, reading each day's reports in the papers but unable to face the ordeal in person – unable even to 'accept that Sandra is dead'. A few months before, Sandra had told her that Lady Lucan was more like a friend than an employer. 'That's why it is so distressing that I have heard no word from Lady Lucan,' Mrs Hensby was quoted as saying.

Throughout the hearing, Kait made copious notes. She sat in sandals and a summer dress with two pairs of spectacles slung on chains around her neck. Slightly deaf, and more so in later years, she craned forwards to hear the evidence. Next to her, grim-faced and silent, sat Sally Gibbs. Alongside them were Bill and Christina Shand Kydd. In the row behind, never exchanging a word, a smile or a greeting with her relatives, sat Veronica – alone but for her police guard, Sergeant Graham Forsyth. According to journalist James Fox: 'The courtroom bristled with the hostilities of Lady Lucan's relatives towards her.'

At that stage it would not have been surprising if some of John's family and friends were bristling with hostility towards James Fox as well. Only a week before the inquest, at what was clearly a highly prejudicial time, an article by Fox entitled 'The Luck of the Lucans' appeared in print. The fact that it was published in the prestigious *Sunday Times Magazine*, that it was embellished with previously unpublished Lucan family photographs apparently from Veronica's albums, and that Fox had interviewed several of John's friends as well as Veronica, gave it added weight. Indeed, other Pressmen and even Gerring hung onto the article later, apparently as a handy reference. Reporters were finding that trying to get interviews with those in the Lucan inner circle was like trying to find 'a traitor in Colditz'. But Fox had somehow penetrated the 'wall of silence', and his copy was a good read. However, the piece, as a whole, was in Veronica's favour.

Among the prejudicial statements it contained was a ludicrous claim, attributed to Dominick Elwes, that *John* was paranoid! Claiming that two of John's friends had confirmed 'that he was developing an exaggerated interest in the latest bugging devices', Fox then quoted Dominick as saying: 'It was the dark side of the moon. It wasn't the Lucky I knew. It was perhaps a classic case of paranoia.' Whether Dominick meant that the way Fox took it, whether he was misquoted, or whether Fox simply got the wrong end of the stick is not clear. Before I could check, Dominick had met his own tragic death.

In a furious response, in a letter printed in *The Sunday Times* the following week under the headline 'Lucan a Press victim', Bill Shand Kydd declared: 'Some time the whole story must be written, exposing the misleading allegations made in the Press, if only that eventually the children, in common with today's readers, will be able to form a balanced view of the facts behind the tragedy, and understand that their family love, care and suffer for them, and will continue to do so.'

But the damage had already been done. 'The Luck of the

Lucans' had had its effect, according to Fox, who recalled in *The New Review* magazine later, with apparent pride: 'By the time we assembled in court . . . there was a marked shift of feeling towards Lady Lucan by the reporters present, as a result of the facts in [my] article . . . She was now the lonely, hard-done-by martyr and mother . . .'

For the Pressmen covering the inquest, Veronica remained the focus of attention.

One reporter recorded: 'She sits staring ahead. She invariably wears the same dark coat, the same white turban and the same blank expression.' Another observed that in court Lady Lucan was 'emotionless – sitting with her eyes drawn through lack of sleep, sometimes yawning, sometimes looking around her defiantly, outstaring those prepared to play the dangerous game of trying to catch her eye. She is a woman deeply alone.'

She looked pale and tense as the coroner went through the preliminaries. Addressing the jury, Dr Thurston recalled that Sandra Rivett had died aged twenty-nine in November 1974 and that the cause of death had been given as blunt injuries to the head. Warrants had been issued for the arrest of Lord Lucan for the murder of Mrs Rivett and the attempted murder of his wife.

'You will note,' he said, 'that Lord Lucan disappeared and was last seen at 1.30 a.m. on the morning of 8 November last. I have deliberately delayed this inquiry for a long time in the hope of something more concrete turning up.'

After 'a great deal of very anxious consideration,' he said, he had decided to call Lady Lucan as a witness. A wife could give evidence adverse to her husband when he was alleged to have assaulted her – and the assault on Lady Lucan, Dr Thurston said, was bound up with the death of Mrs Rivett. He pointed out that the case had attracted enormous publicity and said it was his duty to tell members of the jury that they must only reach a conclusion on the evidence before them. Their task was to decide who the deceased was; how, when and where she met her death; and the person or persons, if any, to be charged with her murder or manslaughter.

Sandra's estranged husband, burly security officer Roger Rivett, aged thirty-four, of Brighton Road, Coulsdon, Surrey was the first witness. He said he had last seen Sandra alive towards the end of April 1974 when he had left her. She had kept the use of their flat in Valley Road, Kenley, Surrey. He said he didn't know where Sandra had been living but had been told that she lived at 46 Lower Belgrave Street and worked as a nanny. He agreed with the coroner that Sandra was 'rather a small lady' of 5 feet 2 inches.

P.C. Patrick Sullivan then explained a plan of the murder house to the court. He pointed out that the door leading from the hall to the basement stairs was open, hooked back; and that someone in Lady Lucan's bedroom on the second floor could not be seen by a person in the adjoining bathroom.

Michael Eastham QC, who told the coroner that he appeared for the Dowager Countess of Lucan, asked the policeman during cross-examination: 'As you walk along Lower Belgrave Street, can you see into the kitchen?'

'Provided there is a light, you can see into part of the kitchen,' the policeman replied.

Mr Eastham told the court: '[The Dowager Countess] wishes me to represent Lord Lucan's interests as best I can because the jury could reach a decision which could bring stigma to his name.'

The next witnesses were police photographers who had taken pictures of the scene of the crime, of the bloody body of Sandra Rivett at the public mortuary and of Lady Lucan at St George's hospital. The colour photographs were not a pretty sight. The exhibits officer in the case produced, carefully preserved in plastic bags, exhibits C.10, C.11 and C.12, the three letters John wrote after the murder to Bill Shand Kydd and Michael Stoop, plus the envelopes for two of them; and the gruesome exhibit C.13, the bloodstained sack in which Sandra Rivett's body had been found.

At eleven o'clock, Veronica was called. She moved to the

184

witness box at the front right-hand side of the courtroom, a tiny, frail-looking figure, painfully thin. She took the oath and was then allowed to sit, rather than stand. At one stage during her evidence, a reporter noticed her rocking her body backwards and forwards in her seat. But any other signs of tension were obscured from even the most eagle-eyed observer: above the varnished wood panelling of the witness box, only her head and shoulders were visible. With her hair drawn back under her white hat, however, her forehead revealed traces of scars from injuries which she was to tell the coroner had been inflicted by John.

To the left of her was the bespectacled Dr Thurston, his white hair balding. He sat in authority on a maroon leather chair, on a raised dais beneath the lion and unicorn on the wall. From his gentle approach and appearance, however, he seemed more like a favourite uncle than a cold inquisitor. Throughout the inquest, he made notes in longhand.

Veronica was to be in the witness box for over two hours. Shafts of sunlight fell through the high, glass-domed ceiling as the assembled Pressmen, policemen, lawyers and others hung on to her every word.

After preliminary questions, Veronica told the coroner that from 18 July 1974, apart from a telephone conversation with John about Camilla, who had chickenpox, she had had no contact with her husband at all.

'So he could not have threatened you?' Dr Thurston asked.

'No,' she replied.

'Did your husband know Sandra Rivett?'

'He met her when he collected the children for access and brought them back.'

'That was all, as far as you are aware?'

'As far as I'm aware, yes.'

Later, during cross-examination, Veronica said there had been three access weekends while Sandra was at number 46.

Dr Thurston asked: 'Did your husband have any connection with Newhaven at any time?'

'Not that I know of,' she said.

'He had a powerboat at one time?'

'When he had a powerboat he kept it on the Hamble. That boat sank and another one was dropped on a quay and smashed. That was some years ago.'

'Did you know much about your husband's financial situation?'

'I have read a bit about it,' Veronica said. 'I read an article in the *Daily Express* which suggested he was in financial difficulties but I don't know from my personal knowledge.'

'How many · nannies had you had in the last six months?' Dr Thurston asked.

'Including temporaries?'

'Yes.'

Veronica's reply could have been 'Seven' or 'Several'.

'When did Sandra Rivett come?'

'I think she came early in September. One particular woman provided all the women I had.'

'An agent?'

'An agent who was a friend.'

She had seen no references for Sandra, she said later. She had taken the friend's recommendations, which were well founded.

'Did you get on well with her?' the coroner asked.

'With Sandra? Yes I did.'

She had an even temperament and was cheerful, Veronica said.

'Did you know whether she had any men friends?'

'She talked of two.'

'You knew she was separated from her husband?'

'Yes I did.'

'Had any man friend come to your house?'

'No.'

'Or had she asked for one to come?' Dr Thurston asked.

'No,' Veronica said.

Frances had in fact told relatives that 'Ray' had come to

the front door of number 46 to pick Sandra up when they went out together. Maybe Veronica wasn't aware of that.

'What was her usual day off?' the coroner asked.

'Thursday.'

During cross-examination afterwards, Veronica said that Sandra wouldn't be back until very late on her days off.

Dr Thurston continued: 'Can you say anything about her stature?'

'Her husband described her as 5 feet 2 inches and I am 5 feet 2 inches,' Veronica replied. 'She once tried on a dress given to me by another woman. It was too large for me. It fitted Sandra. She was a fuller build than me.'

The dress was a size 10, she said later, adding: 'I am a size 8.'

The coroner turned to the evening of the murder: Thursday, 7 November 1974. Though it would normally have been Sandra's day off, she was actually working at number 46 that day.

'Her current boyfriend had his day off on Wednesday,' Veronica explained, 'so she asked if she could change hers to Wednesday as well so that she could go out with him.'

It was the first week the nanny had taken Wednesday off instead, she said later during cross-examination.

At the house that evening were herself, Sandra and the three children. The front door had a Yale lock and usually a brass chain was put up as well after 6.00 p.m. – but it wasn't that evening because, Veronica told Dr Thurston, she 'hadn't thought to do it'. In the basement there was a door leading out of a passage from the kitchen, which was used every day to take the rubbish out. That was bolted. In the breakfast room there were the French windows and there was the other [back] door to the side.

'Are these windows and door kept locked?' the coroner asked.

'They are,' Veronica said.

If someone wanted to leave the house through the garden by climbing the wall it would be a prickly business, she suggested, because there was the rose trellis and bushes and similar things. It would be difficult to climb the wall and there was no other regular means of getting in or out of the house.

From about 8.00 p.m. that evening, Veronica said, she had watched television in her bedroom. Frances was with her, she said, but Mrs Rivett was not.

'When did Mrs Rivett look in?' Dr Thurston asked.

'At about five to nine,' Veronica said.

'What did she say?'

'She put her head round the door and asked: "Would you like a cup of tea?"'

Veronica added: 'I had the habit of getting myself a cup of tea at that time. It was a thing I had been doing since the separation. It was not usual for Sandra to offer me tea, but I accepted her offer. My bedroom is on the second floor. I was lying on the bed, my daughter also. I can place the time from the TV programme.'

In cross-examination later, she suggested that it would be expected that she would be in the kitchen on a Thursday evening, not Sandra.

The coroner continued: 'Did Mrs Rivett take some crockery with her?'

'I don't know that she did.'

Veronica was shown exhibit C.14, the cups and saucers which had been found dirty and scattered in the pool of Sandra's blood at the bottom of the basement stairs.

'I recognise the crockery,' she said. 'I am told that these were taken by Mrs Rivett. She may have had them in her own room.'

'And then you went on watching the news on television?'

'Yes.'

'When did you begin to wonder about the tea?'

'At about quarter past nine.'

'Had you heard anything unusual during that time?'

'Nothing unusual.'

'What did you do then?'

'I decided to go downstairs and find out what had happened to the tea.'

Veronica told the hushed court how she had descended the stairs to the ground floor to look for Sandra.

'What did you do when you got there?'

'I looked round the stairs leading to the basement. There was no light on at all anywhere in the basement.'

'I believe there is a two-way switch?' the coroner said, referring to the switch at the head of the twelve steep stairs.

'You switch on the light by leaning forward through the doorway at the top of the basement stairs,' Veronica said.

'Did you try to turn on the switch?' the coroner asked.

'No,' she said. 'I just saw that it was dark and thought she couldn't be there.'

Was it possible to see the scattered crockery and the pool of blood in the shaft of light thrown by the street lamp outside? Dr Thurston didn't ask.

'Did you call out?'

'I called her name.'

'What did you do then?'

'I heard a noise.'

'What sort of noise?'

'Just a noise of somebody or something in the downstairs cloakroom.'

The 'downstairs' cloakroom? What did she mean by that – the one in the basement?

'That is where there is a wash basin and lavatory?' Dr Thurston asked.

'Yes.'

'And what happened next?'

Veronica closed her eyes and said: 'I moved towards the sound.'

'And what happened then?'

'Somebody rushed out and hit me on the head.'

Dr Thurston asked: 'Did this happen in the area at the top of the stairs, approximately?'

'Approximately.'

That meant she was talking about the cloakroom in the hall – *not* the one in the basement, as Hugh had assumed when she talked to him earlier from her hospital bed.

'Was there more than one blow?'

'About four.'

'Did you hear anybody speak at that time?'

'At the time I was hit on the head, no,' Veronica said. 'Later I did. I screamed.'

'And then what?'

'The person said: "Shut up!"'

The person? According to an interview she'd given to the *Daily Express* back in January, in the darkness at the time she had originally 'thought it might have been one or two people . . . perhaps burglars'. If there *were* two people around, what certainty was there that the person who said 'Shut up!' was the same person who had hit her over the head? She had already made it clear elsewhere that she did not *see* the attacker in the darkness, which also meant she might not have seen someone else – perhaps John coming to the rescue.

The coroner asked: 'Did you recognise the voice?'

Veronica took a deep breath and answered: 'Yes.'

'Who was it?'

She fingered the scar at the centre of her forehead. 'My husband,' she said firmly.

'What did you do then?'

'He thrust three gloved fingers down my throat and we started to fight.'

This was another change from the interview in the *Express*. In the newspaper, she had been quoted as saying: 'The man then thrust three gloved fingers down my throat and said "Shut up".' This implied that she heard John saying 'Shut up' *after* her throat had been attacked. Had the passage of time played a minor but significant trick with her memory? Were the exact details of that night likely to be most fresh in her mind two months after the murder, when she spoke to the *Express* – or at the inquest, seven months after the crime?

As Veronica herself was about to remark, remembering everything after so long was not easy.

But there was another point. By the time Veronica had three gloved fingers thrust down her throat, the attack on her *with the weapon* had clearly ceased. But why? Why would an attacker already wielding a lethal weapon to good effect suddenly stop using it – unless he was *forced* to? It didn't make sense.

'What happened during the fight?' Dr Thurston asked.

'It is very difficult to remember – it was seven months ago,' Veronica said. 'But during the course of it, he attempted to strangle me from in front and to gouge out my eye.'

As they struggled, she went on, they fell in through the basement doorway onto the basement stairs. She suggested that the broken support on the wrought iron banister rail could have been dislodged by her foot as they fought.

'I was on the ground by this time,' she said. 'I remember sitting up somehow sideways between his legs. Then he desisted.'

Later on, during cross-examination, Mr Brian Watling, for the police, asked: 'When you were struggling with your husband, is it right you grabbed hold of him?'

Veronica agreed that she did.

'By his private parts?'

'Yes.'

'What effect, if any, did that seem to have on him?'

'He went back. He moved back.

'Did he say anything to you at that stage?'

The coroner refused to allow Veronica to answer the question. Despite the headline on that morning's *Daily Express*, she never did get the chance at the inquest to 'name the "killer"'.

During cross-examination, however, she did describe the 'instrument' used in the attack on her.

'I was hit with an object,' Veronica said. 'It appeared to be slightly curved and hard.'

She agreed that she had told the police: 'I know it sounds silly, but it felt bandaged.'

Handed a photograph, she remarked: 'That seems to fit the description of what I was hit with.'

Oddly enough, according to her *Daily Express*

191

exclusive in January, Veronica had actually *touched* the so-called 'murder weapon'.

'My hand fell on to a heavy object on the floor . . . it seemed to be metal covered in bandaging,' she was quoted as saying.

Continuing her answers to the coroner's questions, Veronica said she asked if she could get a drink of water and went into the hall cloakroom, where there was only hot water. It was dark in there, she said. (That was where the shaving mirror strip-light was on when Sergeant Baker entered the house later.) With John, she then went upstairs.

Veronica's evidence was now beginning to match what John had said. But it still raised queries. If she'd touched the weapon, why hadn't she grabbed it and used it in self-defence? While she was in the hall, only a few feet from the street, why hadn't she made a run for the front door? Why had she made escape more difficult by going upstairs with John to her bedroom? And if he was the attacker, why hadn't he killed her and what on earth was he doing helping her upstairs?

Frances, who was in the bedroom on the second floor watching television, was sent up to bed. The Lucans went into the adjoining bathroom, Veronica said, and 'together we looked at my injuries'.

'After that,' she told Dr Thurston, 'I think I said: "I don't feel very well." He laid a towel on the bed and I got on it. The towel was placed on the pillow.'

The coroner asked: 'Did he say anything about helping you further?'

'Very vaguely. I understood he was going to get a cloth to clean up my face.'

'And for this he would have gone into the bathroom?'

'Yes,' Veronica said.

'What did you do then?'

'I heard the taps running and I jumped to my feet and ran out of the room and down the stairs.'

She said she ran about 30 yards down the street to the Plumbers Arms. Assistance was sought and she was taken to St George's hospital, where she stayed for just under a week.

Dr Thurston asked: 'Have you seen your husband since the time he went into the bathroom from your bedroom?'

'No,' she replied. 'I have not.'

'You have no doubt it was he?'

'I have no doubt,' she said. 'No doubt at all.'

19

Cross-examining Veronica, Michael Eastham QC leapt straight to John's defence. He was never to get beyond his first major question, but it was a stunner. Having established that the Lucans separated on 7 January 1973, he said to Veronica: 'Even before that, you entertained feelings of hatred for your husband, did you not?'

Before Veronica could answer, her counsel, Mr Bruce Coles, jumped to his feet and declared to the coroner: 'I don't see how this can help your inquiry.'

'I was thinking that myself,' Dr Thurston replied.

To Mr Eastham, the coroner said: ' "Hatred" is a very strong way of putting it.'

Michael Eastham patiently referred him to the letters John had written on the night of the murder.

He told Dr Thurston: '*You* know, although the jury does not know, that in two written accounts, or chiefly in one written account, the absent earl is saying in terms: (a) that he was not the attacker, and (b) that Lady Lucan is deliberately making it look as if he was the attacker. In these circumstances the relationship between the two of them must be relevant as to whether [Veronica's testimony] is an honest recollection of this witness or a fabrication.'

He added: 'I don't enjoy my task but I would not be doing my duty in accordance with my instructions if I do not pursue the line I am pursuing.'

John's main letter to Bill Shand Kydd, written at Uckfield, was now read out in public. For the first time the jury, the Press and the rest of the world could hear his version of the events in his own words. The relevant phrases referred to by Mr Eastham (marked by my italics) rang round the silent courtroom. The letter, written on Susan Maxwell-Scott's writing paper, was dated '7th Nov 1974' and read:

7^t Nov. 1974

Dear Bill,

The most ghastly circumstances arose tonight which I briefly described to my mother. When I interrupted the fight at Lower Belgrave St and the man left Veronica accused me of having hired him. I took her upstairs and sent Frances up to bed and

tried to clean her up. She
lay doggo for a bit and
while he was in the
bathroom left the house.
The circumstantial evidence
against her is strong in
that V will say it was
all my doing. I also
will lie doggo for a bit
but I am only concerned for
the children If you can
manage it I want them to
live with you — Coutts (trustee)
St Martin Lane (Bishopsgate) will
handle school fees.. V. has

demonstrated her[2] hatred for me in the past and would do anything to see me accused. For George & Frances to go through life knowing their father had stood in the dock for attempted murder would be too much. When they are old enough to understand, explain to them the disease of paranoia, and look after them.

Yours sincerely,

John

Dear Bill,

The most ghastly circumstances arose tonight which I briefly described to my mother. When I interrupted the fight at Lower Belgrave St and the man left *Veronica accused me of having hired him.* I took her upstairs and sent Frances up to bed and tried to clean her up. She lay doggo for a bit and when I was in the bathroom left the house. *The circumstantial evidence against me is strong in that V will say it was all my doing.* I also will lie doggo for a bit but I am only concerned for the children. If you can manage it I want them to live with you – Coutts (trustees) St Martins Lane (Mr Wall) will handle school fees. *V. has demonstrated her hatred for me in the past and would do anything to see me accused.* For George + Frances to go through life knowing their father had stood in the dock for attempted murder would be too much. When they are old enough to understand, explain to them the dream of paranoia, and look after them.

Yours ever,
John.

The tall, angular handwriting had already been identified by Veronica as John's. Though his writing had often been hard to decipher, it was no more so than usual in this letter. However the word taken to be the 'dream' of paranoia could have been 'dreams' or something else: perhaps the 'dilemma' or 'disease' of paranoia.

There was a pause as the words sank in. From the use of the term 'ghastly circumstances', the coroner remarked, Lord Lucan sounded under stress.

As was soon to become clear, Michael Eastham was in a classic 'Catch 22' situation. At a trial in a proper court of law, allegations made by a witness can be effectively challenged by producing evidence to cast doubt on the character, truthfulness or testimony of that witness. But the same situation did not apply at inquests. To give the jury enough information to understand the background to the case meant delving into evidence about the Lucans' history. That meant asking Veronica questions which would clarify the situation – but which, by their nature, might be seen as an attempt to discredit her. *That* was forbidden at inquests. Yet without posing the questions, John's name could not be fully defended.

Mr Eastham explained his situation to the court. He told the coroner he was aware that questions aimed at discrediting witnesses were not allowed at inquest proceedings. What he wanted was to ask Lady Lucan questions directed to establishing the relationship between her husband and herself. This, he said, was 'not for the purpose of discrediting her but to assist the jury' when they came to consider what had happened on the night of 7 November.

'That involves,' he said, 'the inescapable and unpleasant duty of suggesting that what she is saying she knows to be untrue.'

He referred to John's secret tape recordings of Veronica put forward for the custody case.

'There is a tape of what this lady said about her husband which has been used in other proceedings,' he said.

Mr Eastham told the court that he had a heavy responsibility on his shoulders because the only case he could put forward was based on what Lord Lucan had said to his mother and to Mrs Maxwell-Scott and written in his letters. He would undertake to the coroner to limit his questions as far as he could but it was essential, he said, that he got out sufficient evidence for the jury to properly realise the 'issue' they would have to consider.

Without further evidence, he said, the reference in Lord Lucan's letter to 'paranoia' would be 'totally inexplicable' to the jury.

(The only previous public mention of 'paranoia', of course, had been the ridiculous suggestion in James Fox's *Sunday Times Magazine* article that Lord Lucan was 'paranoid'.)

'It's very difficult,' the coroner said.

Members of the jury were directed to leave the

courtroom while Dr Thurston heard further submissions. Michael Eastham said his instructions were that by the beginning of 1973, Lady Lucan quite definitely hated her husband. He could prove that thereafter there were long proceedings held *in camera*. What he would like to have in evidence, he said, was that there was a suggestion Lady Lucan suffered from paranoia; and that the situation further deteriorated in view of the long proceedings, which had gone on for eleven days. The main issue was who should have care and control of the children. Allegations of a most far-reaching kind were made. At the end of the day, it was Lady Lucan who gained care and control of the children, subject to stringent conditions. If what Lord Lucan said in his letters had any basis in reality, then for a wife to invent such a story would be a terrible thing.

Dr Thurston remarked that the present hearing was an inquiry, not a trial, and said: 'There will be other evidence.'

Mr Eastham commented: 'None of the scientific evidence will show the lady's feelings towards her husband or her mental condition.'

But he got nowhere.

As far as the coroner was concerned, evidence about the Lucans' relationship was outside the terms of his inquiry.

That extraordinary decision had a profound effect on the hearing. Given the opportunity, Kait could have told the court about the history of the marriage and about Veronica's previous accusations against John. But when she gave evidence later on, she was not at liberty to do so. Both Bill Shand Kydd and Michael Stoop could have filled in background details and explained to the jury exactly what references in John's letters to them meant. Instead, they were restricted by Dr Thurston's ruling to unilluminating 'Yes/No' answers which hardly explained anything. Instead of the jigsaw being pieced together, major pieces were withheld by order. How were members of the jury supposed to get a clear view of the full picture – by guesswork? To insiders who *knew* all the background, doubts about the Lucan case flew in like vultures at a kill. But the jury members weren't even going to hear of Veronica's psychiatric treatment. How could they possibly be expected to reach a reasonable verdict without possession of all the facts?

Michael Eastham's attempt to defend John's name in his absence had been strangled at birth. The injustice of it was breathtaking.

Vanquished hardly before he'd drawn his sword, when the jury returned Mr Eastham told the coroner: 'In view of the ruling you have given in the absence of the jury, I do not think I can assist the jury at all and I do not wish to ask the lady any questions.'

Facing Veronica, Dr Thurston posed a final couple of questions himself. When she put her head round the top of the basement stairs and called Sandra's name, had she seen anyone else?

'Did anybody rush past?' he asked.

'I saw nobody else,' Veronica declared. 'Nor at any other time that evening.'

And with that she stepped down from the witness box.

Members of the jury had heard that Veronica did not recognise the sack. But, unlike *Daily Express* readers months before, they had not learned that the attacker had grabbed at the diamond and sapphire pendant necklace she was wearing, or that she had said to him that evening: 'Oh dear, what shall we do with the body?'

At Guilsborough shortly after the murder, Frances had spoken of the events of the night Sandra died. What she said at the vicarage coincided with what she later told the police. Her police statement disagreed with three points in her mother's evidence, most significantly on the vital question of time. But the police did not take Frances's statement until 20 November, eight days *after* they had obtained warrants for John's arrest. And at the inquest, the relevance of the conflicting evidence about the timing of the events was not emphasised to the jury. Indeed, Frances was not even called to give evidence in person.

Instead, Woman Detective Constable Sally Bower, who took Frances's police statement, read it out to the court. The policewoman told the coroner: 'I think she was telling the truth as she saw it. She was quite clear and composed.'

The statement said:

I live at [46 Lower Belgrave Street] with Mummy, my brother George, my sister Camilla, and whoever is looking after us. Mummy and Daddy don't live together, but I usually see Daddy every other weekend. We stay the weekend with him at the Gibbs's house in Northampton or with the Shand Kydds or with a friend of Daddy's, Lord Suffolk, who lives in Wiltshire at a place called Charlton Park. George, Camilla and I spent the weekend of 2nd/3rd November 1974 with Daddy at the Gibbs's house in Northampton. Daddy took us home to Lower Belgrave Street at 5.30 p.m. on Sunday 3rd November 1974. The last time I saw Daddy was on Thursday 7th November 1974. On that day I didn't go to school because the bus didn't come for me, so Mummy said I need not go. Camilla and George went to school as usual. I spent the day at home with Mummy and Sandra, our nanny. As far as I know nothing unusual happened that day and nobody came to visit us at home.

On Thursday evening we, that's Mummy, George, Camilla and Sandra and I, all had our tea together. I think that was sometime around 5.00 p.m. or 5.30 p.m. After tea I played with one of my games in the nursery. Then at about 7.20 p.m. I watched *Top of the Pops* on the television in the nursery. Mummy, Camilla, George and Sandra were downstairs in Mummy's room. They were watching *The Six Million Dollar Man*. I went downstairs and joined them at about 8.05 p.m., and we all watched the television in Mummy's room. When the programme finished at 8.30 p.m., I went back upstairs to the nursery and played a little more with my game.

Sandra brought George and Camilla upstairs and put them to bed. I had had a bath before I started watching television and I was wearing my pyjamas after my bath. I stayed in the nursery for about five minutes only, then I went downstairs again to Mummy's room. That would have been about 8.40 p.m.

I asked Mummy where Sandra was and she said she was downstairs making some tea. I didn't see her go downstairs so I don't know if she took any empty cups with her. I didn't notice whether or not there were any empty cups in the room. After a while Mummy said she wondered why Sandra was so long. I don't know what time this was, but it was before the news came on the television at 9.00 p.m. I said I would go downstairs to see what was keeping Sandra but Mummy said no, she would go. I said I would go with her but she said no, it was OK, she would go. Mummy left the room to go downstairs and I stayed watching the television. She left the bedroom door open, but there was no light in the hall because the light bulb is worn out and it doesn't work. Just after Mummy left the room I heard a scream. It sounded as though it came from a long way away. I thought maybe the cat had scratched Mummy and she had screamed. I wasn't frightened by the scream and I just stayed in the room watching television. I went to the door of the room and called out 'Mummy?' but there was no answer so I just left it. At about 9.05 p.m., when the news was on the television, Daddy and Mummy both walked into the room. Mummy had blood over her face and she was crying. Mummy told me to go upstairs. Daddy didn't say anything to me and I didn't say anything to either of them. I don't know how much blood was on Mummy's face, I only caught a glimpse of her. As far as I can remember, Daddy was wearing a pair of dark trousers and an overcoat which was full length and was fawn-coloured with brown checks. I was sitting on the bed as they came in the door and I couldn't see them very well. There were two lights on above Mummy's bed and one other sidelight on. I didn't hear any conversation between Mummy and Daddy. I couldn't see if Daddy's clothes had any blood on them. I wondered what had happened but I didn't ask. After Mummy told me to go upstairs I got straight up and went upstairs to my bedroom, which is on the top floor of the house. I got into bed and read my book. I didn't hear anything from downstairs. After a little while, I don't know how long because I don't have a clock in my room, I heard Daddy calling for Mummy. He was calling out: 'Veronica, where are you?' I got up and went to the banisters and looked down and I saw Daddy coming out of the nursery on the floor below me. He then went into the bathroom on the same floor as the nursery. He came straight out and then he went downstairs. That was the last I saw of him. He never came up to the top floor of the house that night, either to look for Mummy or to say goodnight to me. I didn't notice at any time whether or not Daddy was wearing gloves. The last time I saw Sandra was when she took George and Camilla upstairs to bed. I was very surprised to see Daddy at home that Thursday night, but I never asked why he was there.

During the last weekend we spent with Daddy on the 2nd and 3rd November 1974, Camilla told Daddy that Sandra had boyfriends and went out with them. Daddy asked when Sandra went out with her boyfriends and Camilla said Sandra went out with her boyfriends on her days off. Then Daddy asked me when Sandra had her days off. I said her day off was Thursday.

The next witness, Mr Whitehouse from the Plumbers Arms, told the court that at 9.50 p.m. the pub door 'burst open' and Lady Lucan ran in.

'I gave her assistance,' he said. 'I laid her on the bench. She was head to toe in blood from head wounds but it was crusted. She was quite all right for a few minutes. I covered her with an overcoat. She then started shouting: 'Help me, help me, help me! I've just escaped from being murdered! My children, my children! He's murdered my nanny! He's murdered my nanny!' No name was mentioned. I telephoned for the police and ambulance immediately. The police were ten minutes, the ambulance about twenty minutes. I called my wife down to give medical attention until the ambulance arrived.'

Dr Michael Smith, a police surgeon, said that at 10.45 p.m. on the night of the murder he had been called to 46 Lower Belgrave Street. Near the bottom of the basement stairs he saw a large canvas bag which appeared to contain a human body.

'I also noted bloodstains on the floor,' he said. 'I didn't disturb the bag in any way. I was satisfied that the body was dead and that death was not due to natural causes. I thought death was very recent – within an hour or so.'

Dr Smith couldn't be exact: as we shall see, it is impossible to pinpoint the precise time of death. Nevertheless, there was no way Sandra could have been killed at 9.45 p.m. Chances are she died before 9.00 p.m.

Sergeant Baker, the first investigator on the scene, described his arrival at number 46 shortly after 10.00 p.m. and his search of the house with P.C. Beddick, who echoed much of his testimony afterwards. Sergeant Baker told the jury of his astonishing find – the 'weapon' which inexplicably changed colour.

After recalling how he had found the children upstairs, he told the jury: 'I returned to the ground floor and there I found near the door leading to the basement an object on the floor. I thought it was a doll's leg. It was white. I walked straight past it the first time. The second time I noticed it was bandaged with tape. It was lead piping with tape round it. It had gone to, generally, red. I didn't touch it . . .'

He described finding the body in the bloodstained sack and mentioned the unlocked back door.

'I went through the breakfast room to where there is a

205

safe. There was a door opposite that,' he said. 'It leads into the back yard. I went through it, I think by myself. The door was closed – not locked. I don't know if it could be opened from the outside. There was nobody outside . . .'

Soon after that, he said, he summoned the CID.

The next witness was Dr Hugh Scott, who had been working at the time as a casualty officer at St George's hospital.

'At about 11.00 p.m. I was called to see Lady Lucan,' he said. 'She was very distressed. She was obviously badly injured and had bled a lot from scalp wounds. She had blood on her face and head. She also had lacerations on the inner aspect of her mouth and complained of pain on her neck. Lacerations on the scalp were on top of the head extending down to the hairline on the right side of the forehead, on various parts of the top of the head. There were about seven large lacerations – difficult to be exact, they merged with each other. The lacerations were roughly parallel. The general trend was in one direction from front to back.'

Dr Scott also mentioned 'slight bruising around the left eye', and said that the 'one or two small lacerations on the right palate and on the back of the throat' could have been caused by 'any object', including fingers, 'thrust forcefully into the mouth'. He told the coroner: 'There was no other obvious injury to Lady Lucan. Nothing on her neck.'

Shown photographs, the doctor said: 'A weapon of this sort could certainly have caused these lacerations [to the scalp]. It would be hard to explain them from a fall.' He said he could see 'some similarities' between Veronica's injuries and Sandra's. 'The same instrument could have caused those lacerations.'

The shock of one question to Dr Scott brought a sudden realisation to Veronica.

Asked if Lady Lucan's injuries could have been 'self-inflicted', he replied: 'Yes, but it is very unlikely.'

Years later, Veronica was quoted as telling the *News of the World*: '. . . It was only then I realised that I myself was suspected of murdering [Sandra].'

20

Day Two of the hearing began with evidence from Veronica's bodyguard, Detective Sergeant Graham Forsyth. Summoned from the CID office at Gerald Road, he went to number 46 at 10.20 p.m. on the murder night, he told the court. He described the scene there and mentioned that he noticed a light bulb on a cushion chair by the stairway in the basement. Nearby, outside the kitchen door, there was a birdcage-style light holder without a bulb in it. The court was to hear from Ranson later that the birdcage light was the only one which could be turned on and off from the switch at the top of the basement stairs. When the light bulb was fitted into the birdcage holder, it worked.

Sergeant Forsyth described going to the mews cottage at Eaton Row, where he broke in through an upstairs window, looking for Lord Lucan. He then returned to 46 Lower Belgrave Street, where he saw the Dowager Countess of Lucan.

He recalled: 'She'd apparently arrived a couple of minutes before I got there. I spoke to her in the dining room on the ground floor. I said: "I understand you are the mother of Lord Lucan. I am sorry to have to tell you but your daughter-in-law has been attacked and is at present in hospital. I am still trying to ascertain her condition and I'm sorry to have to tell you that a woman who I believe is the nanny to your grandchildren is dead." She said: "Oh dear."'

Sergeant Forsyth paused and told Dr Thurston: 'Before I continue I am about to bring into evidence certain points which were the subject of submission by Mr Eastham and about which you made a ruling.'

He asked if he was permitted to do so.

Veronica's counsel, Mr Coles, rose to his feet and said:

'I think this evidence would be an embarrassment to my client.'

Michael Eastham countered: 'I think the evidence should go in.'

The coroner agreed with him.

Sergeant Forsyth then repeated to the court the conversation he said he had had with Kait. She was to dispute parts of it later.

(To avoid endless 'I saids' and 'She saids', I have omitted them entirely.)

The detective began: 'Does your son live here?'

Kait replied: 'He's separated. The children were made wards of court and Veronica was told to continue with medical treatment for her mental complaint.'

'What was that?'

'Manic-depressive. Not violent, except verbally. In the original court case it was thought that she was a danger to the children. I knew something was wrong because John telephoned me a short while ago and told me to come here.'

'What time was this?'

'About 10.45 p.m.'

'What did he say?'

'"There has been a terrible catastrophe at number 46. Ring Bill Shand Kydd immediately." He said he had been driving past the house and he saw a fight going on in the basement between a man and Veronica. He went in and joined them. He said Veronica was shouting and screaming. He sounded very shocked. I said to him: "Where are you going?" He said: "I don't know." He then just rang off.'

'Did he say what was wrong?'

'No. I tried to find out but he just told me to get the children out as soon as possible.'

'What sort of car does he drive?'

'A Mercedes, a blue one.'

'Do you know where he keeps it?'

'No I don't – probably at Elizabeth Street.'

'Do you know the address?'

Lord Lucan, 14 July 1971

Sally, John, Jane and Hugh in the
rose garden at Penwood

John as a schoolboy

John, then Lord Bingham, in the
Coldstream Guards

The 7th Earl of Lucan in his
ceremonial robes

Veronica becomes Lady Bingham, 28 November 1963

Veronica with Frances, her first child

Nanny Lilian Jenkins with Frances
and George at St Moritz, Christmas 1968

The Lucans with Frances and
Nanny Jenkins in the garden at
46 Lower Belgrave Street

The Lucans out on the golf course

Frances, George and Camilla

Sandra Rivett, the murdered nanny

Roger Rivett, Sandra's estranged husband

Det. Chief Inspector Dave 'Buster' Gerring

Det. Chief Superintendent Roy Ranson

Four of the 'murder reconstruction' pictures, January 1975. Two months after the murder Veronica retraces her steps for the *Daily Express* (see page 308)

She goes down the basement stairs

and sees the body

Back in the hall she is confronted by an attacker and is knocked back onto the basement stairs during the struggle

Veronica later told the inquest a different version (see pages 188–191)

Christina Shand Kydd

Kait Lucan and Bill Shand Kydd

Professor Keith Simpson, Home Office
Pathologist

Dr Margaret Pereira, the blood analyst

Lady Lucan, 8 December 1975

'Yes – 72a Elizabeth Street.'

'I'd be very grateful if you could take the children. There are many things to be dealt with here and obviously we don't wish to involve them.'

'Certainly.'

Sergeant Forsyth told the coroner: 'Then she went upstairs to the children and they were taken away with P.C. Beddick.'

He described his visit to John's flat at 72a Elizabeth Street, and said later he had taken a statement from Veronica. Later still he had obtained four warrants from the Bow Street magistrate under the Bankers' Book Evidence Act and on 28 November he had checked the state of four of John's bank accounts.

'It was because of the second letter to Mr Shand Kydd that I went to those banks,' he said.

The second letter John had written to Bill from Uckfield on the murder night was headed 'Financial matters' and read:

There is a sale coming up at Christies Nov 27th which will satisfy bank overdrafts. Please agree reserves with Tom Craig.
Proceeds to go to:
        Lloyds, 6 Pall Mall,
        Coutts, 59 Strand,
        Nat West, Bloomsbury branch,
        who also hold an
        Eq. and Law Life Policy.
The other creditors can get lost for the time being.
                              Lucky.

It was interesting that he'd signed the two letters with different names: 'John' when writing about the children; 'Lucky', his gambling name, when writing about his debts.

At Coutts, Sergeant Forsyth told the coroner, he discovered that John had an overdraft of £2,841, at Lloyds an overdraft of £4,379, at the National Westminster an

209

overdraft of £1,290 – and there was an additional overdraft of £5,667 on his account at the Midland Bank in Newgate Street. The total amount overdrawn, he said, came to £14,177.

'Do you know whether there has been any movement in or out of those accounts since November?' Dr Thurston asked.

'I have not personally received any such information,' said the detective, 'but I would have expected to have heard if there had been.'

During cross-examination, Sergeant Forsyth said he didn't know if the kettle on the worktop in the kitchen was full or empty because he 'didn't check it'.

'I saw no sign of disturbance in the kitchen,' he said.

The points Kait disputed were that she had said John was 'driving past' the house, and that the first call from him had come at about '10.45 p.m.'. She believed it was earlier. Sergeant Forsyth said that notes of his interview with her had been made for him by a colleague in his presence while he was asking the questions. He repeated the words he said she had used and told the coroner: 'The Dowager Countess was calm but obviously such news as I gave her must have been a shock.'

Michael Eastham said: 'She will tell the coroner that she is certain she did not say John was "driving past" but "passing".'

Sergeant Forsyth agreed that it would have been impossible for anyone *driving* past the house to have seen into the basement.

Referred to the light bulb he'd discovered lying on a chair near the stairway, he also agreed that lights in the kitchen, in the breakfast room and in the boiler room in the basement all had bulbs fitted.

Michael Eastham asked: 'Have you ever been outside on the pavement in Lower Belgrave Street either when the kitchen light was on or in daylight?'

'Yes,' said Sergeant Forsyth.

'Is it possible to see part of the kitchen from the pavement?'

'It is possible,' he said.

Mr Watling for the police told the coroner: 'Chief Superintendent Ranson has done certain experiments.'

The jury would hear of those later.

Michael Eastham said: 'About a pair of gloves in the main bedroom. Did you find any men's gloves in that room?'

Sergeant Forsyth said he did not.

'Did any police officer find any gloves?'

'I don't think so,' he said.

The pathologist on the case, the eminent Professor Keith Simpson, was next into the witness box. He told the court that he had carried out a post-mortem on Sandra Rivett on the morning of 8 November. Her body was doubled up inside the canvas bag. Her clothing was undisturbed but heavily soiled with blood. He considered death took place before the body was encased in the sack. Mrs Rivett had been a healthy woman, he said. There was no sign of any recent sexual intercourse or of a sexual attack. He had found three blunt injuries to the face, one above the right eye, a second near the mouth and the third over the left eyebrow. There were four splits in the scalp on the front side of the head above the ear, and two other splits near the neck. There was also heavy bruising on the tops of both shoulders, and at the back of the right hand was some superficial bruising likely to have resulted from the hand being used for protection.

On the front of the right upper arm there were four in-line bruises which could have been caused by the rough grip of fingers. There had been a great deal of blood, he said, mostly from the nose and mouth. There was surface and deeper bruising to the brain, and the injuries to the side of the head must have caused more than dazing. It was these injuries, together with the bruising of the brain, which caused death. There had also been much inhalation of blood, and it was this which had made it clear that no further kind of asphyxia followed. The blood, entering the air passages, would have precipitated a difficulty in breathing and had precipitated death.

211

Shown a piece of lead piping, Professor Simpson told the coroner that it was similar to one he had seen earlier except that a surgical plaster strip had been wrapped around it. The one he had seen weighed about 2¼ pounds; and blows, or more particularly split blunt injuries, to the scalp were consistent with such an instrument being used. Other injuries, however, to the eye and mouth, were more likely to have been caused, he said, *by a fist or a hand slap* (my italics). This piece of evidence, which had not appeared in the pathologist's report to the police, was vital – as we shall see. But once again, the significance was not pointed out to the jury.

Professor Simpson was then shown photographs of Sandra Rivett's body and of Veronica's head injuries. The injuries of the two women were of a similar kind, he said, and in his opinion could have been inflicted either by the same blunt instrument or by one similar to the other – not necessarily the same weapon.

During cross-examination, the pathologist said that unconsciousness would result quite quickly if the blows to the head were delivered in quick succession. Unconsciousness would be there at the moment of death.

Kait, an agnostic, affirmed instead of taking the oath. Despite her age – she was a month off seventy-five – she declined the coroner's invitation to sit in the witness box.

'I prefer to stand,' she said.

She told the court that she saw John at fairly regular intervals, on average about once every ten days. From time to time she saw him in the company of his children, chiefly on weekends when he was staying with them at Sally's. His feelings for his children were 'strong and passionate', she said.

Dr Thurston asked: 'Was it a disappointment to him that he did not have custody of them?'

'Yes,' Kait replied.

'When did you last see your son before this incident?'

'I am not prepared to say for certainty, but I think probably the best I can say is that it was on the Sunday before the 7th of November.'

'How was he?'

'He was in a state of great anxiety about the children as in the past, but not noticeably or more obsessionally so than was to be expected.'

'Were the children with him?'

'No. I almost invariably saw him in the evenings.'

Dealing with the events of the murder night, Kait said she first received a telephone call from John when she turned to her flat after attending a meeting.

'It surprised me by its lateness,' she said. 'I put the phone call at between 10.00 p.m. and 10.30 p.m. I don't pretend to exactitude.'

She did not think it was as late as 10.45 p.m.

'What did he say?' the coroner asked.

'He said it was John speaking and he said: "There has been a terrible catastrophe at number 46. Veronica is hurt and I want you to collect the children. Ring Bill Shand Kydd, he will help." He also said: "The nanny is hurt." I said: "Badly?" and he said: "Yes, I think so." That was I think the whole conversation. Detective Sergeant Forsyth's account was substantially correct. It was hardly a conversation I would forget.'

This was a typical Kait Lucan remark. Though no one who knew her would doubt her honesty, she took little account of her age and her self-sufficient demeanour tended to prevent others doing so either. Chief Superintendent Ranson found her 'formidable'. Nevertheless on occasion her memory was less reliable than she assumed. She had already, after seven months, forgotten a few details of this conversation she would hardly 'forget'.

'I first attempted to ring Mr Shand Kydd,' she continued to the coroner. 'I was told he was not available. This was a mistake, although I didn't speak to him. I went to 46 Lower Belgrave Street. I returned to the flat and then there was a second telephone call. This was well after

213

midnight. I got the children to bed first so it was not immediately after my return.'

She paused, remembering something, and said: 'I must add that in the first telephone call he said: "I interrupted a fight in the basement."'

Dr Thurston asked: 'He used those words?'

'Yes.'

'As regards the second telephone call, what did he say to you?'

'He said: "Have you got the children?" I said: "Yes, they are here in bed, and to the best of my knowledge and belief they're asleep." He said: "That's all right." I said: "What do you intend to do?" I got nowhere. I also said: "I've got the police with me. Do you want to speak to them?" He hesitated and then said: "No, I don't think I'll speak to them now. I will ring them in the morning and I'll ring you too." Then he rang off.'

He had sounded very much more 'on all fours' during the second conversation, she said. The first time he rang he had sounded in a highly shocked condition.

'I had the impression the [second] call came from a private house. There were no pips, therefore the implication is that it was from a private house,' Kait said. 'He didn't say where he was.'

She told the court she knew very little about John's income except that he was extremely generous to her.

'His way of life did not suggest penury,' she said. 'I knew more at the time of his succession. I was one of the executors. I knew of the sale of the silver, but not until after the catastrophe. I understand it has now taken place.'

She was asked if John told her how he came to see the fight in the basement.

'No. He said he was passing,' Kait replied. 'This did not indicate whether he paused and peered in or whether it was so obvious on passing. I know he did frequently go past the house and look at it. It was very near his flat.'

Cross-examination was opened by Mr Watling, for the police. Kait was invited to sit down.

'I am perfectly all right standing,' she said.

'I appreciate it is something of an ordeal, and I don't want to increase that,' Mr Watling told her. 'But it is right, is it not, that as Detective Sergeant Forsyth has told us, you made a statement to him?'

'Yes.'

Mr Watling then read the start of Kait's first written statement to the police, reminding her that she had signed a declaration which stated she knew she would be liable to prosecution if she made any false statements. He asked her if she had said in the statement that she received the first phone call from John at about 10.45 p.m.

'I am sure this must be correct because this is the statement I made at the time,' Kait said. 'But I am still under the impression that the hour mentioned is unduly late.'

She was asked if it was correct that she had said in the statement: '[John said]: "There has been a most awful catastrophe at number 46." To the best of my knowledge he said there had been a fight in the basement.'

'I have no recollection of that,' Kait replied. 'But I have no reason to doubt it.'

She was asked if her statement to Sergeant Forsyth had continued: 'This is very difficult for me to remember now but I have the impression there was a third person present but I can't be exact about this.'

'Yes,' she said. 'It was my subjective impression at the time, and it remains my subjective impression now.'

'You have told the jury,' Mr Watling said, 'that in the first phone call you had from your son, he used the words: "I interrupted a fight in the basement."'

'Yes – and when asked to repeat the conversation, in some curious way I failed to explain this quite unaccountably.'

Mr Watling said: 'You see, you didn't use in the statement anything about your son telling you: "I interrupted a fight in the basement", did you? What you said was: "I have the impression that there was a third person present but I can't be exact."'

Kait said: 'The words "I interrupted a fight" were undoubtedly his words and I imagine that when I made this statement that the impression that there was a third person present was an obvious deduction from the statement that he interrupted a fight in the basement.'

'Yes,' said Mr Watling, 'but why did you not tell the police officer that so it could go down in the statement? No deductions, just plain statement?'

'It is a plain statement and this is a plain statement,' Kait said.

She said she thought the upshot of the two was the same.

'That may be a matter for the jury,' Mr Watling responded. 'The point is you did not in that statement use the words which you now tell the jury your son used.'

'Yes, but these are the words which to the best of my recollection he used.'

Mr Watling referred her to a second written statement she made several weeks after the murder.

'In that statement you mention: "I remember he said he had interrupted a fight"?'

'Yes.'

John had said it close to the point in the first telephone call when he had asked her to ring Bill Shand Kydd.

Had she rung Mr Shand Kydd?

'I did subsequently get in touch with the Shand Kydds,' Kait said. 'I spoke to Mrs Shand Kydd and told her Veronica was in hospital. Her immediate reaction was: "Has she attempted to kill herself again?"'

(Christina denied using the word 'again'.)

An objection was being raised when the coroner said: 'I shall not record that – it is prejudicial.'

(After Kait had completed her evidence, Veronica's counsel, Mr Coles, asked Dr Thurston if, in view of the ruling he had given the previous day in the absence of the jury, he would ask the Press not to report the remark. The coroner replied that he had no power to direct the Press not to report it, but he would certainly make a request.)

Mr Watling asked if John had said on the phone who was fighting whom.

'No,' Kait said.

'Did he say how Veronica and Sandra came to be hurt?'

'No.'

'Did you think of ringing the police at this time?'

'It crossed my mind as I drove over as I was aware there had been a violent accident,' she said.

Eventually Mr Watling sat down after declaring: 'I need go no further. The jury will have seen this lady for themselves.'

This time Michael Eastham jumped to his feet to protest.

'That is a most improper remark for any member of the Bar to make and I ask for it to be withdrawn,' he said.

'I will uphold the request,' said the coroner.

Kait asked Mr Watling later: 'I did not hear the comment. What did you say?'

Mr Watling told her and apologised.

Answering questions from Michael Eastham, Kait said that shortly before November 1974 she had lent John £4,000 towards the cost of the custody proceedings.

She was asked whether it would be correct to say that he was 'obsessed' with his children.

'Yes, of late,' she replied. 'I would date his obsession as opposed to a father's normal interest to before the date when the first custody order was made.'

Returning to the dispute over what she had told Sergeant Forsyth, Mr Eastham asked: 'Do you agree that you mentioned the fight?'

'Yes.'

But had she said John had told her he was 'driving past' or 'passing' the house?

Kait told the court: 'This is a fallible memory of seven months. John stated to me that he was "passing" the house. Sergeant Forsyth thinks I said "driving past". I assumed that John was "passing" on foot. This may have been a natural deduction on my part. I agree I may have made a deduction. My memory is not equal to say whether I used the word "driving". I think I said "passing".'

'Were you doing your best to assist the police?' Mr Eastham asked.

'I was certainly doing my best to assist the police and myself.'

'Did you say, during the second phone call from your son: "Well look, the police are here. Do you want to speak to them?"'

'Yes.'

'You said: "That was my son. He won't speak to you now—"?'

'— he would phone the police in the morning and me in the morning.'

She said she very much regretted that she had not pressed the point when he hesitated before saying he would not speak to the police immediately.

During the first phone call, she said, John had muttered quite a bit. The words 'blood' and 'mess' had been used, not as part of a proper sentence or as a coherent statement but as expressions of horror and disgust.

'Some parts I did not follow,' Kait said, 'but I got the impression he could not stand the blood and mess. He was muttering . . .'

'In the mutterings did he mention his wife?'

'No,' she said.

Kait left the witness box after answering questions for just over an hour.

When Mr David Webster, counsel for the murdered nanny's family, got up to speak he sounded disgruntled.

'This inquiry is to discover how, when and where Mrs Rivett met her death,' he said. 'But there seems to be a certain amount of imbalance. How and where is becoming clear. But the person who may be charged may not be clear to the jury.'

After further remarks, the coroner declared: 'You are speaking in riddles.'

Outside the courthouse Sandra's father, Mr Hensby, and his sister-in-law, Mrs Ward, also sounded disgruntled.

'My daughter's name has hardly been mentioned,' Mr

Hensby said. 'Yet she is the reason why we are all here. She was a kind, gentle person who loved children and wouldn't hurt anyone.'

Mrs Ward told Pressmen covering the inquest: 'I am appalled. Sandra is the innocent victim here. She is supposed to be the central figure but her name has hardly come up. It is like the shopgirl and the prince. They make out Sandra to sound like rubbish but in fact she came from a good family background and was very refined. Sandra is in the middle of what seems to be a battle between the two sides of the Lucan family. Meanwhile it is Sandra who died and she is gone and forgotten.'

21

Soft-voiced Susan Maxwell-Scott, smart in a dark suit and wide-brimmed pink hat, took the stand to tell the court what she had learned from John on the night of the crime. She said she had known him for about seventeen years, since just before her marriage.

'He was always a close friend of my husband. I got to know him well when we moved to the country and he and Lady Lucan used to come and stay with us.'

Coming to the evening of the murder, she described how she had been woken when Lucan arrived unexpectedly at the house and rang the doorbell. She got up, let him in and gave him a drink. They sat down in the drawing room.

Asked by Dr Thurston about John's appearance, she said: 'He looked a little dishevelled. When I have seen him he normally looks very tidy. His hair was a little ruffled. He was casually dressed. He was wearing a light blue polo-neck silk or nylon shirt, grey flannel trousers, a sleeveless brown pullover, no overcoat.'

'Was there any marking on his clothes?'

'While he was sitting talking I did notice, but not immediately, a damp patch on his trousers on the right side of the hip – thigh.'

She added: 'I forgot to say that when I let him in, first of all he asked for Ian. I told him that he was in London. When he was sitting down I asked him if anything was the matter and he told me what had happened at his wife's house that evening. I will try to do my best to repeat what he told me but it is seven months ago.'

She pointed out: 'Unlike the police officers, I don't have notes and have to rely on memory.'

She began: 'He said he had been walking past Lady Lucan's house on his way to change for dinner –'

The coroner interrupted to say: 'Now the word "walking" is rather important.'

'Yes, I realise that,' she replied. 'I am almost certain he used the word, but it could be he said that he was "passing". I don't know what my police statement said because that's more likely to be correct.'

'The statement says "walking",' Dr Thurston informed her.

'Well, that would be correct,' she said, 'because that's what I gave two days after. Now it's seven months.'

Mrs Maxwell-Scott, standing with her palms pressed down on the edge of the witness box, continued:

'Through the venetian blinds in the basement he said he saw what looked like a man attacking his wife Veronica. He had started by saying to me that it was "an unbelievable coincidence". I told him I didn't think it so extraordinary for him to be there then because he had told me on a previous occasion that he was in the habit of walking past the house quite regularly and sometimes going in. I said to him that evening: "It isn't such a coincidence to pass your house", and he said: "Well yes, I quite often go in to see if the children are all right." He said he let himself in through the front door – he had a key – and went down into the basement. As he entered he slipped in a pool of blood – as he got to the bottom of the stairs, that is.'

She stressed: 'He was not telling it like a story . . . it came out in bits and pieces. The man he had seen attacking his wife ran off. Whether this was on hearing Lucan coming down the stairs or on seeing Lucan, I am not clear. But the man ran off. And Lucan, perhaps unfortunately, rather than chasing the man, went straight to his wife.'

The June sunshine coming through the domed glass ceiling had increased the temperature in the courtroom. Mrs Maxwell-Scott slipped off her black jacket and draped it around her shoulders like a cape.

'Did he say which way the man ran?' the coroner asked.

'No. He just said the man made off,' she replied. 'Perhaps through the back door, I don't know.'

'He then went to his wife –?'

'–who was covered in blood and very hysterical.'

'Did he say anything further about what his wife had said?'

'What she said at that time, yes. At first she was very hysterical and cried out to him that someone had killed Sandra, or "the nanny". Then, almost in the same breath, she accused Lucan of having hired the man to kill *her*. This, Lucan told me, was something she frequently accused him of – having "a contract to kill". He reckoned she got it from an American TV movie. He said he tried to calm her down; as I said, she was hysterical. I don't know how long all this took because he didn't tell me. He took her upstairs to a room – I assumed her bedroom – where her daughter, Lady Frances, was watching television. Lady Frances went to bed. I thought Lucan said he sent her or took her to bed. Lady Lucan was lying down. Lucan persuaded her to lie down. His intention – this is what he told me – was first to get some wet towels to mop up the blood on her and see how severe her injuries were. He was then going to telephone for a doctor and subsequently telephone the police.'

Referring back to what Lord Lucan had told her of the scene in the basement, Mrs Maxwell-Scott said: 'He certainly saw the sack. I think Lady Lucan indicated it to him. He described the basement room to me as being horrific because of all the blood. He assumed that the body was in the sack, but he did not go and examine it. I think he felt rather squeamish with the blood and didn't want to look too closely.'

'Did he tell you what he did next?' the coroner asked.

'He said he went to the bathroom and started soaking the towels prior to wiping the blood, but while he was there Lady Lucan left the bedroom, ran down the stairs and out of the house.'

'Did Lord Lucan say anything about telephoning anybody?'

'After he left the house he said he telephoned his mother and asked her to look after the children. I think he also told her to notify the police.'

Dr Thurston said: 'Having told you this account, was there anything which gave you any indication of the time?'

'Yes. He looked at his watch and said something about the time,' she said. 'I think it was about 12.15 a.m. He said something like: "Can I phone my mother now?" He used the telephone in the drawing room. He spoke to her in my presence. I asked him if he wanted me to leave the room but he said no. I heard him say something like: "Mother, it's John" and then he asked about the children. I gathered the answer must have been satisfactory because he said something like: "Oh good" or "I'm glad". He then asked: "Has Veronica turned up?" I gathered the reply was that she had been found and had been taken to hospital.

'He said something like: "I will telephone you tomorrow." He then told me he was dialling William Shand Kydd's telephone number, but he received no reply. After that he said could he borrow some notepaper. I'm not sure whether he said he was going to write to Shand Kydd. I gave him some of my own. Some of it is headed, some isn't. I gave him a handful of each, and the envelopes. I don't know what he used.'

Identifying the paper, she said: 'That looks like mine. So is the envelope and indeed the stamps.'

The heat in the courtroom was stifling. Mrs Maxwell-Scott produced a pink handkerchief and dabbed her forehead.

'I asked if he'd like some coffee and I went and made us both some,' she said. 'He wrote his letters and said: "Can you post these for me in the morning?"'

The coroner asked: 'After this there was general conversation, indifferent matters, the children and so on?'

'Yes.'

'Did you offer to let him stay the night?'

'I tried to persuade him to stay the night. I suggested it was a good idea to stay and telephone the police in the morning. But after slightly agreeing he said no. He said he must – and he stressed "must" – get back and clear things

223

up, sort things out. When he said "get back" he did not mention London.'

'What time did he leave?'

'To the best of my recollection it was about 1.15 a.m.'

'Did you see the car he left in?'

'Yes. It was parked on the far side of my own car. It was a dark saloon, fairly ordinary. I did not recognise the make. It was not a Mini or a sports car.'

'What happened then?'

'I went to bed.'

The coroner asked if she had had any communication from John since then.

'None at all. When he left he said he would let me know how things went, but he didn't.'

Had her husband heard from him?

'I know he hasn't,' she said.

The next morning, she recalled, she gave the letters Lord Lucan had written to her small daughter to post, probably on her way to school.

'I stamped the letters. I used my stamps,' she said.

Dr Thurston asked: 'Did he take away any writing material?'

'No. He would have been only too welcome to do so. I had handed him a pile.'

Shown a Lion Brand writing pad found in the abandoned Ford Corsair at Newhaven, she said: 'That's not mine.'

The coroner asked: 'Did he ask you if you had any sleeping pills?'

'Yes, he did,' Mrs Maxwell-Scott said. 'He said he was sure he would have difficulty sleeping and had I got any sleeping pills? I said I did not think so. But I went to have a look. The best I could find was a bottle of 2mg Valium tablets which had four pills left in the bottom. They are not, of course, sleeping pills. They are tranquillisers. I gave him the bottle and he took the four pills before he left with water from a jug I had brought him with the whisky. It was not a very strong dose.'

'Do you know if Lord Lucan had any connection with Newhaven?'

'No.'

'How far is your house from Lower Belgrave Street?'

'Forty-two miles. From my own experience, the journey from Victoria Station, driving at an average speed, would take me about an hour. I normally allow myself an hour and a half in heavy traffic. He arrived at about 11.30 p.m. Lucan tended to drive rather fast, though he was a very good driver. I've been driven by him: it is terrifying. He might take less time.'

Cross-examined by Mr Watling, for the police, she repeated that Lord Lucan had seen the sack at number 46 but had not examined it.

Mr Watling: 'When Lord Lucan left that house, he knew that the nanny had been killed and his wife badly attacked?'

'Lady Lucan told him at the house that the man had killed the nanny,' she said. 'He said his wife was covered in blood. He saw the man attacking his wife anyway.'

'You are no doubt aware that no one has seen Lord Lucan since he left your house at 1.15 a.m. that morning?'

'Nobody has *said* they have seen him,' she replied.

'Is it right you are in fact a trained lawyer, a member of the Bar?'

'I was called to the Bar nearly eighteen years ago but I never practised,' she said.

'Your father was a lawyer?'

'My father was a lawyer.'

Mr Watling asked. 'Is it right that Lord Lucan at no time described to you the man he had seen attacking his wife?'

'Not entirely right,' she replied. 'Lord Lucan did not see him clearly enough to describe him.'

'Did he describe the man to you at all?'

'He said he was large.'

'You told the jury at one stage you tried to persuade him to stay the night and he said he must get back?'

'Yes. He said: "I must get back and straighten things out."'

'Did he also say to you that he would not want his children to see him standing in the dock of a court?'

225

'Yes he did.'

'He wrote two letters. Did you notice when he gave you the envelopes anything on them?'

'There were addresses.'

'You will notice some brown smears. You will hear they are blood.'

'I didn't notice them. The letters were on the drinks trolley. I gave them to my daughter to post.'

Cross-examined by Michael Eastham, she was asked if 'in a slightly roundabout way', when she and John were discussing what had happened, she had asked about the nanny.

'Yes,' Mrs Maxwell-Scott said. 'We were discussing this probable killing and it seemed to me it would be likely to be someone who wanted to kill the nanny. But Lord Lucan said it wouldn't be anyone wanting to kill her. He said she was a "good kid". He told me he'd spoken to the Official Solicitor and said the children had got a nice girl for a nanny and that he was very pleased with her.'

She told the court that the wet patch she had noticed on John's grey flannels 'didn't look like blood'. 'But it did cross my mind that he said he had slipped in a pool of blood,' she added. Perhaps he had 'sponged it off'.

Asked about his condition, she said he appeared shocked but not hysterical.

'He was definitely very shaken when he arrived. He was shocked, but it was controlled shock.'

The words he had used that night were that it had been 'an unbelievable, nightmarish experience', so extraordinary that no one would believe him.

She said: 'I did my best to convince him that people would believe it was quite incredible that he had anything to do with it.'

Recalling what he had said about his final minutes at number 46, Mrs Maxwell-Scott said: 'He told me he heard the front door slam and Lady Lucan outside shouting: "Murder! Murder!"'

'Did he tell you what his state of mind was when he

realised he was alone with a sack, a body and a lot of blood?'
Mr Eastham asked.

'My words are that he obviously panicked and lost his head,' she replied. 'He put it another way. He said he felt there he was alone in the house with all that blood, the dead body, a murderer who had got away, and a wife gone away who would almost certainly try to implicate him. He said he was sure she would try and implicate him. After all, she had already said he had hired the man. He told me he reckoned no one would believe his story.'

One who did was Bill Shand Kydd.

Moving to the witness box, he told the court that he was a company director and that he was married to Lady Lucan's sister.

The coroner asked: 'Did you see Lord Lucan quite frequently?'

'About every three weeks,' he said. 'This was since the children went back to Lady Lucan in the summer of 1973. My opinion is that he was devoted to his children.'

He said he could say 'absolutely nothing whatsoever' about Lucan's debts: he had discovered about the bank overdrafts 'subsequently, but I knew nothing about his financial situation before'.

'When did you last see him?'

'My memory is very unreliable but it was probably about two weekends before November 7th. He normally came down to us every third weekend. He seemed very relaxed. He spent a lot of time with the children, his and mine. He expressed pleasurable anticipation because he was going to have the children that Christmas.'

Asked if Lord Lucan was 'unusually fond' of children, he replied: 'I don't think so. He was very fond of his children. I think he was worried about his children and possibly considered that they were not being properly looked after.'

Veronica's counsel, Mr Coles, instantly objected. The coroner upheld the objection.

On Saturday, 9 November, Bill said, he had a telephone call from Ian Maxwell-Scott at Uckfield.

'I was astounded to find that Lord Lucan had been there on the Thursday night, the night of the murder, and he [Maxwell-Scott] had not known about it until the Friday evening. I also learned that [Lucan] had written two letters to me.'

'What did you do about the letters?' the coroner asked.

'I first of all rang London to ascertain whether the letters had arrived. Then I immediately drove to London and directly I had read them I took them straight down to Chief Superintendent Ranson.'

He was shown the letters and identified the handwriting as John's. Referring to the sale of family silver at Christie's, mentioned in the second letter, Bill told the court that it had now taken place.

'The money is being held in escrow at the moment. The total is in excess of £17,000. It would have satisfied the overdrafts.'

Opening cross-examination, Mr Watling asked: 'When you got the envelopes did you notice the stains?'

'Yes.'

'Did you realise they were blood?'

'Yes. I also pointed them out to Mr Ranson as being blood.'

Questioned by Mr Eastham, Bill said he knew the Lucans' children had had a series of nannies.

'Did Lord Lucan ever say anything to you about them?'

'Yes. I always asked when he visited us. The last time he came down he said that Mrs Rivett was the most satisfactory one so far and he hoped it would last. He said she seemed a very nice girl and the children liked her.'

About John, he said: 'I wouldn't describe him as one of my three greatest friends, but I know him well and liked him.'

Would Lucan have approached him for financial help?

'Only if he had been in really dire circumstances,' he replied. 'I would have been the last person to approach if at all possible – in extremis only.'

Michael Eastham then put to him a series of questions about the main letter John had written to him. In view of the coroner's ruling on Monday – which meant that nothing should be said which might be seen as an attempt to discredit Lady Lucan – Bill was asked to answer either 'Yes' or 'No' but nothing further.

Quoting from John's letter, Mr Eastham read out the phrase: 'Veronica has demonstrated her hatred for me in the past . . .'

He asked: 'Could you, if asked, develop that and tell the jury more about it?'

'Yes,' Bill said, unable to elaborate.

'Could you give evidence of fact?'

'Yes.'

The barrister turned back to the letter, continuing the quotation: '. . . and would do anything to see me accused.'

Mr Eastham asked: 'Could you give evidence in relation to the whole sentence?'

'Yes,' Bill repeated.

Mr Eastham read from the letter again: '. . . When [the children] are old enough to understand, explain to them the dream of paranoia.'

He asked Bill: 'Did that make sense to you when you read it? Did you know what he was getting at?'

'Yes,' came the answer.

'Could you give evidence relating to the sentence dealing with paranoia?'

'Yes,' said Bill.

The next witness, housewife Mrs Eileen Sims, of Norman Road, Newhaven, told the court about the abandoned Ford Corsair. She had noticed the navy blue car parked outside her house at eight o'clock on the morning of 8 November. She had never seen it before.

'We don't often get a strange car,' she said. 'This one was particularly noticeable. It was very dusty, very old. I didn't see anybody park the car, and I didn't see anybody go to it from Friday morning to Sunday.'

Detective Sergeant David De Lima, stationed at Lewes, described how he had come across the Ford Corsair.

'I was on inquiries in Newhaven in connection with a stolen car and I noticed the Ford myself. It was a car which had been circulated. I first received the circular that morning when I made a note of it.'

The locked boot was opened. A photograph of the contents was produced for the jury.

'The photo shows the boot exactly as I saw it,' the detective said, 'including the bar with white tape.'

The bar with white tape? Inside the boot, the police had found a *second* piece of bandaged lead piping – like the one found at number 46! The one in the boot was not bloodstained at all, but as far as Ranson was concerned, it was the clincher.

22

Members of the jury were perplexed. As the hearing began its third day, the jury foreman, Mr William Thomas, rose to his feet and spelled out their puzzlement to the coroner.

'Nothing has been said about the nanny being murdered,' he declared. 'We have heard about Lady Lucan going to the barman at the Plumbers Arms and saying: "He's murdered my nanny!" But how did she *know* the nanny had been murdered?'

It was a question worthy of Perry Mason.

According to Veronica's evidence, she never went into the basement. So how did she know that Sandra was down there dead – especially if her body was already in the sack?

John's version of the events, as told by Susan Maxwell-Scott, meant that Veronica *must* have been down in the basement or he couldn't have seen her through the window. If she was, that would explain how she had been able to tell him that Sandra had been killed.

But if she wasn't, how did she know?

'That is quite right,' Dr Thurston said.

But he shelved the question nevertheless. He said he hoped to satisfy the jury after the rest of the witnesses had given evidence.

First into the witness box on Day Three was retired company director Michael Stoop, owner of the abandoned Ford Corsair, who told the court he had known John for about fifteen years.

'We were both members of the Clermont Club,' he said.

He identified the Corsair from a photograph and told the coroner: 'Lord Lucan had asked to borrow the car. I don't recall the exact date. It was the 21st or 23rd of

October, the night of a dinner at the Portland Club. I had a Mercedes and I suggested he might borrow that. I thought he'd prefer the Mercedes: my Ford is a pretty dirty old banger. But I imagine through natural manners he didn't want to deprive me of my better car. He wanted the Ford specifically for that evening. I didn't ask for any reason and he didn't offer any. I was going home to change for dinner. I left the keys in the car and said that he could collect it when he wished. I left it outside the garage. I hadn't seen the car between then and the incident.

'On the Monday [after the murder] I received letters at my club, the St James's. There was no stamp on one letter. The hall porter had to pay the postage.'

He identified the letter and the handwriting as John's.

'Where is the envelope now?' the coroner asked.

'I think I must have thrown it away,' Mr Stoop said. 'I don't recall the postmark. The envelope was largish. It was a large business-type envelope, white.'

The letter, written on both sides of a sheet of blotting paper, was read out to the court.

It said:

My dear Michael,

I have had a traumatic night of unbelievable coincidences. However I won't bore you with anything or involve you except to say that when you come across my children, which I hope you will, please tell them that you knew me and that all I cared about was them.

The fact that a crooked solicitor and a rotten psychiatrist destroyed me between them will be of no importance to the children.

I gave Bill Shand Kydd an account of what actually happened but judging by my last effort in court no-one, let alone a 67-year-old judge, would believe — and I no longer care except that my children should be protected.

Yours ever,
John.

Michael Eastham was to refer to quotations from the letter later.

Mr Stoop was then shown a photograph of the inside of the boot of his Ford Corsair. He told the court: 'The bits of plastic, the hat and newspapers were not there when I handed the car over. The Simpson's bag and the battery charger are both mine. That's all I can see.'

Handed another photograph – perhaps of the lead piping – he said: 'I have never seen that object before.'

He was then shown the Lion Brand writing pad, and told the coroner: 'I've seen so many of these before. It's possible it was in my car. I can't say whether it was. It's not at all improbable. I have not lent my car to other people. The principal reason is that it was insured in my name only. I advised Lucan of this and advised that he carry out insurance for himself. The car would do about 24 miles per gallon on a long journey. I may be wrong. I don't remember the mileage shown on the meter.'

Answering questions from Mr Watling, he said: 'I offered the Mercedes on the basis of insurance. Lucan said no, he would insure the Ford. There has never been anything like the lead piping in my car before.'

Under cross-examination from Mr Eastham, he said he knew that Lord Lucan was missing when he received the letter on Monday.

'If you had looked at the envelope,' Mr Eastham said, 'and recognised Lord Lucan's handwriting, you would have appreciated it was rather important to keep the envelope?'

Mr Stoop said he couldn't recall if the envelope was handwritten. He had received several letters at the same time, opened them and thrown away the envelopes.

'I was really rather keen to read the letter because I realised it came from him,' he said. 'I got in touch with the police within five minutes of receiving it. I didn't look at the postmark. The envelope would I suppose be in the wastepaper basket. Nobody emptied the wastepaper basket in those five minutes to my knowledge.'

'Are you sure you did not look at the postmark?' Mr

Eastham asked. 'Because it is rather important to establish where he was.'

'I am afraid I did not,' Michael Stoop replied.

As he had done earlier with Bill Shand Kydd, Mr Eastham then put a series of questions to Mr Stoop about information contained in his letter from John.

Because of the coroner's ruling on the first day, Mr Stoop too was obliged to answer with a simple 'Yes' or 'No'.

Quoting from the letter, Mr Eastham read out John's claim that 'a crooked solicitor and a rotten psychiatrist' had 'destroyed' him 'between them'. He followed this with John's suggestion that 'judging by my last effort in court no-one, let alone a 67-year-old judge, would believe' him. Did Mr Stoop understand that both passages referred to court proceedings about Lord Lucan's children?

'Yes,' said Michael Stoop.

Mr Eastham then asked about John's phrase: ' . . . I no longer care except that my children should be protected.' Did Mr Stoop understand what Lord Lucan meant by that?

Michael Stoop replied: 'I cannot deal with that by a simple "Yes" or "No".'

'I know you cannot,' said Mr Eastham, forced to tie himself and others in knots. 'But I am in a difficulty. May I put it this way: if I asked you against what or whom the children were to be protected, could you answer?'

Mr Stoop got no chance to say. The coroner promptly disallowed the question.

In answer to other questions from Mr Watling, Mr Stoop said: 'I think I went to the St James's Club on the Monday at about 4.30 p.m. or 4.45 p.m. I rang Gerald Road a little later. I asked the police if I should bring the letter straight round. They said: "When you next pass." I don't think it's right that I said it was inconvenient at that time. I thought it was three or three-thirty in the morning that I went to the police station.'

The jury heard from a detective later that the police had

234

tried to recover the missing envelope, but dustbins at the club had been emptied by then and the envelope 'must have been on its way down the Thames in a barge' – presumably to a dump or incinerator.

Mr Ian Lucas, a senior fingerprint officer at New Scotland Yard, told the coroner that he had received no prints which were directly traceable to Lord Lucan himself. But a print found on the interior driving mirror of the Ford Corsair and a print found in the flat at Elizabeth Street had probably been made by the same person. He would have to receive a control sample to be definite, he said. At 46 Lower Belgrave Street he had found sixty-two marks, of which forty-six had been totally eliminated from the inquiry, four had been partially eliminated, and twelve remained outstanding – which meant they had not been accounted for. Of seven marks he found on the Ford Corsair, four had been eliminated and three were still outstanding. At 72a Elizabeth Street, twenty of the twenty-nine marks found had been eliminated. Questioned by Mr Watling, Mr Lucas said that all the prints found in the basement at number 46 had come from police officers, one of the children or the victim.

'So whoever attacked Mrs Rivett left no fingerprints?'

'I did not find any,' Mr Lucas said.

He also revealed that he found no fingerprints on a piece of piping he examined.

Referring to the fingerprints which had not been accounted for, Mr Lucas told the court: 'I've been in this work over nineteen years. I've been involved in several murder inquiries in my time. In my experience even when persons are charged and convicted there are still outstanding prints.'

Among the most illustrious witnesses at the inquest was the tall, slim Dr Margaret Pereira, a senior principal scientific officer in the biology division of the Metropolitan Police forensic science laboratory. She had an international reputation as a blood analyst. Indeed, as a result of her successes in the forensic solution of crime, she had been nicknamed 'Miss Murder'. Dr Pereira and her colleagues had perfected a method of analysing even the smallest samples of dried blood. At her laboratory, blood was routinely typed in sixteen different blood group systems. By sifting and sifting through one system after another, it was possible to identify the blood of one person in several million. A person's blood-grouping could be seen to be almost as individual as his or her fingerprints.

After the bloodbath at number 46, she found 'an enormous amount of work' to be done. There were human bloodstains in the form of splashes, spots and smears on floors, walls and ceilings.

Dr Pereira told the coroner that with the exception of bed linen in the second floor bedroom, the bloodstaining at the house was mainly confined to the ground floor, the basement stairway and the basement.

Samples of blood were taken from both women and tested. In the ABO blood-grouping system, Sandra had Group B blood, which was found in about 8½% of the country's population. Veronica's blood was of the more common Group A, shared by about 42% of the population. Their blood was also analysed further in two additional grouping systems. The result of the three analyses showed that Sandra's blood was Group B, Hp 2–2, PGM 2–1 (a configuration found in only about 1% of the population), whereas Veronica's was Group A, Hp 2–1, PGM 1 (found in about 12%).

Dr Pereira told the court that there was light blood smearing on the outer surface of the front door of number 46. Tests on a sample of this proved it to be human blood which gave weak reactions for Group A, Lady Lucan's group. The area around the four little steps in the hall was 'an obvious site of attack', she said. Looking from the direction of the hall cloakroom towards the front door, there was a radiating pattern of blood splashes on the woodwork to the left hand side of the top tread of the steps. Considerable force would have had to be used to cause the radiating pattern, and these blood splashes, she said, were more likely to have come from a weapon striking a wound which was already bleeding. In the same area were many downward trickles of heavy bloodstaining, smears of blood and some hairs embedded in the blood. On the right hand wall by the four little steps were similar trickles and smears of blood, but these were much less extensive. In the 'ante-room' – the area between the steps and the cloakroom at the end of the hall – there were splashes of blood on the ceiling, lampshade and cloakroom door. Some of these indicated clearly that they had been trajected back from the direction of the four steps. Dr Pereira told the coroner that, in her opinion, this indicated that 'a victim' was battered on the four steps by an attacker standing with his back to the ante-room – and that the blood splashes in that room had been thrown off the weapon. Bloodstains on carpet fibres from the steps and blood from the edge of the cloakroom door proved to be of Group A, Veronica's group. The lower part of the door leading to the basement stairs, which was open and hooked back to the wall, was extensively bloodstained. There were smears and downward trickles of blood, with hairs sticking to the blood. In the cloakroom in the hall, there was also a tuft of bloodstained hair sticking to the wash basin.

The samples of bloodstained hairs – from the hall steps, the bottom of the basement door and the cloakroom sink – all proved, in scientific parlance, to be 'similar to' a control sample of head hair taken from Veronica and 'different from' Sandra Rivett's. Curiously, the blood on the tuft of hair from the wash basin turned out to be neither Group A nor Group B but a third (and rare) group: AB, Hp 2–1. Dr Pereira suggested to the court that this could be the result of a mixture of Veronica's blood (A, Hp 2–1) and Sandra's (B, Hp 2–2).

'But I can't prove it,' she added.

Sticking to that tuft of hair were a number of textile fibres, including six dark greyish-blue wool fibres. The jury was never to discover where these mysterious bits of wool came from. But Dr Pereira found more greyish-blue

237

fibres, which were 'microscopically indistinguishable' from the others, elsewhere. There were four of them on a bath towel she examined which was stained with Group A blood, Veronica's group. There were seven of them amid a number of textile fibres found among bloodstained hairs stuck to the piece of lead piping from the hall. And, the expert was to tell the inquest, there were another thirty-two of them in the Ford Corsair abandoned at Newhaven. Of these, twenty-five were present in bloodstaining on the front off-side door. The remaining seven were stuck to a tangle of bloodstained human hairs, found on the car's front off-side floor. These hairs, once again, proved to be 'similar to' Veronica's rather than Sandra's – and showed damage typical of a battering attack to the head.

Dr Pereira found the same kind of damage on the bloodstained hairs stuck to the suspected murder weapon. The lead piping found by the basement doorway in the hall was about 9 inches long, weighed 2 pounds 3 ounces and was 'grossy distorted'. It was bound with two-inch wide Elastoplast-type adhesive stretch bandage with a yellow stripe through the middle, and was heavily and extensively bloodstained. An area of bloodstaining on the bandage gave reactions for Group AB, Hp 2–2, PGM 2–1, which could be the result of a mixture of blood from the two women in which Sandra's blood predominated. Blood on the hairs, however, was Group AB, PGM 1. This also suggested a mixture of blood, but with a higher proportion of Veronica's. Tests showed that the hairs stuck to the lead piping were 'similar to' Veronica's – yet *none* of them was 'similar to' Sandra's hair.

The dirty and rather dilapidated Ford Corsair had extensive blood smearing on the inner surface of the front off-side door, both front seats, the map box between them and also on the steering wheel and dashboard. All the blood tested was human.

Blood on the dashboard proved to be Group A, Veronica's group. Blood on the window of the front off-side door gave reactions for Group B, Sandra's group.

But bloodstaining on the arm-rest of the same door – like the blood on the tangle of hairs on the floor of the car – was Group AB, perhaps a mixture of the two.

Dr Pereira's examination of the lead piping found in the boot of the Corsair revealed that it was about 16½ inches long, weighed 4 pounds 1 ounce and was bound in a similar way to the length found in the hall. But she noted contrasts. There was no evidence of bloodstaining on the piece from the car boot. And there were 'minor differences' in the adhesive stretch bandages which had been used to bind the two lengths of pipe.

Also sent to Dr Pereira was the Lion Brand writing pad from the car. The blotting paper had been torn out, leaving an irregular strip. When matched together, the piece of blotting paper on which John had written his letter to Michael Stoop fitted in place. In the expert's opinion, it had once been part of the same pad. She also carried out tests on traces of blood found on the letters to Bill Shand Kydd. But apart from Group AB blood smearing on the back of one envelope, other stains were either insufficient for grouping tests or gave unsatisfactory results.

But it was Dr Pereira's work in the basement at number 46 which produced perhaps the most intriguing disclosures. She vividly described the evidence she found. On the wall of the basement staircase there were many blood splashes and smears and pictures were hanging in disarray. Towards the top of the staircase a baluster was hanging loose from the banister rail, broken at the base. The carpet was bloodstained. On the staircase wall above the third tread from the top, there was an area of blood smears and downward trickles like that found on the lower part of the hooked-back basement door. Samples of blood from that door, and from the middle and top of the staircase wall, all gave reactions for Group A, Veronica's group. Also on the staircase wall there was a fabric impression in blood. Tests on this showed the blood to be Group B, Sandra's group. But Dr Pereira told the court that in her opinion the fabric print, which could have been left by a finely knitted garment, could not have been produced by contact with the clothes worn by Veronica or Sandra that night or by contact with the mailbag in which the nanny's body was found.

In the breakfast room, at the bottom of the stairs, she found 'another obvious site of attack by battery'. There was a radiating pattern of blood splashes on the floor near the piano and some of the splashes were overlaid by a large pool of blood.

On the staircase panelling beneath the banister rail and on the staircase wall behind, there were numerous blood splashes which appeared to have made contact at an angle of about 90°. There were blood splashes on the wall near the bottom of the stairs, on a radiator and on the lower end of the banister rail. Adjacent to the foot of the stairs was an area of very heavy bloodstaining. On the wall and pictures above the upright piano there were directional blood splashes. In addition there were blood spots on books in the bookcase in the corner and bloodstains on top of the piano itself. Dr Pereira told the coroner that in her opinion these were likely to have been thrown off the weapon with the victim lying on the floor near the piano.

'Also in the breakfast room,' she said, 'there were some indistinct shoe prints in blood going from the large area of bloodstaining near the piano towards the safe which was situated behind the breakfast room. These were unsuitable for any comparative work but in my opinion they were probably made by a man's shoes.'

Samples of blood taken from the stained areas she had described in the breakfast room all proved to be Group B, Sandra's group.

Dr Pereira told the court that she did not examine the garden. But bloodstained leaves were found there by the police. The bloodstaining on one of these leaves was tested and again gave reactions for human blood of Group B, Sandra's group.

In the kitchen there were a few scattered bloodstains on the floor. Samples of some stains close to the sink unit near the cooker gave reactions for human blood but grouping tests produced unsatisfactory results. A blood smear near the doorway from the breakfast room was Group B, Sandra's group. Approximately in the middle of the kitchen floor there were two spots of blood close together. Tests on a sample taken from one spot showed it to be Group B, Sandra's group. But tests on a sample taken from the other spot of blood proved it to be Group A, Veronica's group.

If Veronica didn't go down into the basement that night, how did it get there? Also, how did blood of Veronica's group manage to get onto the murder sack?

Dr Pereira told the coroner that the United States mailbag in which the murdered nanny's body was found was heavily and extensively bloodstained. Six areas were tested and all were human blood. Four areas gave reactions for Group B, Sandra's group. But the remaining two areas tested gave reactions for Group B but with some Group A activity, which suggested possible contamination with blood of Lady Lucan's group.

The clothes Veronica wore on the night of the murder were also examined. There was fairly extensive light bloodstaining on her tights, which were also damaged in several places, but for some reason no grouping tests were carried out. Her brown jumper was heavily bloodstained around the neck region and there were also heavy bloodstains on the sleeves, but again no grouping tests were carried out. On Veronica's green pinafore dress, there was fairly heavy bloodstaining on the right shoulder, and numerous other bloodstains in the form of smears were scattered over the garment. Four of these stains were tested and all were human blood. Stains on the left front side at the top, and again on the left front side at the bottom of the skirt, were Group A, Veronica's group. But a stain on the left side of the back of the pinafore dress below the waist gave reactions for Group B, Hp 2–2, PGM 2–1, Sandra Rivett's groups. Another stain in close proximity gave reactions for Group AB.

Veronica's shoes provided more intriguing forensic evidence. On the upper part of her right shoe there were many light blood smears and there was also a spot of blood near the toe region. In addition there was some bloodstaining on the lower surface in the arch region. Two stains tested gave reactions for Group B, Sandra's group. There was similar 'dumb evidence' on Veronica'a left shoe: fairly extensive light blood smearing on the upper and also bloodstaining on the sole and in the arch region. Three stains were tested and all gave reactions for human blood of Group B, Sandra's group. If Veronica hadn't been in the basement, how did she get blood of Sandra's group on her shoes?

During a summary of her findings for Dr Thurston, Dr Pereira agreed it was fair to say that bloodstains examined from the ground floor and top of the basement stairs were predominantly Group A, Lady Lucan's group, apart from [the Group AB] blood on the tuft of hair which had been found stuck to the wash basin in the hall cloakroom.

That was curious. If the attacker rushed at Lady Lucan from the hall cloakroom as Veronica had said – assuming he had already killed Sandra and bundled her bloody body into the sack in the basement – why hadn't Dr Pereira found Group B blood in the cloakroom?

Continuing her summary, Dr Pereira said that blood found downstairs in the basement was predominantly Group B, Sandra Rivett's group, except for a weak reaction to Group A on the sack in which the nanny's body was bundled, and a sample of Group A from the spot in the middle of the kitchen floor.

The coroner recalled that Sergeant Baker, the first policeman on the scene, had said he went through the house and downstairs, where it was ill-lit. If he had inadvertently picked up blood on his shoes, and had gone from where the body was to the back door, could he have made the bloodstained footprints on the breakfast room floor? To laughter in court, Dr Pereira replied: 'Yes, they could have been from anyone with fairly large feet.' People investigating a crime could distort the picture – blood could be spread around.

But the coroner seemed to have forgotten some of Sergeant Baker's own testimony at the inquest given only

242

two days earlier. Sergeant Baker had told the jury that when he first looked into the basement from halfway down the stairs, there were *already* 'two or three footprints in the pool of blood'. Which meant that whoever made those could also have left the bloody footprints leading towards the safe and the back door – *before* the police arrived. Moreover Sergeant Baker actually told the court: 'I didn't tread in any of the blood.'

Cross-examined by Mr David Webster, for Sandra Rivett's family, Dr Pereira said she would expect the assailant to have blood splashes on his clothing in the same way as on the walls. The attacker's clothes would first be spattered, though this might not necessarily be evident to anyone looking, or even to the attacker personally. If the murderer then put the body into the sack, it was likely his clothing would become heavily saturated in Group B blood.

She said there were corresponding hairs on various articles, notably on the 'bludgeon', though she repeated that no hair of Mrs Rivett was found on it. Blood she had analysed from the bandaged lead piping found in the hall 'could have come from both ladies'.

Mr Webster asked: 'Is there any doubt in your mind that the weapon was used to batter both women?'

'It certainly suggests to me that it was,' she replied.

Regarding the bloodstained leaves found by the police in the back garden, she said that if feet were very bloodstained they could have carried blood onto the leaves.

Cross-examined by Mr Watling, for the police, Dr Pereira said that the tiny greyish-blue wool fibres found on the 'bludgeon', on the bath towel, in the wash basin and in the car could have been left by the same person. They could have originated from the same source. She was asked whether the different bandages used to bind the two pieces of lead piping had been woven on the same loom.

'I didn't go into that degree of detail,' she replied.

Dr Pereira then talked about the bloodstain on the envelope of one of John's letters to Bill Shand Kydd.

'The blood would have had to have been wet to get onto the envelope,' she told the court. 'The source of the blood could have been clotted. A clot is wet for a long time after. Blood is still capable if spread out of making smears whether it is clotted or not. It's difficult to say how long blood remains wet. It may take a few minutes or a few hours to dry.'

Referring to the Corsair, she said there were lots of fibres without hair adhering to the offside car door.

Cross-examined by Michael Eastham, she was asked first to explain the 'minor differences' between the bandages on both pieces of piping.

'They both appear to be of the Elastoplast-type but there was no mechanical fit between the bandages,' Dr Pereira said. 'There was a difference in the degree to which the adhesive was present towards the edge. On the bandage from the piping which is believed to be the weapon, the adhesive was spread over most of the back of the bandage 2 to 3mm from one edge, 4 to 5mm from the other edge. The item from the car had adhesive extending to 2 to 3mm of the edge on both sides of the bandage. The width was approximately the same, but it is very difficult to carry out measurements of something that has been stretched.'

Turning to the bloodstains, she said that she had been unable to identify three stains on the floor in the kitchen near the sink. But one of the samples analysed from a bloodstain in the middle of the kitchen floor was Group A, Lady Lucan's group. Dr Pereira agreed that on the back of the dress Lady Lucan was wearing at the time there was blood of Group B, Sandra Rivett's group. On Veronica's right shoe there were many light blood smears on the upper part and bloodstains on the lower region of the arch; and both of the two stains examined gave reactions to Group B. There were also bloodstains on the upper and also arch regions of her left shoe; and again all three samples tested checked Group B, Sandra Rivett's group.

Since it was established that the heavy Group B blood was concentrated in the basement, Mr Eastham asked the key question. Facing Dr Pereira in the witness box, he said: 'It is very probable that [Lady Lucan] walked through the basement?'

244

'It is certainly a likely explanation,' the expert replied.

Dr Pereira agreed it was 'hardly likely' that Veronica could have got Group B bloodstains on the arches of her shoes as she was being attacked.

Answering further questions, she said that the leaves from the garden were fairly extensively bloodstained – and also that 'the unfortunate victim who died bled very extensively indeed'.

Mr Eastham asked Dr Pereira to assume that Lord Lucan saw his wife being attacked, let himself into the house, ran down to the basement and slipped in a pool of blood. She agreed it was likely he would then have had extensive Group B blood on his clothes. If he then assisted his bloodstained wife, who was still bleeding, he would also have got Group A blood on him. And if he then sat in a car, she agreed, provided there was a mixture of the blood, some of it would come off as Group AB.

The Group AB blood found in the Ford Corsair, she said, could have been a mixture of Group A and Group B blood – or it could have been a third, separate, group on its own. The AB group, she told the court, was rare – and found in only about 3% of the country's population.

Returning to the intriguing question of how blood of Sandra's group got onto Veronica's shoes, and even under the arches, Dr Pereira said: 'I cannot eliminate the possibility of the shoes coming into contact with sodden garments.'

Michael Eastham asked which was more probable: that that had happened, or that Lady Lucan had walked through Sandra's blood in the basement?

'I think that is a difficult question for me to answer,' she replied. 'I really can't express an opinion. Perhaps if I could have the shoes . . .'

Veronica's bloodstained shoes were produced and Dr Pereira looked at them in the witness box.

But she ended up saying: 'I can't tell. The bloodstaining could have come from either source.'

As to the blood of Sandra's group on Veronica's dress, she said: 'It was not heavy – it was smearing. It's consistent with contact with clothing of anyone with that blood on it.'

Dr Pereira's evidence provided one possible answer to the jury's puzzled question: 'How did [Lady Lucan] *know* the nanny had been murdered?'

If John's story was true, then Veronica knew because she had been *in* the basement where Sandra had been killed. The forensic evidence – the Group A blood on the kitchen floor and the murder sack, the Group B blood on her dress and shoes – was indisputable. It was 'a likely explanation' that Veronica had walked through the basement – and probably through the pool of Sandra's blood. Wasn't that, after all, the easiest way to get Group B bloodstains on and under her shoes?

Or did the evidence suggest something different? Perhaps the killer, his clothes sodden with Sandra's Group B blood, transferred some of it to Veronica's pinafore dress while he was attacking her. Perhaps, while they struggled, her shoes came into contact with his clothing and became stained with the Group B blood. But that still left the question of the Group A blood in the basement. If Veronica had not gone down there, how did blood of her group get onto the kitchen floor – and onto the murder sack?

23

Dr Pereira had talked of differences in the Elastoplast-type bandaging bound around each of the two lengths of lead piping. Another expert, Dr Robert Davies, a senior scientific officer at the Metropolitan Police forensic science laboratory, who examined both pieces, found differences in the pipes themselves.

He concluded: 'As a scientist, the highest I could say is that they *may* both have been cut from the same length of piping. But it is highly unlikely that the bit found at number 46 was ever joined on either end of the bit found in the car.'

The next witness was Mr Charles Genese of Bexleyheath, Kent, director of a moneylending company, who said that Lord Lucan had called at his office on 11 September 1974 and asked to borrow up to £5,000. He was perfectly open about his financial commitments, and said that his gross income, payable through trust fund solicitors, was about £12,000 a year. 'I would say that he was living at least on a par if not more than his income,' Mr Genese said. Lucan said he had put some family silver up for auction and from the proceeds later in the year would undoubtedly be able to pay off anything he borrowed. His only mention of further income, Mr Genese said later, during cross-examination, was 'if he was fortunate enough at gambling'.

'First of all I said I couldn't possibly lend him any amount in view of his financial position,' Mr Genese told the court. 'I didn't want him piling on further debts.'

But several days later, after Lucan provided a surety, he agreed to lend him £3,000.

'He had to pay £120 per month, 48% per annum for a period of six months,' Mr Genese said. 'I saw Lucan later the second . . . time on 18 October, two days prior to the first instalment falling due. It was on a Friday. He came in and paid.'

Cross-examined by Mr Eastham, he said the next instalment was due in November, 'by which time these events had occurred'.

The first witness from the staff of the Clermont Club in Berkeley Square was Mr Andrea Demetriou, the assistant restaurant manager.

He told the court: 'I knew Lord Lucan as a client. On November 7th I started work at about seven-thirty in the evening.'

'Did you receive a telephone call from Lord Lucan?' Dr Thurston asked.

'It was at around 8.30 p.m.,' Mr Demetriou replied. 'He asked for Walter, the restaurant manager, who was not available. He said: "I'm sorry about this but could I book a table for four people at eleven o'clock? We're going to the theatre and will be rather late." I entered the booking.'

Was that a slip of memory or not? Had John actually said '*They're* going to the theatre' instead? It would have served no purpose for him to make out he was going when the rest of the theatre party knew he wasn't.

'What happened?' the coroner asked.

'He never turned up. A party of four came in. When we inquired about Lord Lucan they said he was coming later and they asked for a fifth chair.'

Cross-examined by Mr Watling, Mr Demetriou said: 'Mr Greville Howard turned up with three people and asked for an extra space.'

William 'Billy' Edgson, the linkman at the Clermont, who parked and collected members' cars for them, told the court he had known Lord Lucan at the club for about eight years.

'I have also done private jobs for him like taking him to the airport, collecting the children, that kind of thing,' he said. 'On November 7th I came on duty at the Clermont

248

at 8.00 p.m. My partner starts at 9.00 p.m. At about 8.45 p.m. Lord Lucan came to the outside of the club. I'd been on duty a good half hour. It was 8.45 p.m. give or take a few minutes. I'm pretty certain it was the Mercedes he was driving. I know that car quite well. I don't know about my fingerprints on it. He said: "Anybody in the club?" I said: "None of the usual crowd, sir." Then he just said: "Thank you very much," and drove off. He was not with me more than a minute or two minutes. I have driven from the Clermont to 46 Lower Belgrave Street. At 8.45 p.m. it would be very quiet. I have never done it in the evening. In the daytime I could do the journey in less than ten minutes. Ten minutes is not a long time from the Clermont to Lower Belgrave Street.'

During cross-examination Michael Eastham asked: 'When you saw Lord Lucan at about 8.45 p.m., how did he seem?'

'His usual self, not excited,' Billy replied.

Mr Eastham asked how much longer the journey from the Clermont might take if a driver went first to Elizabeth Street and then on to Lower Belgrave Street.

'It's only a difference of three minutes,' Billy suggested. 'It would be another three minutes. It's a very short journey.'

With the inquest now almost over, Mr Watling, for the police, told the coroner he wished to make a submission in the absence of the jury. Once again, members of the jury left their benches and filed out of the courtroom. Mr Watling referred Dr Thurston to a statement which had been made to the police by Greville Howard. He had been due to appear as a witness but Mr Watling said he was 'ill in hospital'. He asked that the statement should be read out in Greville Howard's absence.

'The reason I make this submission is that great play has been made by Mr Eastham of a third person,' Mr Watling said, referring to the alleged intruder. But, he suggested, there was evidence in Greville Howard's statement about Lord Lucan's depressed state of mind. 'That evidence is highly relevant,' he continued, 'and should be before the jury when they make their deliberation.'

Michael Eastham told Dr Thurston that he would 'most strongly object' to the proposal. There would be no opportunity to cross-examine Greville Howard in court on his statement, and its prejudicial effect would outweigh its probative value.

The statement was withheld.

Members of the jury were recalled to the courtroom to hear evidence from the final two witnesses, both of them detectives from the murder squad at Gerald Road. One after another the police officers – Detective Inspector Charles Hulls and Detective Chief Inspector Gerring – described experiments made at 10.00 p.m. on the Saturday after the murder to discover what could or could not be seen through the basement window at number 46 from the street.

Gerring first drove a car past 46 Lower Belgrave Street, about 7 feet from the pavement. There were parked cars on his left, outside the house. Looking towards number 46, he said, he could only see the top of the basement area. 'I could see only level with the pavement.'

Hulls then went into the basement, stood at the bottom of the stairs and moved backwards and forwards a few paces towards the door of the kitchen several times. From outside, Gerring tried to see if he could see his colleague through the venetian blinds on the kitchen window.

When the basement was in complete darkness, all he could see from outside, he said, was 'the red glow of the kettle to my left'.

'When the light over the breakfast room table was switched on,' Gerring continued, 'I could make out the figure of Mr Hulls in the area at the foot of the stairs, but then only by stooping. I stooped fairly well down. My head was between 2 and 3 feet from the ground.

'And then the kitchen lights were switched on, and I could see Mr Hulls at the foot of the basement stairs and about three or four of the steps.

'I then walked past the address and on looking through the slats of the venetian blind, I could only see the kitchen and not the foot of the stairs. That completed my experiments.'

Turning to the night of the murder, Gerring told the court that he went to number 46 at 1.00 a.m.

'To the best of my knowledge, nothing had been moved,' he said. 'I saw a pool of blood and the body in the sack. There was a picture lopsided on a wall coming down the stairs. One saucer was broken lying at the foot of the stairs and half the saucer was on the first step. There was no sign of a fight. Mrs Rivett would have become quickly unconscious. The first time I saw Lady Lucan was at 1.30 a.m. that day, Friday the 8th. With Mr Ranson I saw her at St George's hospital.'

Gerring went on: 'It was obvious she'd have taken a sedative by nature of her injuries. She looked as if she'd taken drugs.'

(According to Veronica in one of her 'exclusives', she had *not* been given a sedative at the hospital because she had drunk alcohol at the Plumbers Arms.)

The chief inspector continued: 'She first made a verbal statement on the evening of Friday the 8th around 6.00 to 7.00 p.m. Her understanding was extremely good. Mr Ranson and I left Sergeant Forsyth to take a written statement after she told us verbally. The written statement was remarkably close to the verbal statement.'

What were the differences – and why were there differences? He did not explain.

Cross-examined by Mr Eastham, Gerring agreed: 'If there was a fight going on in the kitchen, it would be very easy to see from the pavement outside.'

He was then questioned by Mr Watling.

'We have heard that Lord Lucan was able to let himself into the house with a key,' Mr Watling said. 'Have you been able to trace any other person who has a key to the Yale lock on the front door of the house?'

The chief inspector said he had not. He also said that no signs of a forcible entry to the house had been found. How could they tell after the police themselves had forced the front door?

He repeated his view that there had been 'no fight as such' in the basement. What about the broken banister rail and the picture on the stair wall knocked awry?

Mr Watling asked: 'Have you been able to find any trace of a third person in the house that night?'

'None whatsoever, sir,' Gerring replied.

'How long have you been a police officer?'

'Over twenty years, sir.'

'Have you made extensive inquiries to trace Lord Lucan?'

'I have, sir.'

The chief inspector told the court that he had spent eleven days at Newhaven and in the immediate vicinity. Extensive searches had been made of the area, but there had been no contact of any sort with the missing earl. In addition, he said, the police had made inquiries in 'virtually every country in the world following reported sightings'.

But, he said: 'There has been no trace of Lord Lucan.'

The coroner told members of the jury that this was the whole of the evidence they were to hear, and he would begin his summing up in the morning. They were released for the day.

Dr Thurston then sat *in camera* to hear more legal submissions.

The pertinent question the jury foreman had asked that morning: 'How did [Lady Lucan] *know* the nanny had been murdered?' had still not been answered. It was time for the coroner and the barristers to discuss the problem.

To recap, during cross-examination by Mr Watling on the first day of the inquest, Veronica had agreed that she had grabbed John by his 'private parts' and said that he had 'moved back'. The implication was that this had brought the alleged fight between them to an end. Mr Watling had then asked her: 'Did he say anything to you at that stage?' Dr Thurston had refused to allow her to answer that question.

But now, during the course of the discussion with the

lawyers, the coroner remarked: 'I propose to ask her what was said.'

Michael Eastham objected strongly. He pointed out that the strict rules of evidence which applied in a proper court of law were not applicable at an inquest hearing. This of course had already prevented him challenging Veronica's accusations in ways which would have been open to him at a trial. Secondly, he pointed out that a wife was not a competent witness in legal terms when it came to giving evidence concerning her husband and someone other than herself. And thirdly, he said that Veronica's explanation – coming as the last bit of evidence before the inquest jury considered its verdict – would have an 'absolutely devastating prejudicial effect' and could not, in law, be given. If Dr Thurston were to allow Lady Lucan to say in evidence what she claimed her husband had told her, and Lord Lucan were then to reappear, Mr Eastham said it would 'bar him forever from getting a fair trial'.

His submission was supported by Veronica's counsel, Mr Coles.

Mr Watling, for the police, told the coroner that he had a 'neutral line' on the question – but suggested it would be 'wholly wrong' if the jury were 'left with the wrong impression'.

The coroner decided not to recall Veronica. The situation would be explained to the jury the next morning.

Apart from giving evidence, Kait had maintained a public silence throughout the hearing, as indeed she had since the murder and John's disappearance. But finally, in frustration on that third day of the proceedings, she remarked to reporters covering the inquest: 'I do not think this is serving any useful purpose at all.'

Her restraint in the circumstances was amazing. Certainly evidence Veronica might have given about John had been banned: but then so had evidence about Veronica. Witnesses had been gagged. Questions had been disallowed. Sometimes the jury had heard incomplete answers. Though no one was going to accuse the coroner of a deliberate cover-up, nevertheless the *whole* truth stayed hidden.

Without knowing essential facts about the Lucans' relationship and background, no one could be expected to understand all the implications of the case. John had not stood trial in a court of law, nor had his name been allowed a full and fair defence at the inquest. Yet, unaware of the whole story, the jury had a judgement to make. How many people's lives might be irrevocably affected by their verdict? All-powerful, the jury's decision could brand a man, blacken his name and his family's, condemn his children to a lifetime of whispers and pointed fingers, 'punish' by association those whose innocence had never been in question.

The torrent of publicity about the Lucan case – including Veronica's 'exclusives' – had no doubt already influenced the attitude of the general public. But members of the jury were obliged to reach their decision solely on the evidence put before them at the coroner's court. And there was the rub. They had heard about bloodstains and fingerprints. They had heard Veronica from the witness box accuse John of being the man who attacked her. But at no time and in no way had it been proved *who killed Sandra Rivett*. Indeed, the jury members had complained to Dr Thurston through their foreman that they had 'heard nothing about the murder'. Yet the death of Sandra Rivett was supposed to be what the inquiry was all about. And now they weren't even going to have light shed on the puzzle which had prompted the foreman's vital question. Officially the answer was to remain shrouded in mystery.

Where did this leave John? Apart from Veronica's claim that he had attacked *her* – and it had been suggested that she was lying – the evidence against him was purely circumstantial. As the court had heard, he would have been bloodstained at number 46 whether he was guilty or innocent. There were no fingerprints tying him to the bloodstained lead piping, even if that *was* the real murder weapon. No one knew who put the other piece of lead piping into the boot of the Ford Corsair. The police didn't even know who drove the car down to Newhaven and abandoned it.

The one indisputable fact that stuck in the public mind was that Lord Lucan had run away. His disappearance affected the police view too. A detective had told an incredulous Susan Maxwell-Scott: 'An innocent man has nothing to fear from the police.' Would Timothy Evans, hanged for a murder he did not commit, have agreed with that? Or the three innocent boys convicted and later cleared of the Maxwell Confait murder? Or the lorry driver freed after serving eight years in jail for the alleged murder of a woman he said he'd never even set eyes on? The list of injustices down the years hardly makes for such complacency.

Yet despite the chilling catalogue of innocent men suspected, charged, convicted, imprisoned and even hanged, people cling to the popular myth that a man who runs away *has* to be guilty. It is high time this fallacy was exploded. Author David A. Yallop helps in his book *Deliver Us from Evil* (Macdonald Futura Publishers, 1981). Among several men he mentions who took to their heels over the years during murder investigations by the police was a Scotsman named Tommy. Tommy had a twenty-eight-year-old woman friend who lived in Leeds. It was known that they had a furious argument at her home and that Tommy threatened to knife her. He had threatened her before. Eighteen days later she was found dead with multiple stab wounds and her skull fractured. Tommy promptly disappeared. The woman's name was Wilma McCann. She had been killed by Peter Sutcliffe, the notorious Yorkshire Ripper – who was picked up, by chance, by the police six years later. But supposing the Ripper had slipped through police hands yet again? How much would you have given for Tommy's chances if *he* had been picked up? In a country where one can no longer have total faith in justice, or in the police, the decision to stay or flee in such a situation cannot be a simple matter.

Who *did* kill Sandra Rivett? Arrest warrants had been issued for John. The police had searched for him throughout the world. But the evidence given at the inquest, let alone that which the jury never heard, left far more than reasonable doubt of his alleged 'guilt'. The jury could – and in the circumstances undoubtedly should – have brought in a verdict of murder by person or persons unknown.

But one injustice piled high on others. It was not to be.

24

The hearing resumed on the fourth and final day fifteen minutes later than expected. Dr Thurston said that before his summing up, he would deal with the jury's question: 'How did [Lady Lucan] *know* the nanny had been murdered?'

He told members of the jury: 'You will remember before we started this case that I said I had great anxiety about whether or not to call Lady Lucan. Although she and her husband are separated, she is still his wife. In law a wife can only give evidence in a matter concerning her husband where there has been an assault on her. In this context, for any other matter whatsoever, she is not a competent witness.'

Referring to her cry: 'He's murdered my nanny!' the coroner told the jury: 'I'm going to ask you to dismiss it from your minds. You should not speculate as to how it came about that this was said. You should not draw any inference in any direction from this remark. You have of course heard a great deal of evidence in other directions.

'The only person who can clarify this point is Lady Lucan and she is in this context debarred from clearing the matter up for you. Do you understand the situation?'

The foreman, Mr Thomas, nodded and replied on behalf of the jury: 'Yes.'

And that – as far as his vital question was concerned – was that. No answer. No explanation. Just ignore it.

As always, Veronica was accompanied on the final day of the hearing by Sergeant Forsyth. Sally and Kait sat a row in front of them, Kait still craning forward to catch the coroner's words. The tensions between both sides of the Lucan family, which throughout the inquest had produced what reporters described as the 'icy' atmosphere in the courtroom, were mentioned by Dr Thurston at the start of his seventy-minute summing up.

Explaining why the jury had not heard all the available

evidence, the coroner said: 'I have thought fit to exclude affairs which might tend to go towards family tensions. You know that Lord and Lady Lucan are separated. They have been on either side of custody proceedings since 1973. It is fairly clear from the letters written by Lord Lucan that there is existing in the family animosity, tensions and matters which, if aired, could only be prejudicial and cause pain to the people concerned.

'To raise family tensions would not benefit this inquiry. If these matters could further the inquiry into Sandra Rivett's death then I would take a different view. But simply to turn this into a forum for airing family tensions would be a wrong thing, and I do not think justice would be served by doing so.'

Assuming that Dr Thurston himself knew the facts, how he ever arrived at this opinion defies the imagination. Moreover, justice in Britain has not only to be done but to be *seen* to be done. How could any outsider see that justice was being served when crucial evidence was being kept under wraps?

'If a person or persons are to be charged with murder or manslaughter it is a difficult matter . . .' the coroner went on. 'As regards evidence, the coroner's court is not bound by the strict rules of evidence. As [Lord Lucan] is not here, and his conduct is to be considered, it is only right that certain points which he has put in his letters, and what can be learned from hearsay – which is presumably what he would wish to say – should be heard. It is only fair that it should be put to you.'

Reviewing the evidence, he pointed out that Veronica and Sandra were both the same height, 5 feet 2 inches.

He recalled evidence given by Sergeant Baker and Detective Sergeant Forsyth about the scene which greeted them at number 46, and referred to the birdcage light fitting without a bulb – and the light bulb found on a chair in the basement.

'Chief Superintendent Ranson has told you that when he inserted the bulb, it lit and worked perfectly. But the bulb had been removed. We don't know why . . .'

Referring to the suggestion that there was 'no disturbance in the basement', he said: 'Certainly there was a body in a sack in a pool of blood . . . but one picture on the wall of the stairs was upset.'

About John's letters to Bill Shand Kydd, Dr Thurston said: 'In the main one, to "Dear Bill", he writes that "the circumstantial evidence against me is strong . . . Veronica has demonstrated her hatred against me in the past and would do anything to see me accused." The second letter is not so important as the first . . . It does suggest that he doesn't expect to be in contact with his family for some considerable time . . . It is evidence of what was in Lord Lucan's mind when he wrote it.'

But, he said, the jury should not treat the letters as proof of the statements in them.

In the letter to Michael Stoop, written on blotting paper from the writing pad found in the glove compartment of the Ford Corsair, he said, '[Lord Lucan] again refers to a traumatic night . . .'

Evidence had been given that Lord Lucan was 'obsessed' with his children. 'He was absolutely devoted to them and even more so since the case when Lady Lucan was granted custody of the children. He was looking forward to spending Christmas with them.'

The coroner went on: 'Taking [his] letters and the parts about "V has demonstrated her hatred and would do anything to see me implicated [sic]" – you have heard Lady Lucan's evidence. You had her sitting there for two hours. And you yourselves have had the advantage of seeing her and hearing the way she answered questions. She answered very carefully and gave questions a great deal of thought.'

There seemed little doubt whose version of the events Dr Thurston believed.

He recalled that Lady Lucan had told the jury that she came down the stairs looking for Sandra at about 9.15 p.m. (What about Frances's statement read in court, which suggested that her mother must have descended the stairs at least fifteen crucial minutes earlier?)

Lady Lucan had said there was no light on anywhere in

the basement. Dr Thurston briefly recalled her story about being attacked in the area of the hall at the top of the basement stairs. She said she had recognised the man as her husband.

(But not by sight. She did not *see* the person who attacked her in the darkness. And though John's voice may have identified him as the person who said: 'Shut up!', that didn't necessarily identify him as the killer.)

'Lady Lucan said she was taken into a downstairs cloakroom and this has been confirmed – her blood was on the towel,' Dr Thurston said.

(But surely the towel came from her pillow in the bedroom?)

He reiterated the rest of her story about going upstairs with her husband, lying down while he went into the bathroom, then running out to the Plumbers Arms.

He recalled that Lady Lucan had told the jury that it would be unusual to find Mrs Rivett in the house on a Thursday. But she had changed her day off. He reminded the jury that the previous Sunday, Lord Lucan had asked Frances when the nanny had her day off, and she had replied: 'Thursday'.

Mrs Maxwell-Scott had given evidence – and this was hearsay – that Lord Lucan told her he saw through the venetian blind what looked like a man attacking his wife. He let himself in through the front door and went down to the basement.

'Lord Lucan has given no description other than that the attacker was big,' the coroner said. 'There is the question to consider of the possibility of there being an intruder. There is the evidence of Lady Lucan's head injuries. These could be explained either by an attack by an intruder or Lord Lucan at this stage.'

Sounding as if he had already dismissed John's claim that Veronica would 'do anything' to see him 'accused', Dr Thurston asked the jury: 'If, as Lord Lucan says, he was trying to help – and he was obviously giving her succour – would she have run crying: "Murder! Murder!" to the Plumbers Arms?'

The next point that occupied the coroner was why John hadn't phoned the police. 'What is an instinctive reaction for somebody in that situation?' Dr Thurston asked. 'This is entirely for you to decide. Would an instinctive reaction be to do what the barman did when he at once phoned the police and the ambulance? You have got to take these matters into consideration.'

(But the barman didn't instantly phone the police. Judging from his evidence, he first went to Veronica's aid. He laid her down on a bench and covered her with an overcoat. And *then* he rang for help – just as John planned to do before Veronica ran off. According to Susan Maxwell-Scott, John said he had helped Veronica upstairs, got her to lie down, and once she was calm enough to be left, he had gone into the bathroom to get a wet cloth – intending to clean the blood from her wounds and *then* call a doctor and the police. But Veronica ran off, so he fled. Even after that, according to Mrs Maxwell-Scott, he said he had asked his mother to call the police.)

Lady Lucan's evidence, Dr Thurston declared (ignoring the odd bloodstain here and there), fitted in with what had been found scientifically. She was 'remarkably clear' when first interviewed by the police and 'she has never varied her statement at any time. The details have been the same.'

(So why did the police apparently need an additional statement for 'clarification'? And what about the differences between the version of her story the *Daily Express* printed early on and the version she gave later at the inquest?)

Taking John's version of the events, Dr Thurston considered the question of visibility into the basement. 'Sergeant Baker said the basement was in darkness,' he said.

(True, but that was at least an hour *after* the violence.)

The coroner had already reminded the jury of the dispute between witnesses over whether Lucan indicated he had been 'driving past' or 'walking past' the house.

Recalling the experiments performed at number 46 by

Chief Inspector Gerring and Inspector Hulls, Dr Thurston said: 'First of all, Mr Gerring drove his car past the house and said he could not see into the basement.' From the pavement, however, Gerring had said he had been able to see into the basement when he stooped down and when interior lights were on. 'But,' the coroner continued, 'the evidence was that there was no light on.'

(There was of course no available evidence about whether there was a basement light on when Sandra Rivett was killed. But how could the killer possibly have man-handled Sandra's bloody, deadweight body into the sack afterwards *without* a light on? John's initial shocked descriptions of the 'blood and mess' in the basement – the fact that he had even covered his eyes at the memory of the sight when recalling the events to Susan Maxwell-Scott – indicate that a light must have been on at some stage. How could he have seen it all otherwise? Though Kait had forgotten to mention this at the inquest, John had even told her: 'Oh mother, there was something terrible in the basement. I couldn't bring myself to look.' That, presumably, was a reference to the body in the bloodstained sack. Could John perhaps have removed the bulb from the birdcage light himself, just before helping Veronica to her bedroom, to make sure that if the children came downstairs they couldn't witness the bloodbath for themselves?)

Dr Thurston referred to the second part of John's story about interrupting the fight he had seen between his wife and the attacker.

But, said the coroner: 'There was no sign of a struggle. Blood was spread over the wall but there was no sign of furniture being upset.'

(This was a red herring. John never suggested he had *fought* the attacker himself – merely that he had arrived in the middle of a fight and the attacker had then run off. On the other hand, clearly someone had knocked the picture on the stairway wall askew, and broken the support on the banister rail – and they *were* signs of a struggle.)

'We have a question of an intruder,' Dr Thurston said. 'We know Lord Lucan had a key. We know he came into the house. But we have been unable to discover whether anybody else was there at number 46 Lower Belgrave Street. We have been unable to find anyone else with a key. There was no sign of any door being forced.'

(Could the police tell whether the front door had been forced once they had forced it themselves?)

The coroner went on: 'Then there is the question of the escape of the intruder in hearsay. We have not been told which way the intruder went out. It is possible to go out through the door into the garden but we have had indications that it would be extremely difficult to get out of this garden without leaving traces.' No such traces had been found.

(But why were leaves in the garden bloodstained?)

On the first day of the hearing, checking whether any man other than Lord Lucan could have been in the house, the coroner had put a couple of questions to Veronica. When she came downstairs and called Sandra's name, had she seen anyone else? Had anybody rushed past? Dr Thurston recalled: 'Lady Lucan has said: "I saw nobody else. Nor at any other time that evening."'

Turning to evidence about the bloodstains, Dr Thurston said: 'Shall we just for a minute consider what Miss Pereira the blood specialist had to say.' Very broadly, he said, there were two main areas of blood – the Group B blood in the basement, Sandra's group, and the Group A blood, Veronica's group, on the hall steps. But blood could be transferred.

'You have heard in the first instance that Police Sergeant Baker went down the stairs and it was necessary for him to pass through the blood on the stairs.'

From the Group B (Sandra's group) bloodstains on and under the arches of Veronica's shoes, Dr Pereira had suggested it was 'a likely explanation' that Lady Lucan had also walked through the basement.

But, as the coroner remarked: 'This would not be compatible with what Lady Lucan said.'

263

He reiterated that the bloodstaining on the shoes 'could have appeared there from walking through [Sandra's] blood' – or 'it could have come from contact with soggy clothing'.

Dr Thurston went on: 'We must remember that the assailant would have blood splashes on his clothes. And in the act of putting the body in the sack, the assailant would have been saturated in blood.'

(But if John was the killer, if his clothes were 'saturated' in Sandra's Group B blood, how could he have avoided leaving tell-tale Group B bloodstains, drips or smears in the hall, up the stairs, in Veronica's bedroom and bathroom, and in the nursery? And if he was 'saturated' in blood, how could Frances have failed to notice?)

The coroner recalled that Dr Pereira's examination of the bloodstained length of lead piping from the hall showed the blood to be Group AB. This 'could well be from a mixture of blood' of both women and suggested, he said, that the same 'weapon' was used to attack them both.

(But how could it have been if, according to Sergeant Baker, the piping was 'white' when he first saw it?)

Dr Pereira had found that hairs on the piping were similar to Lady Lucan's.

(But why were none of them Sandra's?)

Lord Lucan had left Uckfield at about 1.15 a.m. on Friday, 8 November, Dr Thurston said. A car he had borrowed (a couple of weeks earlier) was spotted parked at Newhaven at 8.00 a.m. The police discovered it on Sunday, and in the boot they found a second piece of bandaged lead piping (without bloodstains). Dr Thurston recalled evidence that there were differences between this 'bludgeon', and the adhesive tape wrapped round it, and the 'weapon' found at Lower Belgrave Street. The jury had heard that the two pieces of pipe *might* have come from the same original length (though they had not been adjacent to each other). There were similarities between blood samples, hair and fibres found in the car and at Lady Lucan's home.

The coroner went on: 'You may feel it is possible that Mrs Rivett was not the objective of the assailant's attack.' (On what evidence?) 'You have very seriously got to consider the matter: was there an intruder? This was mentioned by Lord Lucan . . . The injuries on Lady Lucan and Sandra Rivett are similar. Both could have been caused by the same bludgeon. Lady Lucan describes herself as having been attacked without any doubt whatsoever by her husband.'

Dr Thurston took a sip of water from a glass on his table. Behind Kait and Sally, Veronica sat with her head on one side, listening intently.

'As regards motive, this is a matter for conjecture,' the coroner said. 'There is a question of Lord Lucan's financial situation. There is no doubt that, as a result of the separation, he was having to keep two establishments going with all their outgoings. It could have eased his situation if he had only one establishment instead of two.'

(But that could be said of millions of men. Was that a motive for murder? And anyway, it was Sandra Rivett who had been killed – not Veronica. What possible motive could Lucan have had to kill her? And if he'd killed Sandra by mistake, and Veronica knew it, he *had* to kill Veronica as well. Yet Veronica had survived, and John – as the coroner himself had said – had given her 'succour'. What kind of sense did that make? None of this was pointed out by Dr Thurston.)

The coroner told the jury: 'I am going to ask you to retire. I do not think in this case I can ask you to consider the question of accidental death . . . The circumstances of this are quite clear. If you are satisfied on the evidence that there was an attack by another person, then your verdict would have to be murder.

'I cannot see on this evidence how I can possible offer you any alternative. The second point is that you have got to ascertain the person or persons, if any, to be charged with murder or manslaughter. And on the evidence you have got to decide whether you feel you can name the person responsible. You have got the facts before you, you have the possibility of an intruder, and you have got to consider what a very serious matter this is.'

He referred to the possible 'stigma' that could accompany their verdict, and said: 'I have had anxiety over how to present this case for many months. It is a most unusual and difficult matter.' But now the responsibility for the findings was the jury's. Dr Thurston told them he could accept a majority verdict provided there were not more than two dissentients.

The six men and three women of the jury filed from the courtroom. They were out for thirty-one minutes. It is easier to make quick decisions when you don't know all the facts.

25

Above the glass dome of the coroner's court, the sun rose higher. In a while it would be noon. The jury came back for the showdown.

Dr Thurston said: 'I believe you have reached your verdict?'

The foreman stood up. He spoke quickly and quietly. 'Yes,' he said. 'Murder by Lord Lucan.'

Veronica, listening impassively, drew several deep breaths.

'I will record,' the coroner intoned, 'that Sandra Eleanor Rivett died from head injuries, that at 10.30 p.m. on 7 November 1974 she was found dead at 46 Lower Belgrave Street . . . and that the following offence was committed by Richard John Bingham, Earl of Lucan – namely the offence of murder.'

He told the jury: 'It is a very rare procedure in coroners' courts that a person is named as you have done. It is my duty to commit that person to trial at the Central Criminal Court . . . But in this case there is nobody I can commit for trial because we don't know where Lord Lucan is. There is no doubt that if he turns up he will be charged with the offence. I will keep this on my file until such time as there may be any further developments.'

Dismissing the six men and three women he said: 'What you have observed in the jury room is completely confidential. You must not divulge any of the deliberations. Thank you for your attendance. You are now formally discharged.'

Pressmen scrambled out for telephones to file their copy.

Kait and Sally, the first of the family to leave the court, sped off in a taxi which was pursued down the street by photographers and reporters.

Veronica rose and bowed to the coroner, who had praised the way she gave evidence. She went to thank Chief Superintendent Ranson and Chief Inspector Gerring for their kindness and help. She exchanged a few words with Sandra's father, the first – according to one report – since the inquest had begun.

Mr Hensby, looking pale and sad, went home to his caravan near Basingstoke. From there Mrs Hensby was quoted as saying: 'Thank God. I want Lord Lucan named as the man who killed my daughter. I would like to think he is dead but I believe he's alive somewhere. He has so many friends with so much money. He could be anywhere in hiding, his hair changed, even his face altered. If he's dead then I hope he's rotting in hell. If he's alive then he will have this on his conscience for the rest of his days.'

The sensational end to the inquest produced a wave of reactions.

In a statement issued to the Press through her solicitor, Veronica declared: 'I am obviously very relieved that the coroner's inquiry is over. I intend to put the past behind me so far as I can and continue to lead a family life. As to the inquiry, you have heard my evidence. My husband's interests were represented before the coroner, and the jury have returned their verdict. I cannot say that I am pleased or displeased with the verdict. I was concerned only with establishing the facts.'

Christina was quoted as saying that she felt 'great sadness and sorrow' at the jury's decision. Months before she had told a reporter that, knowing John, she believed everything he had said in his letters 'of explanation'.

From Guilsborough, Sally's husband William told the Press: 'I know Lord Lucan is innocent, I have always known it and nothing has shaken that belief. If the jury has the power to decide who is guilty of a murder, then by what right does the coroner refuse to hear evidence to the contrary?

'In this case the coroner several times prevented questions that would have helped Lord Lucan. To me it is amazing and frightening that a coroner's court jury can name a man a murderer without hearing all the relevant evidence. This is not British justice and therefore must be ignored. I only hope that if Lord Lucan eventually comes forward and is brought to trial the inquest verdict will not prejudice his chances of a fair hearing.'

Susan Maxwell-Scott said: 'I am extremely disappointed that the jury decided he committed murder. I know that he did no such thing. I believe in his innocence . . . I always will.' Asked later why she thought Veronica had accused John, she was quoted as saying: 'I think she believes her evidence. I feel awfully sorry for her. She is a sad person. I steadfastly believe the story Lucan told me.' But as a result of the inquest jury's 'wrong' verdict, Mrs Maxwell-Scott said elsewhere: ' . . . there is no way Lord Lucan could get a fair trial.'

Others agreed – though sometimes from a different standpoint. Publicity given to the case had been prejudicial to a fair trial as well. Even Chief Superintendent Ranson, referring later to examples of individuals who had been 'convicted by the Press prior to the trial', remarked: 'There'd be lots of funny questions you know, there'd be lots of criticism I feel by a defence about this case if it ever came to trial.'

The day the inquest ended, a vigilant, healthy Press could with one cry have lambasted a system which defied the Magna Carta, which allowed a man to be branded a killer without being present, without standing trial, without even the benefit of a full defence. It did not. The evidence cried out for further scrutiny, yet instead of investigation came condemnation. Until he stands trial and is *proved* guilty beyond reasonable doubt, Lucan remains legally innocent. Yet after the inquest, newspapers threw caution – and the libel laws – to the winds and referred to John categorically as the killer. One leader-writer declared in print that his nickname shouldn't have been 'Lucky' but 'loathsome' Lucan. And a veteran news agency reporter who covered the inquest described Kait as 'vicious' for having mentioned

Veronica's 'mental complaint' to Sergeant Forsyth on the night of the murder. 'She would have said anything,' he remarked privately, an assertion that was manifestly untrue but indicative of the climate of opinion against the Lucan 'lot'.

The assumption of John's 'guilt' was so widespread and all-pervasive that his defenders were persuaded that seeking corrections, retractions or apologies in the papers would be a futile exercise. In a land once famed for its 'justice', Lucan and his relatives found themselves virtually defenceless, at the mercy of anyone who cared to burst into print. By contrast, writers leapt to defend Veronica, who had already proved she could take care of herself.

The only early newspaper article in John's defence appeared in the *News of the World* the weekend after the inquest and was based on an interview with Susan Maxwell-Scott. Could Veronica, she asked, have *mistaken* John for the killer?

'A person who's been hit over the head, possibly slightly concussed, within an ace of being strangled and believes she might die, must be confused,' Mrs Maxwell-Scott suggested.

The day the inquest ended, Mr William Thomas, the sixty-two-year-old foreman of the jury, grey-haired and bespectacled, told the Press he was satisfied with Dr Thurston's reply to his question: 'How did [Lady Lucan] *know* the nanny had been murdered?'

'I appreciate that this sort of evidence cannot be disclosed publicly,' he said curiously. 'I do not want to say any more except that the coroner is a gentleman.'

What did he mean, 'cannot be disclosed publicly'? Was he implying that another answer had been given to the jury, or himself, *in private*?

Mr Thomas told reporters that members of the jury were aware of the public interest in the case, and said he thought they had heard enough evidence to return their verdict against Lord Lucan.

Two other jurors – both attractive young female medical students, one tall and dark, the other fair and shorter – were quoted in the London *Evening Standard*.

'We decided only on the facts and were very concerned about the effect on the children and the reputation of the Lucan family and the stigma attached,' said the taller girl from Shropshire. 'We had a great concern for the ordeal of the Rivett family generally. I personally felt very deeply for the Rivett family when forensic evidence was being given. It must have been extremely distressing but there was no doubt we had to hear it. Until the last day nobody had made up their minds. But I think we had a fair idea this morning.'

Asked which piece of evidence led them to their verdict, the two girls were quoted as telling the *Standard*: 'The letter to William Shand Kydd, not the financial one but the other one about the "unbelievable coincidence". There was something about it . . .'

They would not explain further, no doubt recalling Dr Thurston's demand for silence. But there was an error about that report. John had not written the letter about 'unbelievable coincidences' to Bill Shand Kydd – but to Michael Stoop. If the jurors were confused about that, could they have been confused about more important facts?

The evidence which the jury didn't hear about Veronica never did emerge, apart from information she let drop herself in Press interviews over the years. But the banned evidence about John did come out. It could be read in newspapers before and after the inquest.

Question One: How did Veronica know that Sandra Rivett had been murdered?

The jury had heard only John's version in court. According to evidence given by Susan Maxwell-Scott, John said that *Veronica told him* that the intruder had killed the nanny. Veronica then allegedly gestured towards the sack and accused John of hiring the man to kill *her*.

Much later, Mrs Maxwell-Scott said: 'What I imagine must have happened – though not from what John said, he obviously arrived too late – is that Veronica presumably came downstairs to find Sandra and disturbed the killer putting the body into the sack or something. I don't see how else she would have known that the body was *in* the sack.'

Veronica's recollection was different. According to interviews she gave the *Daily Express* before the inquest, she knew Sandra was dead because *John told her*.

The very morning the inquest opened, in her 'exclusive' story splashed across the front page of the *Express*, she had been quoted as saying: 'I shall simply tell the court what happened and, of course, if asked I shall reveal the name of the man who attacked me – the man who sat on the stairs afterwards, cried on my shoulder and told me he had killed Sandra.'

Since warrants had been issued for John's arrest on both charges, since the murder hunt for Lucan had gone on for seven months, and since Veronica then accused John in court that morning of being the attacker, no *Express* reader could have been left in any doubt who the 'killer' was supposed to be.

In another interview Veronica gave to the *Express* five months earlier, back in January, she said she sat on the steps in the hall with the man who had allegedly attacked her and placed her head against his chest. She was quoted as telling the *Express*:

'I asked him: "Where is my nanny?" The answer came: "She's gone out." I insisted: "But she wouldn't have gone out without telling me." Then he muttered: "She is dead." I now knew that I had to play for time and think up some plan for escaping myself. So I replied: "Oh dear, what shall we do with the body?"

'He mumbled: "She is downstairs – but don't look. It is a horrid sight . . . an awful mess." He told me he had to make a quick decision. I pretended to be helpful. I said that as Sandra had no friends and relatives, no one would miss her. By this time I was weakening physically. Would my delaying tactics work? My neck was badly wrenched and ached. All I wanted to do was lie down to take the pressure off my head. My throat was hurting so much from the fingers forced into my mouth. I asked if I could have a glass of water. He let me go into the downstairs cloakroom in front of us where I got a drink. He asked me at that point if I had any sleeping pills. When I replied that I had some he asked me if I would take them. I suppose to finish the job! I said I would. Then he took me up to my bedroom . . .'

Question Two: What had Greville Howard told the police?

This came out in *The Guardian* on 20 June, the day after the jury gave its verdict. According to Peter Chippindale: 'Mr Greville Howard made a statement to the police that he had a conversation with Lord Lucan some months before, in which Lord Lucan had talked about getting rid of Lady Lucan and dumping the body in the Solent.'

The conversation took place one evening when Lucan was very drunk, months before Sandra Rivett was killed.

'Howard told me that Lucan could see no way out of his [financial] problems,' Ranson wrote later in his own newspaper series in the *Daily Star*. 'He was worried his children might one day see him in court as a bankrupt. It would be easier, Lucan said, to get rid of his wife. Howard said it would be far worse for the children to see their father in court accused of murder. Lucan replied: "But I wouldn't get caught."'

Ranson told me: 'I think [Howard] thought it was just [Lucan's] drunken rambling.'

Certainly Greville Howard did not take John seriously.

Lucan's elder sister, Jane, commented: 'I'm sure John was near wanting to get rid of Veronica many times, but I just don't think he'd ever have come to it.'

Wanting wasn't proof of actually doing it.

Kait had never seen her elder son through the usual rosy mists of motherhood. In her word, he had been 'awkward' as a tiny infant, rebellious as a youth. As a man – and 'goodness knows', she said, it had taken him a long time to grow up and mature – there was hardly an opinion she could hold without him taking the opposite view. Politically, he was as Right-wing as she was Left. Almost the only interests they shared were reading whodunnits and playing the piano music of Bach. They could scarcely have been more different. Yet though Kait deplored John's way of life, and declared that any man who gambled was 'a fool', she was certain of one fact.

'My son is not a murderer,' she said privately. 'I am absolutely convinced of that.'

The day the inquest ended, Chief Supt. Ranson told reporters that the search for the missing earl would go on until he was found 'dead or alive'.

'Whatever the verdict had been would not have affected our inquiries into the tracing of Lord Lucan,' he said. 'He will be arrested when we trace him – if we do . . .'

But the trail was completely cold, and the two top policemen on the case didn't agree whether their elusive quarry was alive or dead.

'Alive,' said Gerring. 'Remember, this man was a gambler. He lived by his wits at the tables. It was a job to him, his meal ticket. The whole question of whether he survived in life depended on whether Lady Luck was smiling on him at the backgammon table. I cannot believe that a man who lived this way would suddenly give it all up without a fight, without a gamble. And that means staying alive no matter if it means going to any lengths to change identities and going to live in some remote part of the world.'

'Dead,' said Ranson. 'I believe he would rather die than let his three children see him subjected to a murder trial. I think he went off somewhere to die hoping never to be found again. I believe with someone like him, especially with his background, this would be considered the most honourable thing to do. And I am convinced that the sea somehow holds the secret to his death.'

According to the police chief, John could have obtained

a sixty-hour passport on the quayside at Newhaven, caught the 11 a.m. ferry to Dieppe on Friday, and perhaps thrown himself over the side while crossing the Channel. Because of stomach gases, a body in the sea would surface after two or three weeks, Ranson learned, but wouldn't necessarily be found. He discovered that if fishermen bring up a body in their nets, rather than risk having their entire catch condemned, they might weight the body down, or plunge a boat hook into the stomach, releasing the gases – and send it back down to the deep.

Aspinall also talked of John going to his death from a boat or 'falling on his sword', not that he was likely to have had one handy. Lucan 'wasn't the type' to commit suicide – most people agreed on that. Yet even Kait thought he had killed himself, that the strain and trauma of the murder night on top of everything else had probably been 'too much'. Though she was sure of his innocence, the fact that he never contacted her again as promised seemed to confirm her suspicion that he was dead.

'Everyone meets their Waterloo,' she said sadly.

Dead or alive, the very fact that John had disappeared convinced many people he must be 'guilty'. But as Susan Maxwell-Scott pointed out, guilt wasn't the only reason why a man might flee.

John's main letter to Bill Shand Kydd made it clear he feared he might find himself charged with 'attempted murder'. The swift realisation that he was being sought in connection with the murder as well could only have made matters worse.

Bill said: 'He could have heard or read the news and thought: "J.C.! Now I really *am* in the shit!"'

Wasn't that reason enough to stay 'lying doggo'?

Or could something more sinister have happened? His disappearance was so uncharacteristic that an old friend convinced of his innocence asked: 'Do you think he could have been killed by someone after he left Uckfield?' It seemed preposterous, but rumours flourished. Someone approached the family suggesting John had been spirited away to a hiding place and then killed when he became 'too hot to handle'. There was another theory that he had asked a friend to dispose of his body, once he had committed suicide, to make sure no trace was ever found.

A rumour which circulated among London businessmen suggested that Lucan had been bumped off by 'a Mafia hitman' because of a gambling debt. Equally curious, in June 1979 Sir Rupert Mackeson claimed from Rhodesia that John *had* been murdered – and that his own life had been threatened by 'two East End men, rather rough types who swore a lot'.

'Lucan is dead. I can assure you of that, dear boy,' he was quoted as telling a *News of the World* reporter. '[The] two thugs in London told me: "We've killed Lord Lucan and you will go the same way unless you keep your mouth shut." They mentioned the names of certain City men and said I would be killed unless I laid off. I was bloody frightened and I still am.'

He claimed that he had 'found out' that 'the organised American crime syndicate have taken over the City of London'. Asked if he was 'referring to the Mafia', Mackeson – who finally flew back to Britain in April 1980 – replied: 'Don't be silly, dear boy, I'm up the creek. You don't expect me to explain that.'

Was Lucan dead? Had he committed suicide, been killed by 'a Mafia hitman', by 'East End thugs', by anyone else? Was that why he had vanished into thin air and never reappeared? Or was that all too fanciful? Was he simply living a new life somewhere, quietly 'lying doggo'?

Whatever his fate, in October 1979 Ladbroke's odds expert Ron Pollard gave the odds against Lucan being found as 1,000 to 1. There was a far greater chance, he reckoned, of locating Nessie, the Loch Ness monster, or capturing the Abominable Snowman.

Three months after the Sandra Rivett inquest, Dominick Elwes was found dead at his mews house in Chelsea, sprawled across his bed in his shirt, tie and underpants. There were pill bottles nearby. He had taken an overdose of Tuinal. Next to his body was a suicide note, one of several he had written in red ink on lime green paper. A police officer found the red pen still clutched in his hand.

The inquest on his death took place before the same coroner and in the same courtroom where such a short time before John had been branded a murderer. The Press benches were full. During the hearing, Dr Thurston remarked: 'It sounds as if [Mr Elwes] had a characteristic manic-depressive personality and suicide is always a risk, isn't it?' He decided that Dominick 'killed himself – there is no question of this being an accident'. Dominick was forty-four.

Though he said he had 'never been the same' since the murder and John's disappearance – that the affair had 'shattered' his life – neither the coroner nor the witnesses who gave evidence at the proceedings mentioned Lucan. That was left to Chief Superintendent Ranson and Sergeant Forsyth, unexpected observers at the Elwes inquest, who explained to reporters: 'We have an interest in any of Lucan's friends and will have forever if necessary.'

Dominick had reaped a bitter harvest from his attempts to help John. Along with other friends of John's, he had co-operated with James Fox in the preparation of his article, 'The Luck of the Lucans', but had been very disappointed with the outcome. John Aspinall refused point blank for years afterwards to talk about Lucan to any other journalist, including me. Dominick, who had even painted a picture which accompanied the article, showing John and some of his friends lunching together at the Clermont, claimed that he had become 'a pariah'. After his death, an Atticus column in *The Sunday Times* – in which others besides Dominick who had helped Fox were listed – declared: 'I refer those who are blaming a newspaper article for a personal tragedy to Matthew, Chapter 7, verse 3. "And why beholdst thou the mote that is in thy brother's eye, but considerest not the beam that is in thine own eye?"'

Late that November, four days before meeting his own

death in a plane crash, racing driver Graham Hill was among Clermont friends at Dominick's memorial service in Mayfair, when emotions which had been simmering beneath the surface finally broke through. Kenneth Tynan delivered an apologia for Dominick's life, stating: 'He loved the world of wealth and ceremony far more than it deserved.'

John Aspinall gave a passionate oration, read a poem with the key lines: 'Why did you leave us, Dominick? Why did you die?' and was socked on the jaw as he left the church by the 'very overwrought' Tremayne Rodd – Dominick's cousin, an ex-boxing champion and a former Scottish Rugby international player – who claimed Aspinall had 'ruined the service' with his 'inappropriate' speech. Rubbing his chin ruefully, Aspinall commented: 'I am used to this sort of thing in dealing with wild animals.'

Of the gamblers, it was Dominick who declared that he and John were like 'brothers'. He was one of the few who contacted Kait, who chased off trying to find John, saying he 'knew' he was still alive. According to one report, the floral tributes at Dominick's funeral at Arundel included a wreath signed 'Lucky'.

Back at Uckfield from the Sandra Rivett inquest after John had been branded a murderer, Susan Maxwell-Scott gained little consolation from an unexpected telephone call.

'It was from the man in Market Harborough,' she said. 'He said he was sorry to hear about the inquest jury's verdict. He said he had told the truth from the start about the phone call from his friend saying that another man *had* left the house on the night of the murder. He said he was sure that his friend would come forward if the case ever came to a trial. I know he was dismissed as a "hoaxer", but I think his story was true.'

BOOK FOUR

The Evidence

26

Three people were in a position to know at least part of what really happened at 46 Lower Belgrave Street on the drizzly November night of the tragedy: John and Veronica, whose stories did not match, and Sandra Rivett, who had been murdered. Or were there four? If John's story was true, there was another man at the scene of the crime – the man he saw through the basement window fighting Veronica. The man who fled when John raced into the house to the rescue. The man who had presumably killed Sandra.

John's story was almost a real-life carbon copy of the start of the famous David Janssen American TV series *The Fugitive*: husband on the scene, wife dead, killer fleeing, husband blamed. Except that in this case, another woman had died and the wife was the accuser.

But Detective Chief Superintendent Ranson believed a different version. He had 'no doubt' in his mind that Lucan murdered Sandra Rivett, mistaking her for Veronica – and then, when he discovered his mistake, tried to kill Veronica as well.

To those who knew Lucan best, the idea was inconceivable. John, the 'gentle' giant who 'wouldn't hurt a fly', committing murder? 'Mistaking' another woman for the wife he'd been married to for eleven years? Bludgeoning the nanny to death in a gory bloodbath of a killing when he was 'incredibly squeamish', 'couldn't bear anything messy' and 'couldn't stand the sight of blood'? Committing such a brutal murder when the children he was desperate to protect were in the house and might walk in and witness the scene at any moment? Attacking Veronica as well, but failing to kill her – a man a foot taller, at least twice her weight and powerful enough to lift great logs on his shoulder 'like Tarzan'?

Making such a blundering hash of the whole thing – a calculating, meticulous, well-organised man like John? None of it was in character. None of it made sense.

In the opinion of people who had known him most of his life he was a softie at heart, 'incapable' of murder. But if he *had* wanted to kill his wife, they suggested, chances were he would have succeeded – though the method would have been devious and non-messy, nothing so crude as bludgeoning. Only half tongue-in-cheek they suggested he'd have sent her a poisoned orchid laced with some very weird poison 'no one had ever heard of' and the deed would have been done when he and the children were safely on the other side of the world.

'If something like that had happened,' they said, 'one might have thought twice about it. But there were too many flaws in this to bear any hallmark of John at all.'

Maybe anyone, some people said, could be 'driven' to murder, could go berserk and kill in the middle of a violent row. But if John had argued violently it would have been with Veronica not Sandra – yet it was Sandra who had been killed. In any case few people ever heard him raise his voice in anger, let alone shout or become enraged. He was noted for his great self-control, his poker-player's ability to conceal his feelings and stay cool under pressure.

A friend who had known John since he was a teenager at Eton said: 'He was a very gentle person and a very controlled person. Ranson said one theory was that he was controlled for so long that he suddenly blew his top and snapped. I don't believe that was the case at all.'

Neither did Hugh, who said: 'He had no history of physical violence known to me and I'm certain he could not have resorted to that. People can act strangely under pressure – the police come across this every day – but I'd had lunch with John two or three weeks before and there was nothing about him which suggested that he was becoming more depressed or that he had reached some irrevocable decision. I would have noticed and worried. The police suggested he could have had a brainstorm but they also said the murder was premeditated, and you can't plan to go berserk. Anyway I would find it very implausible that John would crack like that.'

Since it was Sandra who had died, one would have thought that the obvious assumption would have been that she was the intended victim. And if the police were right that the murder was premeditated, that raised the question who *wanted* her dead? Hardly John. She'd only worked at the house for a few weeks and he scarcely knew her, though he said she seemed a 'nice' girl and he was pleased with her work as a nanny. What possible motive could he have had to kill her? And though it might be considered that he had a motive to kill Veronica, if she came to any harm he would automatically become the prime suspect. How could that have helped him regain custody of the children?

As Caroline Hill said: 'To have committed murder would have been to destroy everything: himself, his wife and his children. I am deeply convinced he did not do it.'

Michael Hicks Beach said: 'I was obviously worried about John when I heard about the killing, but it was inconceivable that he had done it. Although he wanted an end to the problem with Veronica, he had told me only the weekend before that he still hoped to bring the custody case back to the courts. I don't think he was capable of murder and I don't think he could have stood the social disgrace of even being *suspected* of being involved in a murder, let alone the effect such a suspicion would have on his children.'

An Old Etonian business friend also thought John was 'incapable' of murder. 'Secondly,' he said, 'John Lucan is a person who has always been extremely well organised, everything well planned. He'd never have done it because it wasn't in his make-up. But if he *had*, he would never have left Veronica half-dead – he would have succeeded in killing her. And he wouldn't have used that method, battering someone to death with a blunt instrument. It's not his scene. The method wouldn't have been messy.'

'I've known John since we were in prams really,' Juliet Hill said. 'I know him as well as if he was a brother, and

I'm convinced he didn't do it, particularly in such a bungling fashion like that. Anything John ever did he knew exactly what he was going to do beforehand, and he did it extremely efficiently. I don't think it's in his character to commit a murder of any kind, but if he had he would have done it in some most devious way when he was abroad with the children, I would have thought. He was the most efficient, punctilious person and I just can't imagine him doing anything so idiotic as that and "mistaking the nanny for his wife" and all the rest. It's just totally out of character. I can't see that he would do it with the children in the house either. He had them every other weekend, so it would be completely mad to do it when they were there. And he was squeamish. He had a lovely habit of wrinkling up his nose and saying "Yeuk!" If he was going to kill, he wouldn't have used that gory method.'

Her husband, Robin, added: 'And I don't think he would have taken a risk of that sort which would obviously rebound on his children.'

'It was inconsistent with his character,' John Wilbraham said. 'Battering someone to death is certainly not John's scene. The mess is not him either, and it must have made a hell of a mess. And he certainly wouldn't have blundered – that's the thing that utterly amazes me. He'd have got the right person for Christ's sake. He wasn't a fool, far from it. If he'd wanted to kill Veronica – which I certainly don't believe he did – I am sure he would have succeeded. These things have never tallied.'

From the very beginning, people who knew John raised doubts, though these were apparently not shared by the police. If Lucan had gone to number 46 that night specifically to murder Veronica, why hadn't he done it? If he had killed Sandra Rivett 'by mistake' and Veronica knew it, he *had* to silence her forever.

So why had he done the opposite – helped her upstairs to her bedroom and given her 'succour', as the coroner put it? Why did he then allow her the chance to 'escape'? And when she did disappear from the bedroom, why did he go further *upstairs* to look for her, calling: 'Veronica, where are you?' That action spoke volumes. Wouldn't a guilty man have recognized the danger immediately she vanished – and reacted instinctively by chasing after her *down* the stairs? Going *upstairs* carried the clear implication that he thought Veronica knew she had nothing to fear from him. But did she? In her shocked and confused state, did she run off because she genuinely believed he was the killer, and thought that her own life was still in danger? Or could there have been some other reason?

Whatever had taken John to number 46 that night, whether he had simply gone to keep an eye on the house as usual, or something more sinister, Veronica said later that she was 'glad' he was there.

Her feelings about her husband were capable of swinging from one passionate extreme to the other.

Christina recalled: 'Sometimes she said she loved John, sometimes she said she hated him. Sometimes she said she loved him when she married him, sometimes she said she hated him when she married him. Totally inconsistent.'

Long after John disappeared, however, Veronica was quoted as saying: 'We were joined together by an incredibly strong emotional bond. To say I love him is to denigrate love. It is more than love.' Most of the time, she said, he had shown her 'more kindness than anyone else' in her life. He had been her 'only friend'. And on the night of the tragedy, she still wanted him. She was quoted as saying: 'I had wanted him to come back and there he was . . .' With her again at number 46, the house they had once shared . . .

Veronica's appeals to her husband over the previous twenty-two months to return to her and be reconciled had fallen on deaf ears. Several months before the tragedy, he had told Nanny Jenkins: 'She wants me back but it can never be.' He had also told Hugh: 'It must not be.' But on the very night of the murder, according to Veronica herself, the subject of a reconciliation cropped up again.

285

After the violence, when John helped Veronica upstairs and Frances was sent to bed, the Lucans apparently spent between about twenty to forty minutes in Veronica's bedroom. What they were doing during that period remains a mystery. Indeed, the ' "missing" forty minutes' were to perplex Chief Superintendent Ranson. John spoke later only of 'calming' Veronica, and getting her to lie down on her bed. The only physical clues found later were that the bedding had become rumpled, and a couple of the bedroom lights had apparently been switched off after Frances left the room. Was it during this curious period that the subject of reconciliation was once again raised?

Part of Veronica's recollection of the conversation, which she revealed later in a Press interview, went:

'I said: "Why didn't [sic] you come back?"'

'He said: "No, Veronica. That can never be now . . ."'

An echo of the very words he had used months before. 'It must not be.' 'It can never be.'

Veronica also described to the Press the moment she decided to run off, after John went into the bathroom.

'I had a choice for about four seconds,' she was quoted as saying. 'What I did then caused him to do what he did afterwards.'

But having run off, there was the question of her curious hesitation at the Plumbers Arms. Contrary to Press reports, Veronica did *not* run into the pub screaming. According to the barman's testimony at the inquest, having arrived at the pub, Veronica 'was quite all right for a few minutes. *Then* she started shouting . . .' (my italics)

Why didn't she cry out for help from the second she burst through the pub door? In an emergency, why delay?

27

What foxed Chief Superintendent Ranson were the times. They didn't fit.

He wasn't convinced that Veronica could have spent forty to sixty minutes talking to her 'attacker'. And the only explanation he could fathom was that she must have spent some of the time unconscious.

'You see,' he told me shortly after the inquest, at his base at Cannon Row police station, close to the Houses of Parliament and Big Ben, 'there's no doubt at all that Lady Lucan must have had periods of unconsciousness she doesn't recollect. You take the sequence of events. The time is rather fluid, but there's little doubt that Sandra went to make tea at about nine o'clock and Lady Lucan gets rather cross with the non-appearance of the tea and goes down, she estimates, towards the end of the news. Well, the news on BBC television is twenty-five minutes, so let's say she went down between quarter and twenty past nine. In the meantime, Sandra's been killed and put in the sack. So what happened for the next –? She didn't run into the pub until about ten o'clock, shall we say a few minutes either way, so there's forty unexplained minutes.'

This ignored the fact that Frances placed the key events earlier. By her recollection, Sandra must have gone downstairs to make the tea at some time between about 8.30 p.m. and 8.40 p.m., and Veronica went to look for her *before* 9.00 p.m. Which meant there were more like sixty unexplained minutes.

'And if Frances's times were correct instead,' I said, 'there was even longer, wasn't there?'

'Well . . .'

'More like an hour?'

'Yes, there's an hour,' Ranson said. 'So what happened

[in] that time? There's no doubt that Lady Lucan escaped as soon as she possibly could, in my mind anyway. What happened during the twenty [sic] minutes? I think there's no doubt at all – I'd be surprised if there wasn't a period of unconsciousness from Lady Lucan, considering her injuries. And what happened during that?'

'That's the only reasonable explanation, is it?'

'Yes,' Chief Superintendent Ranson said. 'She tells her story as though it's a continuing sequence of events. But it can't possibly be, because there wouldn't be [that] forty minutes.'

But by accounting in such a way for those 'forty unexplained minutes', the head of the murder squad automatically blasted a gaping hole in the police case against John. Because Veronica *survived*.

Take it step by step.

If Lucan went to the house that night to kill his wife and murdered the nanny 'by mistake', he had to murder Veronica as well. According to Dr Pereira, the blows Veronica was dealt with the weapon were delivered with 'considerable force'. In other words, whoever wielded that weapon wanted her dead. The radiating pattern of Group A blood splashes by the four little steps in the hall indicated that Veronica had been felled during the attack. Evidence about the nature of her head injuries was to suggest the same. If, as the police chief believed, Veronica became unconscious, she also became defenceless. Therefore she could not have fought back. *So why wasn't she killed? What made* the attacker stop?

I posed the question.

There was a long pause before Chief Superintendent Ranson replied. It was not the first point in the interview which had caused difficulty.

Going over the evidence at another stage he had remarked: 'All you can do is guess and try and make intelligent guesses.'

The pause came to an end.

'Again,' he said finally, 'you can only guess, can't you?'

What was the most intelligent guess? Veronica had

been attacked and yet she had survived: that was fact. If she was unconscious she must also have been defenceless: that was obvious. If John had killed Sandra he *had* to kill Veronica too: and if she was unconscious, there was nothing to prevent him. Yet whoever attacked Veronica with 'considerable force' had suddenly, inexplicably, stopped. Why? If John was the killer, it made no sense. But if someone else was the killer the answer was clear: Veronica survived *because* John ran into the house to the rescue. Just as his story implied.

In terms of Sandra Rivett's death, Lucan was the least likely suspect. He wasn't related to her, he hardly knew her and though he liked her the idea of anything 'going on' between them was a non-starter.

'With a *nanny!*' protested Bill Shand Kydd.

Class distinctions were not dead, even though poor Sandra was.

So why were the police so sure of Lucan's 'guilt' that they had started looking for him 'instantly'?

'It's a matter of access,' Chief Superintendent Ranson said. 'And he wasn't available even at that stage – he'd disappeared already. We knew there was trouble between husband and wife. So many murders are a triangle – most murders, I would say 90% of murders if you take it countrywide, are family murders. They're husband and wife or husband and boyfriend or boyfriend and wife. Right from the off there was talk of the husband straight away.'

Ranson's three points were each worth examination.

By access he meant that there was no evidence of a break-in. Ten years earlier there had been no sign of a forced entry when a burglar had stolen the jewellery from the Lucans' bedroom. And there was equally no sign of a forced entry on the night Sandra Rivett was killed a few feet from the safe by an intruder Lucan claimed was probably 'a burglar'. Apart from Lucan, who'd always had a key, that suggested three possibilities:

1 The killer knew someone at the house who let him

in. Might that explain why the security chain wasn't in use on the front door that evening?

2 The killer had a key. That meant he probably knew someone who lived or had lived at the house – like the jewel thief in 1964 who was thought to have obtained a key from one of the Lucans' early employees.

3 The killer was a professional burglar, or someone with a skeleton key, who was able to break in without leaving trace, and might have taken the mailbag with him to carry his loot.

Over the years there had been a long succession of nursery and other staff at number 46. Sandra Rivett had a key, which suggested that some of the others had probably had one as well. A key can easily be duplicated. The police were sure they had traced all keys to the house, but how could they be certain?

It's by no means unknown for professional thieves to go out armed and prepared to commit violence if disturbed. Belgravia is a high-risk area for buglaries. According to one self-confessed thief: 'Every burglar is a potential killer.' So what were the possibilities?

1 The intruder at number 46 that night went there specifically to kill.

2 He went there to see Sandra, had a row, went berserk and killed her in a fit of passion.

3 He went there to rob the safe or the house and turned violent when he was disturbed.

It left the field wide open.

There were four oddities that night. Could they have been linked?

First there was the change in Sandra's day off. She had had several boyfriends since her husband had left her seven months before. During her employment at number 46, Thursday was her regular day off – the night she saw them. But that week she had taken Wednesday off instead to see her latest love, the Australian barman John Hankins. According to Frances, Sandra had split up with her previous boyfriend only 'a few days' before she was killed. Other reports suggest he wasn't the only man she'd ditched. If any ex-boyfriend knew she'd been out with John Hankins on Wednesday, might he have wanted to see her on Thursday evening, perhaps to patch up a row or attempt a reconciliation? Or even wreak revenge?

Second, it was unusual for Sandra to offer to make Veronica a cup of tea at that time in the evening. Veronica said as much at the inquest. Why had the normal routine changed? Could Sandra have had a special reason for offering to make the tea?

Third, although the two women were spending the evening upstairs, although they were going to drink their tea upstairs, although the cups and saucers were already upstairs, and although the tea could have been *made* upstairs by the nursery, Sandra inexplicably went all the way down towards the kitchen in the basement. Why?

Fourth, did the intruder know that Thursday was usually the easiest night to get into the house? Because the nanny was usually out then, the chain on the front door was normally left off on Thursday evenings so that no one had to get out of bed to let her in if she arrived back late – as Sandra did. Anyone bringing her home late on a Thursday night, or watching her arrive back, might have known that.

But because that week Sandra had changed her day off to Wednesday, the door chain should have been up on the Thursday evening she was killed. If it had been, no one would have been able to get through the front door, even with a key. So why was the chain left off? That afternoon, Sandra had taken Frances out to the post office to post a letter, and by the time they arrived back at the house, the children's tea was ready. Was getting them in to tea the reason why Veronica 'hadn't thought' to put the chain up once they were back? Was it a simple oversight? Or could Sandra have put the chain up automatically, then taken it down again that evening when someone arrived at the front door?

'The girl must have let someone in. That's the first thing I thought,' said Miss Lilian Jenkins, the former nanny. 'Why go all the way down to the kitchen when she could have made tea in the nursery?'

The same thought occurred to Bill Shand Kydd, who said: 'I never did understand why she went downstairs when there was every facility to make tea upstairs.'

The distance between the nursery and the kitchen was four floors and sixty-six stairs. Because of the obvious inconvenience of carting food and drink up and down, a baby Belling cooker had been installed years before just outside the nursery on the third floor. This enabled the resident nanny, whoever she was, to prepare tea on the spot.

On the evening of the murder, Sandra offered to make tea and collected the tea things. The cups and saucers were dirty because they had been used earlier and had not been washed since. They were already upstairs but it's not clear where: perhaps in Sandra's bedroom on the fourth floor, in the nursery on the third or in Veronica's bedroom on the second. Sandra put them on a tray. Then, instead of staying upstairs and using the baby Belling, she unaccountably began her long and difficult descent.

She set off to go down eighty-two, sixty-six or fifty-one stairs, depending on where she collected the tea things – presumably planning to carry the scalding-hot tea all the way back up fifty-one stairs to Veronica's bedroom afterwards. To make matters worse, the stairs are steep and she was wearing high-heels; she couldn't watch her step because she was carrying the loaded tray; and she had to go part of the way in darkness because the old lightbulb in the hall had not been replaced.

In the event, she apparently never even reached the kitchen. The police found the dirty cups and saucers scattered in the pool of Sandra's blood at the foot of the basement stairs.

But why had she made that inconvenient, unnecessary journey in the first place? Why go downstairs at all when the alternative would have been so quick and easy? Was there a hidden reason?

Had someone been in touch with her, perhaps by phone? Had a boyfriend or an ex-boyfriend, who possibly knew she'd seen John Hankins the night before, perhaps pleaded to see her for five minutes? Had she agreed to see him briefly on the quiet? Was that why she suddenly offered to make Veronica a cup of tea? Was it an excuse to spend ten minutes downstairs? Was that why she went down instead of using the nursery baby Belling? Was that why the door chain was down – because someone had entered the house? And if Sandra did let some man in for a secret assignation, what happened next? Did she tell him she didn't want to see him or anyone else because she had fallen for John Hankins, whom she hoped to marry? Did a jealous row break out which turned violent? If that was the case then there was no question of her being a 'mistaken identity' victim: whoever killed her *knew* who he was killing.

Chief Superintendent Ranson said that most murders were family affairs between 'husband and wife ... or boyfriend and wife'.

'Right from the off,' he'd said, 'there was talk of the husband [sic] straight away.' (He meant Lucan.)

'Presumably [Sandra's] boyfriends, Hankins and whoever the others were, all had cast-iron alibis for that night, did they?' I had asked the police chief.

'We checked them all out, every male acquaintance of Sandra's,' he said.

'She must have had an awful lot of boyfriends by the sound of it,' I said, recalling lascivious comments one of Ranson's officers had made.

'Well, I would say not, not an exceptional amount of boyfriends you know for a mature sexual lady,' Ranson said.

According to Ranson, the Australian barman John Hankins was 'top of the pops' with Sandra at the time of her death.

'He was very well regarded ... There was talk of marriage between her and Hankins and going to Australia.'

John Hankins last spoke to Sandra when he telephoned her at number 46 at 8.00 p.m. on the murder night, shortly before she was killed.

'In the initial stages [of the investigation], he wandered into Gerald Road police station,' Ranson said. 'He wasn't interviewed by me – I was too busy. And he had to sit there until I had time to [talk to him].'

'So you never actually roped him in?'

'No, we wanted a statement from him.'

'Nobody else ever got roped in under suspicion?'

'No,' Ranson said. 'Oh you know, there was so much background . . . You get involved in all sorts of things that we haven't got interest in really.'

'Was Sandra actually in the process of getting a divorce from her husband?'

'Inquiries were being made about it by her,' Ranson said. Then he added: '[Roger Rivett is] a strange chap you know. There's no doubt he could have made money out of this, sordidly made money out of this. He could have given interviews with papers, he could have supplied photographs of his wife. And he's the only person [sic], the only witness in the case that we've said: "Well, don't talk to the Press since the matter is *sub judice*" [and] he did exactly as we said. All these other people . . . gave interviews and appeared on television and did all sorts of things.'

Talk of 'triangles' was meaningless in terms of Lucan – the police got nowhere delving for 'crumpet' in John's life. He had been seeing Andrina Colquhoun for six months, but only, she said, on a friendly basis.

'He was terribly shy,' she said. 'I used to see him for dinner or lunch about once or twice a week. I'd never seen him with any other girl.'

After the murder, however, Andrina said the police suggested: 'Well, it could have been a crime of passion! He could have been killing her in order to marry you!'

But, she said, they never came close to discussing marriage because they were only friends.

As for Veronica, one friend claimed that John would have been delighted if she'd found someone else to marry.

Kait remembered Veronica in the past being 'worried about a letter she'd written to some man'.

'But John couldn't have cared less,' Kait said. 'His attitude was hardly that of a jealous husband.'

Access. Unavailability. Domestic problems/eternal triangle. Ranson's three key points. Certainly John had had access to the house, since he still had a key. There was no denying he had disappeared. And the Lucans had undoubtedly been under tremendous domestic pressure. But *murder*?

'John was very cool under pressure,' Bill Shand Kydd said. 'The only way he could have done it was if he had had a complete brainstorm, if he had been insane at the time. But there is nothing which has ever suggested that he was capable of such insanity and people who saw him very very shortly beforehand found him perfectly compos mentis.'

The tests carried out by the police proved that if John had been in Lower Belgrave Street, as he said, he could have seen into the basement provided a light was on.

Ranson's attitude was that it would have been 'a miracle' if John had happened to be peering in at precisely the time when Veronica was being attacked.

Said the Chief Superintendent: 'You imagine, he happens to be going past and he happens to see a man . . .'

But Lucan made a *point* of going past the house every night. Several people could have testified to that in court. And when he did pass the house, it wasn't in the course of taking a simple stroll or drive. He went there with a purpose. As the inquest jury had learned from the information Kait gave Sergeant Forsyth on the night of the murder: 'In the original [custody] case, it was thought that [Veronica] was a danger to the children.' The whole point of John's regular trips to Lower Belgrave Street was to snoop around outside number 46, to peer in – and, if Veronica wasn't there, sometimes go in – in order to find out what was happening and reassure himself that Frances, George and Camilla were all right. So it wasn't in any way unusual that he should have been outside the house on that fateful night. Certainly it would have been 'an unbelievable coincidence' if he happened to peer in at exactly the moment Veronica was being attacked. But those were the very words he had used himself. No wonder he thought no one would ever believe his story.

Though 'unbelievable coincidences' may seem improbable to people who've never experienced one, they do happen. During the world-wide hunt for John, the police in Australia nabbed two suspects. In the backwoods of Goondiwindi, excited Aussie cops arrested a 6 foot 3 inch Englishman with 'a public school accent' and 'lily-white' hands who they felt sure was the missing English aristocrat. He turned out to be an unemployed boilermaker from Essex – which meant, according to one wit on a British radio show, that he probably *was* an aristocrat in Australian terms. The other suspect the Australian police caught, allegedly thinking he was the missing earl, turned out, by coincidence, to be the fugitive British politician John Stonehouse, who had also disappeared in November 1974. If that wasn't an 'unbelievable coincidence', what was? Unbelievable, but true.

28

Nobody believed that Lucan had any motive to kill Sandra Rivett. Therefore the only way the police case against him made any kind of sense was if he *had* murdered her by mistake. But how likely was it that a husband would confuse another woman for the wife he'd been married to for eleven years?

The two women, apart from their height, did not look remotely similar. Sandra's hair was red. Veronica's at the time was brown. Their facial features were so different that no one could have failed to tell them apart. If there had been a light on in the basement when the murder took place, there could have been no possibility of a mistaken identity killing.

And if it was dark? The police and Veronica pointed to the fact that both women were petite, only 5 feet 2 inches tall. But their build was so dissimilar that, as Veronica told the inquest jury, they even wore different size dresses. Sandra weighed 8 stone and had a fairly average build. But Veronica weighed only about 6 or 7 stone and looked skinny.

'John wouldn't have bashed Sandra Rivett, you know,' Christina said. 'He wouldn't have made such a mistake. Even in the dark, if he'd grabbed her arm, he'd have known it wasn't Veronica. Veronica's arms were so *thin*.'

Michael Stoop said: 'There are so many ways by which a man knows his wife: the cadence of her footsteps, the smell, everything . . .'

The possibility that John could have blundered so badly and killed the wrong woman – and then failed to kill the 'right' one – was quite unacceptable to many of those who knew him.

But the police thought he'd have had little chance to realise he was 'attacking' the 'wrong' woman. This, according to a detective, is how the murder went:

1 The killer waited in darkness beside the banister rail at the bottom of the basement stairs with the weapon poised for attack.

2 Sandra appeared, came down the stairs and was struck on the back of the head with the blunt instrument.

3 She died immediately from that first blow without ever fighting back, though the killer kept on battering her afterwards in a frenzy.

The theory was that John had got into number 46, gone down to the basement and lain in wait for Veronica to come down and make some tea. Veronica maintained it was her practice since the separation to make a drink for herself around that time in the evening. Nobody would have expected *Sandra* to come down on a Thursday instead.

But how valid was this idea? John didn't need to be told that there were facilities upstairs to make tea. He would have known nobody needed to come down to the kitchen to boil a kettle. How could he possibly be sure on any given night if or when Veronica would come down?

'He could have stood down there for two weeks without anybody ever coming downstairs to make a cup of tea!' Bill Shand Kydd said.

And if he thought Sandra was out on her night off, why wait for Veronica in the basement anyway? If she was alone, why not simply clobber her upstairs? Not that he'd have done anything in the house while the children were there.

Indeed, evidence gleaned from an examination of Sandra's injuries by the pathologist, Professor Keith Simpson, disproved or cast doubt on virtually the whole of the detective's theory on how the murder went. This emerged when I interviewed the professor at the City of London mortuary.

For a start, the first blow probably wasn't delivered to the back of Sandra's head.

Injuries provide a form of dumb evidence to experts who know how to read them – like bloodstains to Dr Pereira. Head wounds from an attack with a blunt instrument can be 'scattered' across the head or they can be in 'parallels', otherwise called 'couples'. What this means is simple.

'[It's] a matter of common sense,' Professor Simpson explained. 'If the body [of the victim is] conscious and moving, your blows may land anywhere . . . scattered, more wide apart. Whereas if [the victim is] lying still, you deal repeated blows in the same place.'

And in Sandra's case?

Said the professor: 'I think that where you see blows coupled, as you have on the right side of [her] head, and above and in front of her ear and on the back of [her] head, you can be pretty certain [she wasn't] moving. Whereas when you see scattered blows like you have over the front of [her] face, with marks on [her] arm and hand looking like protective marks, they're likely to be early ones – while she's still able to move and ward off injuries.'

So the injuries to her face probably came first. Which made sense of course. Was a killer likely to batter a victim unconscious from the back and then deliberately turn her over to injure her face too?

Secondly, self-evidently, the killer attacked Sandra from a position ahead of her.

'If the blows to the face were the initial blows,' I said, 'that presumably must mean that the attacker attacked her from the front and not from behind?'

'Yes,' said Professor Simpson.

'So a suggestion that she was attacked as she actually came down the stairs from behind . . . doesn't stand up, does it?'

'[It] doesn't look as if it accords with my ideas about the order in which the injuries were sustained,' he said.

Thirdly, Sandra didn't die immediately.

Professor Simpson said: '[My report to the police] says [that] "considerable bleeding had taken place from the nose into the main air passages", and that means that [Sandra] was still bleeding and had remained alive for some time . . . In fact the amount of bruising over her brain showed that she was alive, she didn't die at once . . .'

Fourthly, Sandra tried to defend herself, perhaps even fought back.

Chief Inspector Gerring told the inquest there was no sign of a fight in the basement – despite the broken baluster, the picture on the stairway wall knocked awry, the scattered cups and saucers. Chief Superintendent Ranson also thought there were no grounds to believe there had been a tussle.

But Professor Simpson's report mentioned 'superficial bruising' on the back of Sandra's right hand, which indicated that she had 'tried to ward off' blows. It also mentioned four 'in line' bruises at the top of her right arm – marks probably left by the killer's fingers when he gripped her forcefully, perhaps to steady her body for more blows. In other words, some kind of hand-to-hand struggle took place.

Professor Simpson said: 'There had been some little fracas . . . probably. She was capable of trying to ward off the injuries that were being dealt . . . [It looks] as if she was involved in some sort of scuffle before or during the course of her receiving [the] head injuries.'

And fifthly, the attacker was unlikely to have been waiting with the weapon poised, ready for someone to appear.

The pathologist had told the inquest that a couple of Sandra's (earliest) injuries, to the face, were more likely to have been made not with a weapon but with a hand or fist. And that suggested that the killer set about Sandra first with his hand or fist and then picked up the weapon to finish her off later, didn't it?

'Oh yes,' the professor told me. 'Oh yes. Certainly.'

I double-checked.

'There is a possibility that the weapon could have been picked up *after* the fight had begun?'

'Yes, during the course of the fight,' Professor Simpson said. '[It] may not have been used in the early stages of the fight.'

If that was the case, then clearly the killer hadn't been lying in wait with the weapon poised ready for the attack.

Which meant either that Sandra had *surprised* him in the basement, where he'd been on other business. Or that whoever killed her became enraged, went berserk, lashed out at her with his hand or fist – and then picked up the nearest object to hand and used it as a blunt instrument to batter her to death. Both those possibilities suggested that the murder was not pre-planned. And that the murderer killed the person he meant to kill.

The final question was one of visibility. No one but Sandra and the killer knew whether the basement lights were on or off when she came down the stairs and was attacked. The prospect of the nanny attempting to negotiate her way down that tricky staircase in darkness wearing high heels and carrying the loaded tray of cups and saucers makes it seem unlikely. But even if the lights *were* off, it still wouldn't have been pitch-dark down there because of the street-lighting coming in from the lamp post opposite the house.

Indeed, if the killer had been waiting by the banister rail at the bottom of the basement stairs – as the detective at Gerald Road had suggested – he would have been 'spotlit' by the beam of light from the lamp post.

Whoever killed Sandra saw her clearly enough to aim hand and fist blows to her face, to grab her arm, to batter her to death with some sort of blunt instrument – and to bundle her bloody body into the sack afterwards, assuming that was done by the same person. According to Professor Simpson, the murder and the bundling up of the body could have been carried out by a man or a woman of Sandra's own height or taller.

If John was the attacker, if he was fighting Sandra face-to-face, hand-to-hand, at arm's length or less, was it likely he could have 'mistaken' her for Veronica? And if the lights were *on* in the basement at the time, was it likely anyone could have killed the 'wrong' woman?

Then there was the blood which appeared to be in the 'wrong' places. Like the spot of Group A blood, Veronica's group, on the floor in the kitchen close to other

301

bloodstains which could not be identified. And the two areas of bloodstaining on the murder sack which gave reactions for Group B but with some Group A activity – suggesting 'possible contamination with blood of Lady Lucan's group'.

Lucan's blood group was not known, but the police were certain that he was not wounded or bleeding at number 46. So whose was the Group A blood on the sack in which Sandra's body was found?

The detective at Gerald Road suggested: 'That's Fanny-Anne's, Lady Lucan's.'

But if Veronica didn't go down into the basement on the murder night, how did it get there?

'You've got police officers and dogs and cats running round the house and blood can easily be transferred,' he replied.

Cats and dogs? It turned out there wasn't a dog in the place. And the Group A bloodstain on the kitchen floor wasn't a pawmark or smear. According to Dr Pereira it was a spot, which meant it had 'quite likely' been *dripped* onto the floor. Was a cat, or a police officer, likely to have been dripping with Group A blood? Sergeant Baker had opened the sack and taken out Sandra's lifeless arm to see if he could feel a pulse. But any blood he might have picked up doing that would have been Sandra's group, Group B.

I raised the question of the Group A blood with Chief Superintendent Ranson, mentioning his colleague's answer about police officers, dogs and cats.

'Is that how you think it got there?' I asked.

'It must be something,' he said reasonably. 'There's no doubt that Lady Lucan after she was assaulted didn't go down the cellar [sic] because she'd have been dripping blood everywhere . . . Had she gone down there we'd have found large amounts of her blood, once she was attacked. She says that directly she got to the head of the stairs she was attacked by this intruder, who she later said was Lucan. She was immediately attacked. If she'd have gone down the cellar, gone down the basement breakfast room,

302

she was losing so much blood there would have been blood everywhere.'

But that wasn't necessarily so. If Veronica was 'dripping blood everywhere' she went, then according to Ranson's theory, 'large amounts' of her Group A blood should have been found in the hall cloakroom, in Veronica's bedroom, in the adjoining bathroom, on Veronica's bed and all the way up the stairs from the hall to the second floor. Yet Dr Pereira's report made no mention of such findings – presumably because there weren't any. And if Veronica could move elsewhere in the house after being attacked without leaving massive traces, there was no reason to suppose she'd have left 'large amounts' of her blood if she'd gone down into the basement.

The police chief went on: 'You see when Margaret Pereira talks about traces of blood on the sack, it was so . . . they talk about traces, but it's just a reaction . . . It could be a smear, you see. The body, Sandra's body, was removed from the basement in the sack and it could have been a transference off a wall, at the head of the stairs, you know . . . [carrying it] out through the house.'

'You mean the police might have got it there?'

'You see, taking the body out of the house we had to leave her in the sack, well, we *did* leave her in it. You couldn't . . .'

'But that was done the next morning. The blood would have been dry by then, wouldn't it?'

'Well, there would be sufficient . . . although it's dry you could still get a transference.'

'You mean it might have brushed against that door [from the hall to the basement] for instance?'

'Mn.'

I mentioned the same point afterwards to Dr Pereira, who told me:

'The blood on the stairs would probably have dried, except on the carpet, within the hour I would say. Rather longer down in the basement because it was so thick and heavy in the region near where the body was found.'

She agreed that Ranson's 'transference' theory was

possible to the extent of saying: 'The sack would still have been wet and that could have picked up dried blood.'

She added however: 'I don't *know* that, mind. It can only ever be a theory. You can't prove how – especially when you've got multiple layers of blood, as you probably have in that case – you can't really prove how it all got there.'

Transference or not? Early on the morning after the murder, when Sandra's body was carried out of number 46 in the sack to be taken to the mortuary, a Press photographer was 'doorstepping' the house to record the scene. He told me that when the bloody sack was manhandled out through the front door, the whole thing for obvious reasons was wrapped in protective polythene sheeting. If it had been carried up from the basement that way, which seems highly probable, then Group A blood on the walls or basement door *couldn't* have been picked up by the sack inside. So how did it get there?

Even if it had been transferred to the sack in a different manner, another question was left begging.

'. . . That still wouldn't explain the [Group A] blood in the kitchen, would it?' I asked Ranson.

'Well again,' the police chief said, 'these, you see we examined the kitchen but these blood spots were so small we never noticed them. It wasn't until we got Pereira down there that these were realised to be blood. You know, in a kitchen you get gravy stains and things like that, and these stains that she was talking about in the kitchen weren't as big as the end of that pencil . . . They were so minute, these little tiny spots . . . You see we don't know what Lucan did, do we?'

'No,' I had said. 'It's just that although it all seems so obvious that Lucan did it, there are these funny little things that come up. You know, like this blood that doesn't appear to have any way of having got down there, *being* down there.'

'Did [my colleague] tell you that the cats were licking the blood?'

'Ugh!'

'Yeh,' said Ranson, laughing at my reaction. 'We had to chase these cats away. They were young, there were two cats there. One was very young, just out of the kitten stage, and he was lapping, licking the blood.'

'One of them? You mean by the sack?'

'By the pool. In the dining [sic]' (i.e. breakfast) 'room'.

'This was when the police arrived was it?'

'Mn.'

'So presumably that cat had blood all over it? You must have had a lot of catty bloodstains.'

Obviously not.

'You see,' the police chief replied, 'cats don't like getting their feet wet.'

'Don't they?'

'Have you never noticed a cat walk round a puddle? You know, they won't walk through a puddle, they'll walk *round* it. And I wouldn't think the cat would walk through a puddle of blood.

'But they were very frisky cats and if you went to grab them they'd dart away, they'd run away, you see. And then, that is when they might go into the blood and take it elsewhere. The cats were running all over the house. We had to remove them.'

'There was a dog too?'

'No dog.'

'Just the two cats in the house? You had to remove them when the police arrived?'

'Well they weren't removed for a day or so. Three days, but we eventually removed them.'

'Doesn't make your job any easier, does it?'

Coming back to the bloodstains on the kitchen floor, some of which Dr Pereira had been unable to group, I asked: 'In other words, they could have been put there by the cat?'

Ranson said: 'Well, there's I would say a feasible explanation as to how they came there considering . . . although the only thing, being quite fair about it, these were blood *splashes* shall we say. They weren't smears of blood they were splashes, although they might have *dripped* off something . . .'

305

I found it almost impossible to take the cat theory seriously. For a cat to be dripping with blood, wouldn't it have had to be rolling about in a pool of blood, or doing something similar to get its fur sodden? And how likely was that? Sandra's black cat Tara was one of the two cats at the house. But Kait had caught Tara, at Frances's insistence, to try and take the pet back to St John's Wood with the children, and she noticed no blood on it whatsoever. Even if Sooty or Tara had picked up some of the blood from the pool, it would have been Sandra's Group B blood – not Group A. And the stain on the kitchen floor which was so perplexing was Group A, Veronica's group.

I asked Ranson: 'If [Lady Lucan] had actually been hit down there, would that be consistent with those –?'

'No.'

'It wouldn't?'

'No,' he said. 'If you're struck with a weapon, you don't get little round droplets of blood. If I strike you with a weapon like this, this is where you get the directional splashing, from the head of the victim or from the weapon as it's [brought down and up again] ... You saw the photographs ... So if she was attacked you get directional splashing from the attack or the area she ... and she was struck so many times ... Up on the ground floor where the weapon was drawn back, the splashes are on the ceiling, you see. So you can read the scene of a crime, and you'd get similar blood splashes there [in the kitchen].'

'So you don't think there's any way ... I mean just supposing things hadn't happened the way they said they happened, there's no way those splashes (i.e. that splash or spot of Group A blood) could have got down in the kitchen if she'd actually been hit [there]?'

'She wasn't attacked downstairs,' Ranson declared. 'And if she'd gone downstairs, the amount – you saw the photographs of her – the amount of blood she was losing you'd have *pools* of blood from her, I'd think, if she went and stood there ...'

Back to that argument.

'You know what it's like when you have a nose bleed

and the amount of blood and the amount of mess you make from a nose bleed,' he went on.

But the point wasn't valid. If Veronica didn't leave 'pools' of Group A blood everywhere she said she went, there was no reason to suppose she would have left 'pools' if she'd gone down to the basement.

Indeed, in view of the fact that Veronica had Sandra's Group B blood on and under her shoes, it was 'a likely explanation', as Dr Pereira said at the inquest, that she did walk through the basement.

Oddly enough, some of the earliest news stories about the murder suggested that Lady Lucan *had* been down to the basement that night.

One report read: 'Police believe she may have come face to face with the killer while he was trying to drag the canvas sack containing the murdered woman across the room.'

Another read: 'Bloodstains up the staircase and on the ground floor could possibly mean that Lady Lucan disturbed the attacker, who then followed her as she tried to escape upstairs, stunned her and got away.'

Yet another read: 'In a five-hour statement to Murder Squad detectives, she has said that she managed to calm the killer *when she discovered him with the nanny's body.*' (My italics.)

Only a week after the murder, the *Daily Express* went so far as to publish a huge front-page 'murder reconstruction' drawing. This showed Veronica reaching the bottom of the basement stairs, and coming face to face with the killer – a figure clearly drawn to resemble John – and the sack, drawn with one arm sticking out of it. The splash story alongside contained the line: 'Halfway down the basement steps, she was attacked and beaten about the head.'

Crime reporters covering a case liaise closely with the police officers concerned, so one can only assume that these reporters from four newspapers got their information from police sources.

Equally curious was a series of 'murder reconstruction' photographs taken later at number 46 with Veronica's co-operation by ace *Daily Express* cameraman Harry Dempster, who became very friendly with her. The object of the exercise, Harry told me, was for Veronica to retrace her steps on the murder night for his camera. One of these pictures – along with other, general, snaps – accompanied Veronica's first 'exclusive' revelations about the murder night in the *Express* on 20 January 1975. Harry's 'murder reconstruction' photographs showed these scenes:

1 *Veronica standing at the bottom of the basement stairs.* Harry said Veronica told him she came down to the basement looking for Sandra, and saw her body lying on the floor. (Which indicates that a light was on and that the body was not yet in the sack.)

2 *Veronica standing at a spot near the piano in the basement, by the kitchen doorway.* The *Express* printed this picture. Part of the published caption read: 'Lady Lucan stands at the spot where Sandra Rivett's body lay.'

3 *Harry Dempster posing as Sandra to show the position in which her body lay.* Harry said Veronica described the position to him.

4 *Veronica returning back up the basement stairs towards the hall.*

5 *Veronica in the hall confronting an attacker (posed by another Express man), coming towards her from the direction of the cloakroom.*

6 *Veronica lying on the top part of the basement stairs, her foot hooked into the banisters.* Harry said she told him she had been knocked back through the basement doorway from the hall by the attacker.

However, in the story the *Express* ran, Veronica made no mention of going down to the basement, seeing Sandra's body on the floor, and then returning to the hall. Only the last two of the 'murder reconstruction' pictures coincided with the *Express* story – and with the evidence she gave at the inquest later.

So if she *didn't* go down to the basement that night and see Sandra's body before she was attacked herself, why did she pose down there for Harry's 'murder reconstruction' pictures?

And what *had* John seen through the basement window? Or was that tale concocted?

29

'You see,' Chief Superintendent Ranson told me, 'basically he's stuck with a story that he tells on the spur of the moment in a letter and on the telephone . . . and Lucan, assuming he's got an ounce of good sense, is aware that this story can't stand up. You see that story's destroyed forensically, isn't it?'

'Is it?' I asked. 'How do you mean?'

'Well,' Ranson said, 'he says: "I saw my wife being attacked by an intruder in the kitchen" or "in the basement" of Lower Belgrave Street. There's no forensic evidence at all bloodwise to say that Lady Lucan was attacked in the basement, is there? None at all.'

But there was a flaw in that argument. Dr Pereira's analysis of the bloodstains at the house supported the evidence Veronica gave at the inquest about being attacked in the hall. But it did not necessarily tell the full tale.

The particular Group A bloodstains found just beyond the basement doorway heading towards the front door showed that the short flight of four steps in the hall was 'an obvious site of attack'.

There was the radiating, almost circular, pattern of bloodsplashes on the woodwork to the left of the top tread of the steps. There were hairs 'similar to' Veronica's stuck to the wood. And there were trickles of blood running down the woodwork too.

What would that mean?

'Well,' said Dr Pereira, '[the trickles are] where there's been somebody leaning up against [the woodwork] with blood literally pouring out of their wounds . . . You know, very heavy bloodstaining on the wall which would have then run down in trickles which was either due to continuous contact with her head or contact which left a great dollop of blood which then flowed down the wall.'

'Is that spraying effect indicative of the fact that she [Lady Lucan] did actually get a bash with a weapon at that point?'

'Yes. She did. Probably repeated blows,' Dr Pereira replied.

'More than one?'

'Yes,' said Dr Pereira, 'because you have to get the blood flowing before you start to get the blood splashing out. It won't happen – you won't get much splashing the first time, but once you start hitting . . .'

If the bloodstains proved that Lady Lucan had been attacked in the hall, how could John have seen 'what appeared to be' Veronica struggling with a man in the *basement*?

It was a good question – but there was an answer. The clue lay in Dr Pereira's last words. An attacker has to get the victim's blood 'flowing' before it starts 'splashing out'. The point Ranson had missed.

I asked Dr Pereira: 'If she had been hit before she ever got into that area [in the hall] and therefore there was a kind of wound, and then she was hit [again] –?'

'I should think the most likely explanation was that she was hit several times in that area probably,' she said. 'I don't know.'

'But the effect would be the same if she had been hit before she got there and the blood had come to the surface and she was then hit again?'

'Mn.' Dr Pereira nodded in agreement. 'You've got to get the blood welling up in the wound before you start getting the splash.'

The Group A blood splashes and trickles – together with directional blood splashing apparently thrown backwards off the weapon towards the cloakroom – indicated that the short flight of steps in the hall was the spot where the attack on Veronica got fully under way and probably ended. But there could be no forensic proof to show in which part of the house the attack on her had *started*.

When I saw Professor Simpson, I re-checked the point with him.

'Dr Pereira explained to me that when you hit the first blow, you don't get any directional splashing [of blood] because —'

'You don't get *any* splashing,' the professor said instantly. 'When you strike a clean scalp, there's no blood until the weapon has bounced off the head and blood starts to well up.'

'And then if you hit it again —?'

'Then,' he said, 'if you strike that again, of course, you get splashing.'

'How long would it take after you'd struck the first blow for the blood to well up, that first time?'

'Oh within a second blood is welling up much into —'

'Really?'

'Oh yes. So if you strike again within a couple of seconds you've got a bloody patch you're striking. You've got to strike the same *place* of course.'

'Supposing I move from point A to point B —'

'Yes.'

'— and I've received the first [blow] at point A —'

'Yes.'

'— I then get to point B before I'm struck again —'

'You'd expect to see blood dripping between the two . . . If your head is struck with a bottle and your scalp is split open, you won't move very far before blood's dripping over your shoulders and down to the ground, if it's clear —'

'But if it all happened in a matter of seconds, and you're sort of running away from the attacker, and then he finally gets you and clobbers you all in one position — ?'

'Oh then, *then* of course,' Professor Simpson said, 'I mean if it's going to be a second or two before blood starts pouring down your face, you could move a few yards away, couldn't you?'

'Yes.'

'That's quite true,' he said. 'Yes.'

' . . . Presumably then the scientists could arrive and find that the signs of the site of the attack were at one position?'

'Certainly.'

'It wouldn't necessarily mean the attack had *begun* there?'

'Certainly,' Professor Simpson said. 'You would expect blood to start dripping on the shoulder. It wouldn't necessarily drop all over the ground and provide a trail between one point and the other.'

'So there wouldn't, forensically, necessarily be any evidence to show *where* the attack began?'

'No,' Professor Simpson declared.

The short flight of steps in the hall was the place where Veronica appeared to have been caught by the attacker, stilled, felled, perhaps even knocked unconscious. It was where she had 'probably' been dealt 'repeated blows'. Blows which, once she was no longer moving, would in all likelihood have fallen in 'parallels' or 'couples'. The doctor who examined her at St George's hospital said that she had about seven large lacerations on her head which were 'roughly parallel'.

Speaking generally, Professor Simpson told me: 'It is not a matter of certainty, but where wounds are parallel and set close together, it is more likely that the victim lay still ... held still or unconscious.'

But Veronica's head injuries, according to the professor, who saw photographs of them, also included 'isolated singles' – single, scattered blows.

He concluded: 'It seems far more likely that she was moving than in the case of Sandra Rivett.'

In other words, it was possible that Veronica had been struck by the weapon and immediately moved away from the attacker in an attempt to escape. If she moved away, the attacker's second blow with the weapon was more likely to have landed at random. And though the blood would have begun to well up from the initial injuries – perhaps smearing any surfaces she brushed against in an effort to get away – it would not have started to splash round the walls and ceilings until the attacker had got her into a position where he could deal repeated blows on wounds which were already bleeding.

She had escaped as far as the four little steps in the hall, presumably trying to reach the front door and help. But where had she moved *from*? There was no forensic answer.

Veronica told the inquest that she had been beaten over the head by a man who came rushing out at her from the hall cloakroom. But that was very curious. Because if the attacker had already killed Sandra, and bundled her body into the sack by that stage, his clothes would probably have been heavily saturated with Sandra's Group B blood. So why hadn't Dr Pereira found ample evidence of Group B blood in the cloakroom? Didn't that suggest that the attacker was never in the cloakroom at all? And if he wasn't in the cloakroom, where *did* he first come face to face with Veronica and start to attack her?

Dr Pereira concluded from the dumb evidence of the Group A blood splashes in the area that Lady Lucan had been battered on the hall steps by an attacker who was facing the front door, his back to the cloakroom. That matched Veronica's testimony about the man rushing at her from the cloakroom.

But if the attacker had chased up the basement stairs after her, he would have ended up in exactly the same position. Veronica had talked of struggling on the basement stairs. And indeed, apart from the picture on that stairway wall which had been knocked awry, and the baluster on the banister rail which had been prised loose, Dr Pereira also found forensic evidence which suggested a fight on the basement stairway.

She discovered Group A blood on the wall about halfway down the twelve basement stairs. If it had been smeared there from Veronica's bleeding head wounds, that meant Lady Lucan's feet could have been within inches of the breakfast room floor and the pool of Sandra's Group B blood. Dr Pereira also found Group A bloodstains and trickles on the staircase wall above the third tread from the top of the stairs. And more Group A blood smears and trickles at the bottom of the basement door, which was hooked back against the wall. *All these stains could presumably have been made as Veronica fell, fighting, down the stairs – or indeed as she fled from the killer UP them.*

If John told the truth about seeing what appeared to be a man fighting Veronica in the basement, he may have seen the beginning of an attack which had *started* in the basement.

What might have happened? Wherever the violence began, the evidence of the Group A bloodstains meant that Veronica must have been wounded on or before she reached the basement stairs. Let us suppose for the sake of argument that the attack on her did start in the basement, and that she tried to escape up the stairs towards the hall and the front door. Maybe her blood had welled up enough to smear the Group A stain on the staircase wall about six steps from the bottom. A fabric print which Dr Pereira found on the same wall in Sandra's Group B blood might perhaps have been left there by the killer's bloodstained clothes as he grappled to pin Veronica down. The picture on that wall could have been knocked askew in the struggle. Clutching at Veronica's clothes to try to prevent her escape, the killer could have left that mark on the back of her dress which looked, to Dr Pereira, as if it had been made by a 'bloody hand' reaching out to grab her.

Veronica herself said she had been as 'slippery as an eel'. Others in the past remembered her ability to move 'as fast as lightning'. She could have reached almost the top of the basement stairs before the killer perhaps landed the next 'isolated' blow. By now her blood might have been flowing more freely, running down her face and dripping onto her shoulders. Perhaps pushing her foot against the baluster for leverage in a desperate attempt to reach the open doorway to the hall, Veronica could have been shoved down by the attacker – breaking the baluster loose. At the same time her injured head could have come into contact with the staircase wall, leaving the Group A blood smears and trickles above the third tread from the top. The similar bloodstaining on the bottom of the basement door could have occurred in the same manner. Urging herself on through the doorway, turning left into the hall, Veronica could have reached the short flight of four steps before the killer finally caught and stilled her. Facing the front door, and using what Dr Pereira described from the evidence of the blood splashing as 'considerable force', the killer probably rained repeated blows down on her with the weapon – sending blood splashes flying back towards the cloakroom and ceiling, while more blood poured from Veronica's head wounds in trickles down the woodwork at the side of the steps. Without remembering it later, she might have sunk into unconsciousness – as the police believed and the forensic evidence implied. She had already received about the same number of weapon-blows that had killed the nanny. Within seconds Lady Lucan too might well have been dead. Except that suddenly, miraculously, the violent attack *stopped!*

If Lord Lucan's story was true, there was a clear reason why. Because by then, if he had seen part of the struggle through the basement window, enough seconds would have elapsed for him to find his key, open the front door and run down the hall to the rescue. The killer, confronted by another man – and a big one at that – would obviously have run away from John rather than towards him. There was in fact only one direction he could have gone: straight back through the doorway and down the basement stairs. While John followed in hot pursuit, the killer could have 'made off' – disappearing from sight while John's attention was distracted by slipping and falling into the pool of Sandra's blood at the bottom of the stairs.

John presumably assumed the killer had fled, and turned his attention to Veronica.

Though Veronica only remembered sustaining 'about four' blows from the killer's weapon, she had actually received about seven. Let us assume that after that fourth blow she lapsed into unconsciousness, and remembered nothing more until she heard John say: 'Shut up'.

She would therefore have been unaware that John had raced in to the rescue, unaware that the killer had fled, unaware that John had chased into the basement after him, and unaware that the man who had tried to batter her to death with the weapon had now been replaced in the house by the husband whose arrival had saved her life.

She would also have been unaware of *the gap* between the time when the attack on her *with the weapon* had ceased, and the moment when she heard John's voice say: 'Shut up'.

She would therefore have assumed – as she apparently did, judging from her testimony at the inquest – that the assault on her was *a continuous attack by one man*, first wielding a weapon, and then, inexplicably, using his hands instead.

Clearly, Veronica couldn't have fought the killer off if the blows from the weapon left her unconscious and therefore defenceless.

So the logical explanation is that there were *two separate fights*, with a short time lag in between.

The first would have been the fight between Veronica and the killer, who battered her into unconsciousness with the weapon and would undoubtedly have killed her if John hadn't arrived in the nick of time.

The second, after Veronica had regained consciousness, could have been when she heard John say: 'Shut up', mistook him for the killer and started fighting *him*.

How could this have come about?

Let's assume that after the killer vanished, John went back up to the hall to attend to Veronica, who by that time had come round, injured, shocked and confused, and was screaming hysterically.

John apparently said: 'Shut up.' Maybe he tried to silence her screams by putting his hand over her mouth, and maybe Veronica misunderstood.

Not knowing that the killer had fled, and assuming in

the darkness that John *was* the killer, maybe *she* started to fight *him*, believing that her life was still in danger.

The 'fight' Veronica described ended when she grabbed John's 'private parts' and he 'moved back' and 'desisted'.

If John was fighting Veronica, or indeed fighting her *off*, it might explain why, in his main letter to Bill Shand Kydd later, John made it clear he feared he would be accused of 'attempted murder'.

Veronica's theory – convinced as she was that her husband *had* tried to kill her – was that he hadn't succeeded because he was 'emotionally exhausted'. But how likely was that?

A man of John's size and strength could obviously have overpowered, or indeed killed, Veronica had he wanted to. And the fact that he *hadn't* was the clearest possible sign that that was not his intention.

Whatever happened – and John of course made no mention later of being involved in *any* fight – the Lucans then apparently talked to each other.

Afterwards Veronica got a drink of water from the hall cloakroom – probably leaving that tuft of her bloodstained hair which Dr Pereira later found stuck to the wash basin – and John then helped her up to her bedroom.

Was that what happened that night?

Such a sequence of events would be consistent with the forensic evidence.

And if another man *was* the killer, he had now unwittingly been left free to make good his escape.

What evidence might the killer have left?

Chief Inspector Gerring had told the inquest that there was 'no trace' of another man at number 46 that night. Yet among the discoveries made there by the forensic experts were:

* fingerprints which could not be identified or eliminated from the inquiry
* tiny dark greyish-blue wool fibres
* and Group AB blood.

Senior fingerprint officer Ian Lucas had told the inquest that about a dozen fingerprints found at the house could not be accounted for.

Chief Superintendent Ranson had told me at Cannon Row: 'There are so many things in a murder investigation that you never get an answer for. It's like outstanding fingerprints. We threw that fingerprint witness in to make it quite clear we had fingerprints there that we couldn't eliminate. But I would say that every murder I've been on we've lifted fingerprints that you never get, even though you've convicted a man and everything. You can never find out. People say: "This is strange. You've got fingerprints here which you can't eliminate." But you can't say to them: "Well, Lady Frances had a party and twenty-six kiddies came there" – and these are upper-class children and can you imagine us trying to get elimination fingerprints from twenty-six ten-year-olds without having a kick from their parents? And somebody went to the house to collect those children, so if you say twenty-six by twenty-six you've got fifty-odd people whose fingerprints [they] may be. I think there's little doubt that some of them are Lucan's, which of course doesn't mean anything anyway because he's got lawful access to the house.'

The experts fingerprinted the house even though Veronica said that the man who attacked her wore gloves. As far as I could discover, no bloodstained gloves were found at number 46 or in or around Lower Belgrave Street. Had the killer run off still wearing them? And if he'd gone to the house wearing gloves, did that suggest he might be a burglar?

Then there were those mysterious little dark greyish-blue wool fibres Dr Pereira found – all of them associated with bloodstaining and/or bloodstained hairs 'similar to' Veronica's. The fibres were on the tuft of bloodstained hair sticking to the wash basin in the hall cloakroom. On a bathtowel stained with Group A blood, perhaps the one John put down for Veronica on her pillow. Amid a number of textile fibres found among bloodstained hairs sticking to the length of lead piping found in the hall. Stuck to a tangle of bloodstained hairs on the floor of the Ford Corsair. And, most of all, in a patch of 'extensive blood smearing' on the inner surface of the Ford Corsair's front off-side door. Presumably anyone who had got involved in the mess at number 46 could have picked up hairs and fibres as well as blood, but where had the fibres originated?

According to Professor Simpson, talking generally: '... Fibres may come away if ... clothing [is] struck. That could certainly result in fibres adhering to a weapon.'

So the fibres might have come from clothing worn by one of the people at the house that night.

Veronica sometimes wore a blue velvet headband. In fact she wore it when Harry Dempster of the *Daily Express* took his 'murder reconstruction' photographs of her. Something like that might have left fibres on bloodstained hairs, on a weapon used to inflict head injuries, on a towel on which she rested her head – perhaps also on the clothing of anyone who fought her or helped her. But if she wore a woollen headband that night there was no mention of it in Dr Pereira's report. Nor, from the various descriptions given, were any of the clothes known to have been worn then by Veronica, Sandra or John made of dark greyish-blue wool. Had someone *else* worn greyish-blue wool – the killer?

The rare AB group bloodstains Dr Pereira located could have resulted from a blending of the Group A and Group B blood of the two women. Or they could have come from another person with Group AB blood. Lucan's blood group was unknown, but since the police were quite certain he wasn't injured or bleeding the AB stains couldn't have come from him anyway. So could they have come from a fourth person – the killer? Both women had fought back. Was it likely he could have killed one and attacked the other without being scratched, marked or cut himself?

Fingerprints, fibres and AB bloodstains ... The

possibility of another man having been at the house could not be discounted.

But how had he got away? Was there a clue?

30

Whoever battered Sandra Rivett to death, according to Chief Superintendent Ranson, would have been 'covered in a very fine spray of blood'.

'Fine spray' sounds mild. But Bill Shand Kydd told me he'd once battered a wild animal to death in Africa rather than leave it injured after it had accidentally been run over by a safari vehicle.

'I didn't notice at the time,' he recalled, 'but when I got back I found I was *smothered* in blood.'

If the killer then bundled Sandra's body into the sack, his clothing would probably have become heavily saturated with blood.

'You've got to realise that the body was in a sack, which would have meant an enormous amount of manhandling of a very bloody body,' Dr Pereira told me. 'So therefore the clothing of whoever did it, although they might have evidence of a fine spray of blood in some cases, was probably sodden with blood.'

And if the killer's clothes were sodden – or, according to Professor Simpson, if his hands were heavily bloodstained – he could have been *dripping* with Sandra's Group B blood too.

In which direction would he have tried to escape? Not towards the front door or he'd have run slap-bang into John. There were only two other outer doors to choose from, and both of those were in the basement. The one at the front, where the milk was delivered and the rubbish was put out, was still locked when Sergeant Baker arrived on the scene. So, as Ranson agreed, the killer hadn't gone out there. Which left only one escape route – the back door to the garden, opposite the safe. The door to which the large bloodstained footprints on the floor led. The door which was invariably kept locked, but which Sergeant Baker found mysteriously *unlocked*.

Was it the killer who had unlocked it?

Chief Superintendent Ranson read out the relevant part of Sergeant Baker's statement:

'"I immediately went to the rear yard with P.C. 720 to look for the person responsible." This is having found the body ... blah, blah, blah. "The door to the yard was closed but unlocked. There was no person in the yard."'

But of course there was no one in the yard. By then enough time had gone by for the killer to get clean away.

'I just wondered,' I suggested to Ranson, 'whether there was any chance somebody had sort of skedaddled out of that door and perhaps made their getaway after everybody had left?'

For a moment he didn't take the point.

'The yard or the garden at the rear of the house was paved, a patio type,' he said, 'with pots and shrubs, not very well kept, with a bit of garden furniture. There's at least a 15-foot wall with roses and ramblers, you know, it's a very untidy garden. The walls are, well it's a very old brick, I won't say moss-covered but they're certainly covered in the staining of years. And had anybody gone over those walls or come in via those walls you *must* have seen it. There were no ladders there – he wouldn't stop to take a ladder with him – and there was a trellis fixed for the roses, not protruding but nailed onto the wall at the top ... ramblers ... and there was no disturbance of any sort at all. You know, it would be impossible to get out there with[out] leaving a mark.'

But the killer didn't *need* to go over the wall. All he had to do was to hide in the garden until the coast was clear. Then he could have crept back in to the breakfast room, nipped up the basement stairs and escaped into the night through the front door.

'What I was really wondering,' I said, 'was if somebody could have opened the door, waited in the yard until in fact Lucan and Lady Lucan had run out – she'd gone to the Plumbers Arms, he'd got alarmed and run off – and then come back through the house before the police arrived?'

322

Ranson laughed.

The police chief had a habit of emitting a dry laugh at moments like this. It seemed that he had not considered this serious possibility.

At the time we talked, I was still unaware of some of the evidence which had come out at the inquest. Nevertheless, there was one way of testing whether my theory was likely. If the killer had been dripping with Sandra's blood, he might have left traces of it in the garden.

'Presumably my idea falls flat anyway,' I said, 'because if there was anybody who had skedaddled into the yard, there would presumably be blood in the yard?'

'Well,' Ranson said quietly, 'there *was* blood in the yard . . .'

Suddenly I was excited. Blood in the back yard was the vital clue. Who else but the killer would have gone out into the garden that night dripping the murdered girl's blood? Sandra herself had been killed before she apparently got further than the bottom of the basement stairs, so it couldn't have been her.

Veronica said she did not go into the basement at all. And even if she did, she would hardly have wandered into the garden in the middle of all that violence. Certainly some of Sandra's Group B blood was found on Veronica's clothes. And though Dr Pereira did not, for some reason, carry out tests on all the bloodstains on the clothes she was wearing, it is extremely unlikely that Veronica would have picked up enough Group B blood to drip any. Veronica did of course have Sandra's Group B blood on and under her shoes. But there was apparently no sign of small, ladylike footprints in blood on the floor leading towards the back door. And if her shoes didn't leave bloody prints on the way out of the breakfast room, they would hardly have carried blood into the garden either.

Then there was John. He had admitted to Susan Maxwell-Scott getting blood on himself at number 46. If, as he said, he slipped and fell into the pool of Sandra's blood as he ran into the basement, and later helped Veronica upstairs, he could hardly have avoided getting Group B and Group A blood on him. Maybe that's how blood got into the Ford Corsair. If it was John who left the two spots of blood beneath Mrs Florman's doorbell, maybe they dripped from a cuff or the underside of a sleeve, which could easily have dipped into the thick pool of blood when he fell. Maybe that's also how remaining traces of blood got onto his letters to Bill Shand Kydd. But if his clothes, rather than patches, had been *saturated* with the murdered nanny's blood, how could Frances have failed to notice the fact? And why hadn't he left ample evidence of it? He'd helped Veronica up to her bedroom on the second floor, and then gone further upstairs to the nursery floor, yet no evidence had been given of Group B blood in Veronica's bedroom, in her bathroom, in the nursery or on the stairs. In any case, what reason would John have had to go out into the garden – unless he was looking for the killer? Veronica herself accounted for John's movements after the attack on her. And after she fled from the house, it would be absurd to imagine he tried to 'escape' through the garden, knowing it would mean scaling a 16-foot-high wall. But would a *stranger* to the house have known that?

Long after the murder, after number 46 was sold, the first new owners surprised a burglar trapped on the premises. By coincidence, the back door to the garden was the only one *he* could get out of. But even though he'd had the luck to find a ladder left by builders, he *still* hadn't managed to escape over the garden wall.

Where was the blood in the back yard?

'There was a bloodstained leaf. There was a leaf with a spot of blood on it,' Chief Superintendent Ranson said.

In fact Dr Pereira's report to the police showed that two or three such leaves had been picked up from the ground in the garden and sent to her for analysis. She described them as 'extensively bloodstained'. Tests on one of them gave reactions for Group B, Sandra Rivett's blood group.

How did the blood get there?

'Again,' Ranson said seriously, 'we must say it's the animals.'

Back to the cats. But even the most agile cat was incapable of opening, let alone unlocking a door . . . and it couldn't have gone into the garden otherwise.

'You don't think your man Baker could have trodden on a leaf when he went outside? Did he have blood on his soles?'

'Well, we didn't examine his soles,' Ranson said. 'We had no reason to.'

Nor was the back door examined to discover whether whoever opened it had left bloodstains.

'I didn't really look quite honestly, no,' Dr Pereira said.

In fact Sergeant Baker said he was careful not to tread in any blood. And even if he, or another officer, did, Dr Pereira told me that the blood had not been trodden onto the leaves. It had most likely been *dripped* from something or someone. Who else but the killer, trying to get away from Lord Lucan?

As things turned out, once he was through the back door and out in the garden, he would have been safe – because, instead of pursuing him further, John went to help Veronica and took her upstairs. All the killer had to do was to wait until the house was quiet – in all probability after both Veronica and John had fled – and then come back through the basement, up the stairs and out through the front door to freedom.

And curiously enough, if that's what he did do, the killer could well have rushed out into Lower Belgrave Street at about 9.50 p.m. About the time Frances heard the curious 'banging' noise. And the very time when, according to Michael Fitzpatrick, his Irish friend said a man came out of the house, bumped into him and said something like: 'Get out of my way, you damned fool!' A man who was *not* Lord Lucan.

In the Lucan case, the times were crucial. Knowing what time Sandra Rivett died would help identify the killer.

But, surprisingly perhaps to readers of fictional whodunnits, in real life experts cannot pinpoint the exact time of death. A police officer, not Ranson, explained this to me at Gerald Road police station.

'Was the actual time of death established – the exact time?' I asked.

'No,' he said.

'Nobody knows if it was between –?'

'You asked me if the *exact* time was –'

'Well, is there a near time?' I asked.

'Well,' he replied, 'we can establish that, you see, because of the witnesses. You know, Lady Lucan saying she comes downstairs at a certain time, I think you know just after nine o'clock –'

'Yes, but her times are different from her daughter's times, aren't they?' I said.

'Well,' he said dismissively, 'her daughter's only ten!'

Can't a ten-year-old child tell the time? Nanny Jenkins certainly regarded Frances as a reliable child, not one to make up stories. As she once remarked about something else: 'If Frances said it, I wouldn't question it.'

I persisted: 'Yes, but there's a big difference in the times they give, isn't there?'

'Well yes,' said the police officer, 'but not to a great extent because we've also got the link-man at the Clermont Club [Billy Edgson] who says that he saw Lucan about half-past eight to a quarter to nine.'

That response was disturbing. If Lucan was outside the Clermont when Sandra was killed, obviously he could not have been the killer. Yet the policeman seemed to be implying that because Lucan must have been the killer, the murder could not have taken place until after he'd left Berkeley Square and had had time to get to Lower Belgrave Street.

'If you take the two different times,' I said, 'you've got two different times when the murder could have happened. I wasn't sure if the doctor had been able to say the murder was within this ten minutes or that ten minutes?'

'No,' said the policeman. 'In fact medical people find it extremely difficult. Do you know how they work it out?'

'No.'

'Well, your body temperature is 98.4 isn't it? ... Now when you die, your temperature goes up. It could go up to 104°. Now, then it comes down. And it comes down according to the heat of the ambient temperature, which is the temperature in the room. And it comes down so many degrees. You know, it may well come down ten degrees in the first hour – there's a set formula for this.'

'So they can work it out from how much it's gone up or gone down?'

'Yes,' he said.

Then, glancing round the room, he added: 'You see the trouble is this. Now supposing these windows were closed, that door was shut and that heater was on, and I murder you. Particularly with strangling, the temperature goes way up. So then I leave you dead, I walk out and the body's there. When the police come and they open the door they may well open the windows. So that the ambient temperature, the temperature of the room, then goes down.'

'But if they know that,' I said, 'surely they wouldn't touch anything until the doctor's come, would they?'

'What I've said is what it says in the good book,' the police officer said. 'But what happens in practice, of course, is completely different.'

'So that they haven't –?'

'– You *cannot*,' he said. 'It's very difficult to determine the exact time of when a person died.'

Though a doctor called to number 46 at about 10.45 p.m. found Sandra's death to have been 'very recent, within an hour or so,' other evidence meant she must have been killed much earlier than 9.45 p.m.

Frances and her mother judged the times they gave for the relevant events from the television programmes they watched.

Frances was quite clear that Veronica left the bedroom to look for Sandra 'before the nine o'clock news came on television'.

Veronica, on the other hand, said she didn't leave the bedroom until about 9.15 p.m.

But the most significant fact was the one on which both mother and daughter agreed – that Sandra herself went downstairs *before 9.00 p.m.*

Frances said she last saw the nanny just after 8.30 p.m. when Sandra took the other two children up to bed. By the time Frances returned to Veronica's bedroom at about 8.40 p.m., Sandra had already disappeared. Frances said her mother told her that the nanny had 'gone downstairs to make tea'.

Veronica said that it was about 8.55 p.m. when Sandra put her head round the bedroom door, said 'Would you like a cup of tea?', and disappeared to make one.

Either way, that meant Sandra went downstairs before 9.00 p.m.

The police believed that the killer was already lurking in the basement when Sandra descended the stairs. That meant the killer must have got into the house before about 8.30–8.40 p.m., taking Frances's times, or before about 8.55 p.m., taking Veronica's.

But Billy Edgson said he spoke to John outside the Clermont Club at about 8.45 p.m., and the other Clermont employee told me he saw John on the step there at 9.00 or 9.05 p.m. – *which ruled Lucan out completely as the killer. There was no way he could have been in two places at the same time.*

For Sandra to have collected the tea things, gone down to the kitchen, made the tea and taken it back to Veronica's bedroom would have taken no longer than ten minutes. Therefore, if nothing had happened, she could have been safely back with the tea before 8.50 p.m., taking Frances's times, or by about 9.05 p.m., taking Veronica's.

But she wasn't. She had been killed at the bottom of the basement stairs, apparently before she had even reached the kitchen. That suggested the murder took place within a minute or two of her leaving the bedroom, sooner rather than later – and almost certainly before 9.00 p.m.

For John to have driven straight from the Clermont in Berkeley Square to Elizabeth Steet, where the police later found the Mercedes parked with its engine cold and its battery flat, could have taken him seven to ten minutes depending on the traffic. He apparently then went into his flat because his car keys – presumably for the Mercedes – were found there afterwards. How long he stayed there before going round to number 46 is not known. But maybe he decided to make one of his regular checks on the house before having a bath and changing to go out to dinner. If he went straight from 72a Elizabeth Street to 46 Lower Belgrave Street, it could have taken him another one to five minutes, depending on whether he drove there or walked. It is not known whether he went by car or on foot, though Susan Maxwell-Scott said he told her was 'walking' past the house.

Therefore – *even without taking into account time spent at 72a* – if Lucan was still outside the Clermont at 9.00 p.m., he could hardly have arrived outside number 46 before about 9.08 p.m. by car, or 9.12 p.m. on foot *at the earliest*. And if he was still at the Clermont at 9.05 p.m., he couldn't have arrived at the house earlier than about 9.13 p.m. by car, or 9.17 p.m. on foot. *Which again means that Lucan could not have been the killer.*

31

But if John didn't commit the murder, what was the second piece of 'bandaged' lead piping doing in the boot of the borrowed Ford Corsair?

There was no certainty that he had driven Michael Stoop's car that night to number 46, or that it was the car he drove to Uckfield. There was a further question mark over who drove the Corsair to Newhaven, where it was found abandoned. However, the letter to Michael Stoop, written on the sheet of blotting paper from the Lion Brand writing pad found in the glove compartment, suggested it was John. And the discovery of the second piece of piping in the boot – even though it wasn't bloodstained – delighted the police.

'You can imagine our pleasure when we saw that weapon in the car down there,' Chief Superintendent Ranson told me. 'It's a very conclusive piece of evidence . . . How is it that a piece of lead piping appears in the boot of that car?

'[Lady Lucan] didn't know that [Lucan] had this car, the man who owns the car said: "It wasn't there when I lent it to Lucan", and so the assumption is that the weapon in the car was put there by Lucan and therefore the assumption is that the weapon in the house also originates from Lucan.'

Years later, Ranson said he considered the second piece of piping to be 'the most vital evidence in the whole case and, indeed, it was the first – apart from Lady Lucan's story – which firmly pointed to the 7th Earl of Lucan as being a murderer.'

News of the discovery caused a stir at the inquest. Lucan nailed by his own negligence! What a fool to leave the second piece in the Corsair! If he *did*. But did he?

Why would anyone bother to 'bandage' a piece of lead

piping? To get a better grip? And why would he want *two* pieces? Did he think he'd drop one or lose one on the way?

'What about him having two?' I asked Ranson. 'Why should he need two weapons?'

Ranson laughed his dry laugh once again.

'Have you ever come across people with two bits of lead piping before?'

'Well,' he said, 'you come across people with two guns and two knives, but . . .'

'You do?'

'Yes . . . Sometimes there's several weapons used in battering someone to death. But you see one is 8 inches – one's longer than the other.'

(What could possibly be the significance of that? This emerged years later. In Ranson's view, finding one piece 'too long to wield in a confined space, he taped the shorter piece'. What *that* meant, probably, was that Ranson must have noticed how low the ceiling was in the hall near to the cloakroom at number 46. Around the spot where the attack on Veronica was supposed to have begun. So low – at about 6-foot 6-inches – that a 6-foot 2-inch tall man standing upright would have found it impossible to stretch his arm straight above him, let alone wield a length of lead piping with considerable force. In any case if he planned to kill her in the basement – as the police believed – where space wasn't confined, why should he bother to design a shorter piece for the hall? It didn't make sense.)

'It does seem sort of, talk about the cautious man!' I said. 'I mean to actually take *two* with you seems a funny thing to me.'

'Well, he didn't take two,' Ranson said. 'He made two.'

'How do you know he made them?'

'Well –'

'Are there fingerprints on them?'

'No,' said Ranson – and back came that dry laugh.

'You know one of these went to the atomic lab somewhere? Did they show fingerprints or anything else?'

'They showed finger marks but not fingerprints. This doesn't help at all.'

In the background Big Ben chimed across the road.

'We tried something that's never been tried before,' he said. 'We tried to get it examined down at Harwell to see if there were latent fingerprints on it. And although there's finger marks ... it's thwarted by the stretching [of the adhesive tape]. You see it's stretched and bound round that pipe.'

The binding of the adhesive material had stretched any fingerprints out of recognition.

'And presumably nobody knows where [the two pieces of lead piping] came from?' I asked.

'We tried to find out,' Ranson said, 'but you're looking for ... you know when you consider the lengths of lead piping that there are scattered about ...'

(The origin of the mailbag, which he said was 'foreign' to number 46, was never discovered either. Later on the police chief suggested that yachtsmen sometimes use such bags to store their sails. Or could the bag have been brought into the house as an afterthought after the murder, in the hope of disposing of the body? During Nanny Jenkins' years at number 46, she remembered that people often left mailbags draped over the pillarbox close to the house. But an *American* mailbag?)

Of the two pieces of lead piping, Chief Superintendent Ranson said: 'We'd have loved to have the forensic man come up and say: "Yes, this piece came off the same as – this was originally one piece and he chopped it in half." But we haven't got that evidence.'

'What kind of adhesive was it?' I asked.

'Well, it's just this surgical tape that they'd use to bind you with if you had cracked ribs, you know they use it in hospital ... It's not Elastoplast as such but something similar to that.'

'Could I go out and buy it?'

'Yes, you could go and buy it from any chemist.'

'Any chemist? The chemist in Lower Belgrave Street

presumably didn't say whether Lord Lucan bought some from him?'

'No.'

Dr Robert Davies, the scientist who examined the two pieces of piping, made it clear at the inquest that there was no certainty they had ever been part of the same original length.

'As a scientist,' he told the court, 'the highest I could put it is to say that they *may* have come from the same length of pipe.'

But they were 'most unlikely' to have been adjacent pieces, one piece lopped off the other. In most respects the two pieces of pipe did not correspond, and a difference in corrosion suggested they had had different usage.

In addition Dr Pereira had testified that there were also differences in the batches of adhesive material used to bind both pipes. The same tape had not been used for both pieces. One lot had been used to bind one length of piping and a second, slightly different lot of adhesive, had been used to bind the other.

What this all boiled down to is the fact that the two 'weapons' could have been made at different times *by different people*. One could have been a copy of the other.

But why would anyone do that – unless they wanted to make it appear as if John was the killer?

Bill Shand Kydd said: 'I was quite clear before the inquest that the police had one piece of evidence which was linked with the "murder weapon" and was found in the car. Now I wasn't told what it was. I assumed obviously that it was connected with the bit of lead piping, but quite frankly without that one single piece of evidence there was nothing else that could have convicted John of anything. They had no other evidence at all apart from Veronica's statement and the matching piece of lead piping in the car.

'And my only thought is that here's an intelligent chap who's very cool under pressure, so if you want to go and bump somebody on the head first of all why make the mistake of taking two pieces? Secondly, having done the deed and ditched the car, I mean the *last* thing you do is leave the other piece in the boot! So the question is how the hell did that other piece get there?'

How indeed. Especially if the lead piping found at the house *wasn't* the real murder weapon . . .

There was no doubt at all that Sandra and Veronica had both been battered with a blunt instrument of some kind, perhaps the same one. But the experts couldn't say for certain what the blunt instrument was. Therefore – although Ranson was convinced it was the lead piping – the murder weapon could have been some implement which had never been found.

It was Veronica who said, oddly, that the weapon used to hit her 'felt bandaged'. In her *Daily Express* exclusive two months after the murder, she was quoted as saying: 'My hand fell on to a heavy object on the floor . . . it seemed to be metal covered in bandagings. I also felt a clump of hair on the floor. I actually thought at the time: "That can't be mine," but it was.' Why she didn't pick the heavy object up and use it in self-defence, she did not explain.

But even if the lead piping in the hall had been used on her, which could not be proved beyond doubt, was it also the weapon which had been used to kill Sandra? Dr Pereira's examination revealed an extraordinary fact. Something she might well have expected to find was not there.

What evidence would usually be found on a weapon used to batter someone over the head? For a start, some of the victim's hairs.

I asked Professor Simpson: 'There were hairs, weren't there, adhering to the weapon?'

'Oh yes,' he said.

'Would that happen automatically as part of the attack?'

'Exactly,' he said. 'You've only got to strike a scalp with a weapon to have scalp hair, and if [the wound] starts to bleed and you strike again, blood – and sometimes little particles of skin stuck to the weapon.'

'You would anyway?'

'Oh yes,' he said.

The Nob Squad were fortunate to have the services of Simpson and Pereira, both tip-top professionals. Ranson regarded Professor Simpson as 'a very eminent man', and the professor himself rated Dr Pereira as 'absolutely first class, quite the tops'. Her examination of the bloodstained lead piping was undoubtedly most thorough.

Yet, despite that, *not one single hair from Sandra Rivett's head was found on it!*

The piping was about 9 inches long, weighed 2 pounds 3 ounces and was 'grossly distorted', Dr Pereira reported. It was 'heavily and extensively bloodstained' and tests produced a reaction for human blood of Group AB. Tests on some of the hairs found sticking to the piping showed 'damage typical of that resulting from a battering of a head', and all the hairs examined proved to be 'similar to' Veronica's and not Sandra's. As Dr Pereira repeated during cross-examination at the inquest: 'There was no hair of Mrs Rivett on the bludgeon.'

If the piping was the murder weapon, how could that be?

But there was something even more suspicious about it. According to Sergeant Baker, the first investigating policeman on the scene, the 'bandaged' lead piping had changed colour. On oath at the inquest, he testified that the first time he saw the object in the hall, it was 'white'. When he noticed it again later, it had turned to 'red'. In other words, the piping had *become* bloodstained since he first set eyes on it! That perplexed Chief Superintendent Ranson no end, as well it might.

'You see,' he told me at Cannon Row, 'then you get a curious twist of evidence which I can't believe – the sergeant saying when they saw that weapon first it was white, and then it changed to red!'

He laughed his dry laugh. Then he hazarded an explanation.

'You see,' he suggested, 'which would be indicative of that weapon having been *washed*. It's a possibility that

335

after attacking Sandra, that may be what Lucan was doing in the [hall cloakroom] – washing the weapon before he took it away with him.'

That didn't figure.

'But how would it then become red afterwards?' I asked.

'Well,' he said, 'the blood would seep back through again.'

But even as he said it, Ranson wasn't convinced.

He added: 'But of course if he'd washed it and [then] attacked Lady Lucan with it, you'd think the blood would be smothered there anyway.'

Of course.

'It would *have* to be red if he'd attacked Lady Lucan with it afterwards, wouldn't it?' I said.

So much for that. But later the police chief returned to his theme.

'See, was he washing his hands in that back cloakroom?' he asked. (Why, if the killer was supposed to be wearing gloves?) 'He had the weapon up there, which we're told changes from white to red. Was he washing the weapon there? Had he washed the weapon for some reason or other?'

'Are the policemen sticking to that story?'

'Oh yeh,' he said.

'Somebody's presumably said to them: "Have you got your facts straight? How can you possibly say the weapon was white and went red afterwards?"'

'Mn.'

'And they still claim it was white and went red?'

'Oh yes. Yes.'

'This is Sergeant –?'

'– Baker.'

'Is Baker a reliable man? Far be it for me to [query] one of your staff, but you obviously –'

'We pursued this with him,' Chief Superintendent Ranson said. 'It seems a stupid thing but . . .'

'It's a very curious thing, isn't it? . . .'

'You see this may be an illusion he had about this,'

Ranson said. 'He's dropped into a pub and somebody's said, you know: "He's killed the nanny" or something like this, and he's looking for a body somewhere and he hasn't found it and there's also the possibility of an intruder still being in the house. So you can imagine he's very keyed-up and the significance of that weapon –'

'Did he say it was a "weapon"? Because he must have thought it was white because he said he thought it was a [doll's leg].'

Ranson said: 'There's no doubt that when he first saw that lying there he had no reason to believe that it was a murder weapon. There's no doubt it never really registered. He might have thought: "Oh, there's a doll's leg" and gone past it and then later the significance of it becomes apparent and by that time it's smothered in blood, it's completely red.'

Which is exactly what did happen.

'Do you think in fact he made a mistake?' I asked. 'Or do you think that somebody *had* tried to wash the blood out?'

'You can only . . . Let's assume he was wrong. That's the answer to that. But let's assume he's right,' Ranson said. 'Well, assuming he's right, *an* explanation for that is that it's been washed but the blood had seeped through again.'

'Why would anybody do that?'

'Well, if he wanted to take it away with him, put it in his pocket. You wouldn't want to put a bloody piece of piping in your pocket. Whereas if you say: "Well, let's wash the worst off anyway" . . . you do this with vegetables don't you? You wash the worst of the dirt off and later when you're going to cook it you really wash it.'

Ranson theorised that the killer was in the hall cloakroom perhaps washing the lead piping in preparation to leave the house when Veronica came along the darkened hall calling Sandra's name. The police chief painted a vivid imaginary picture of what the killer's possible reaction might have been.

'Can you imagine the state of mind of a person who has committed murder?' he asked. 'Let's assume, let's say it's Lucan and [he thinks] he's killed his wife. He's put her in the bag . . . Imagine his state of mind when he's successfully done this dreadful deed . . . and suddenly he hears his wife saying: "Sandra, Sandra." Can you imagine what went through his mind? There's three things, I feel, that went through his mind – he felt that Lady Lucan had got out of the sack and was coming up the stairs shouting out for help: "Sandra, Sandra"; he thought it was a ghost, if you believe in ghosts; or at that stage he realised he'd killed the wrong woman.'

What next?

According to Ranson's theory, the killer would then have rushed out of the cloakroom – wearing gloves and wielding the washed or unwashed weapon – and attacked Veronica with it.

But what if that's what did happen, then the 'bandaged' lead piping would have become bloodstained again immediately. And it would have *remained* bloodstained until the police arrived to investigate.

Even if the piping was washed *after* the attack on Veronica – which she made no mention of and which is thoroughly unlikely anyway – enough time had surely elapsed between then and the arrival of Sergeant Baker for any blood left at the centre of the 'bandaging' to seep through again. Yet it hadn't, presumably because there was none.

Years later, Ranson compared it to an adhesive plaster wrapped round a cut finger which you wash and the blood then seeps back through. But that only happens when the wound is *still bleeding*, and lead piping doesn't bleed.

A killer would hardly bother to wash a bloody weapon before putting it into his pocket if his clothes were already saturated and dripping with Sandra's Group B blood. The only place on the ground floor where he could have washed the weapon was in the hall cloakroom. And the apparent lack of Group B blood in the cloakroom suggested that the killer never went in there after the murder.

(Discussing the violence on an LBC radio show in October 1987, Veronica said: ' . . . my husband *leapt out of a cloak cupboard* and hit me on the head . . .' (My italics.)If she meant the cupboard in the anteroom outside the cloakroom, this would have been an even more unlikely place for anyone to 'wash a weapon'.)

The washed weapon theory did not make sense.

If, as Sergeant Baker testified, the 'bandaged' lead piping was 'white' when he first saw it, more than an hour after the murder took place, that meant only one thing. *It could not be the murder weapon.* The fact that no hairs from Sandra Rivett's head were found on it confirms this.

So how did the lead piping *then* turn 'red' – and why? How did it get not only Group AB blood but also fibres and Veronica's hair on it? Did that 'evidence' get onto the piping by accident, or was it put there deliberately?

Consider the facts. There was bloodsoaked carpet in the hall, where the lead piping was found. And lying around, according to the forensic evidence and Veronica herself, were some of her hairs. Probably they were damaged and bloodstained, and possibly they had some of those curious unidentified 'dark greyish-blue wool fibres' sticking to them. Also on the lead piping Dr Pereira found some unexplained 'fabric fibres'. Could they perhaps have been fibres from the stair or hall carpet?

It seems likely the killer would have transferred some of Sandra's blood from the bloodbath in the basement to the hall. But could hairs from Sandra Rivett's head have been transferred there as well – especially *after* her body had been bundled into the sack? They were the key 'evidence' missing from the 'weapon'.

How did the blood, the wool and the fabric fibres, and the hairs 'similar to' Veronica's get onto the lead piping? In the early confusion of the police investigation, could someone have kicked the piping accidentally into a position where the 'bandaging' picked up the evidence from the floor by itself – and turned from white to red?

Or, unthinkable though it was, had someone deliberately doctored the thing – smeared it with blood and the rest to make it *look* as if it was the murder weapon?

If that was the case, then the discovery of the second piece of lead piping in the boot of the abandoned Ford Corsair had to be suspect too. Even Ranson himself, in yet another article by James Fox – in *You, The Mail on Sunday Magazine*, in October 1984 – was quoted as saying: '... I suppose the cudgel in the boot of his car could have been planted.'

If it *was*, that suggests someone wanted to frame Lord Lucan. But who would have wanted to? And who might have been in a position to do so?

32

What might the real murder weapon have been? Shortly after the inquest, I had asked Chief Superintendent Ranson: 'Remember [Professor Simpson] said various injuries [to Sandra] had been made by a blunt instrument? Is that blunt instrument, by the way, bound to be the lead piping, or is there any possibility it could be something else?'

Ranson's reply came like a bolt from the blue.

'It could be a truncheon,' he said. 'It *could* be a policeman! No, you see [the experts] won't commit themselves. You see, he couldn't say *those* injuries were caused by *that* blunt instrument. With a bullet-hole, you could possibly say: "Well, that bullet came from that gun," but when you've got injuries of that nature . . .'

At the unexpected mention of a truncheon, *I* had laughed. The idea was fantastic. A fugitive peer branded a killer and hunted by police forces throughout the world for a murder which had actually been committed by a *policeman!* Who'd ever believe it? Not me. Not then.

But later, as I dug into the research and intriguing facts emerged, I began to wonder.

Shortly after the murder, a man who announced himself as a CID officer called to see Nanny Jenkins. She was out, on her day off, but he told the woman who employed her then that he would return. He did, and Miss Jenkins noted his visit down in her diary. The man asked her first why she had not come forward to give evidence. She explained that she had not worked for the Lucans since December 1972 and therefore knew nothing of the events at number 46 on the night of the murder. He took a statement from her anyway. Then, as their interview came to an end, he said: 'I really came about the letter Lady Lucan wrote to you.' 'She never wrote to me,' Nanny replied.

Then she remembered a letter Veronica had *handed* to her, which she was told to get to the Commissioner of the Metropolitan Police if Veronica was ever 'mugged or found dead'. Nanny had been given the letter one day after she had sat up until 1.00 a.m. waiting for Veronica to return from a visit to the mews cottage at 5 Eaton Row. Handing it over, Veronica told Nanny she had been 'indiscreet with a policeman' by showing him 'the family jewels'. According to Nanny, Veronica's letter mentioned 'corruption' in the police force.

'Lady Lucan was very serious about it,' Miss Jenkins recalled. 'She thought the police were going to rob her of her jewels.'

This incident may have begun a period when Veronica appeared afraid of the police, when she told Kait to dodge round corners whenever a police officer approached. Nanny herself remembered Veronica commenting anxiously when a pair of policemen simply passed number 46 while on their beat.

After the Lucans separated, when evidence was being gathered for the custody case, Nanny Jenkins told John about Veronica's 'mugged or found dead' letter and the circumstances surrounding it. John tried to find out more. According to Christina, he tried to track down a particular police officer, but got nowhere.

'There was something very funny happened there and none of us know,' Christina said. 'John never got to the bottom of it either. But I know that Veronica was worried about the policeman. I seem to have in my mind that it involved only one night. And Veronica rang the next day to try and get hold of him and the police station said that he wasn't there any more. And whether she had tried to attach herself to him, or something had occurred and he'd gone straight to his superiors and said that he was in a very difficult situation, and they covered for him in some way, or whatever, I don't know. But I know that none of us ever found him, and it was Veronica's story not John's. Veronica told me long before John even knew about it. But she must have told him too because he went looking for the policeman. He was told that the policeman had been at whatever his local station was but had now been moved to another police station. They refused to say where he was and so John could never find him or speak to him. It was very peculiar, the whole thing was very odd. But Veronica was very worried about the policeman, there's no question of that. *Something* had occurred.'

Miss Jenkins said: 'I mentioned the letter to Lord Lucan after the separation and said Lady Lucan told me she'd been "indiscreet with a policeman" and Lord Lucan said: "He's no longer in the force."'

Had the policeman so suddenly left his station or the force? Or was that a white lie to keep John off his trail? And if so, what did the officer have to hide?

Nanny Jenkins recounted all the details to her visitor. The man listened intently. He seemed in a hurry and said he had to meet another police officer somewhere. He made a telephone call.

'I may have to come back,' he told Nanny as he left.

But she never saw him again.

Who was the police officer John tried to find? What had happened or been said between him and Veronica? Why had she been so afraid? Why had she written about 'corruption' in the police force? What made her fear that one day in the future she might be found 'mugged' or 'dead'? What connection did it have with the Lucan jewellery? And could there have been any connection at all between that episode and the tragic later events at number 46?

Let's suppose for the sake of argument that a policeman or ex-policeman was involved in the murder of Sandra Rivett. Perhaps he knew there was valuable jewellery and silver at 46 Lower Belgrave Street. Perhaps he went there with the intention to rob. Would any of the facts fit?

John said the killer was 'large'. Veronica agreed that the man who rushed out and hit her over the head – a man she did not *see* in the darkness – was much taller than she was, which a policeman necessarily would be. Dr Pereira said that the footprints in blood leading towards the safe and the back door had been made by someone with big feet.

If Sandra disturbed a policeman trying to burgle the house, perhaps a local cop she recognised, there was a clear reason why she had to be killed. And why Veronica, arriving downstairs, had to be silenced. Having escaped from the house, a policeman could have covered himself perhaps by cleaning up, changing his clothes and *returning* to number 46 – or, more likely, getting a colleague in league with him to go there for him. By then, Sergeant Baker and P.C. Beddick had already forced the front door, so there would be no problem gaining entry. Who would stop another policeman from helping to 'investigate' a crime – especially in the early flap? Ranson himself had talked about the initial confusion caused by so many police officers flooding in, wanting to see the body and be among the first on the scene. If all this sounds fanciful, consider one thought. If, as Sergeant Baker indicated on oath, the lead piping didn't become bloodstained until *after* the police started arriving, who but a policeman *could* have made it bloodstained? Mingling with colleagues, he would hardly be suspect. And if the lead piping was tampered with, was it also a policeman who made and bound the second piece of piping and planted it to be 'found' in the boot of the Ford Corsair? Who was in a better position than a policeman to throw suspicion in another direction?

And who was more convenient to blame than Lucan, who'd turned up unexpectedly – and caused the killer to flee empty-handed, without even the diamond and sapphire pendant necklace he'd tried to grab from around Veronica's neck? Lucan, who'd had trouble with his wife. Lucan, who'd been on the spot. Lucan, who might have glimpsed enough of his face to identify him in the future as the killer . . .

Less than an hour after the emergency call from the Plumbers Arms – long before Ranson had even been told of the murder – Sergeant Forsyth and some of his colleagues were *already* looking for Lucan. They searched for him at the mews cottage – and that was extraordinary. Because when Forsyth spoke to Kait shortly after, it became clear from his questions that he knew nothing about the Lucans.

He didn't know they were separated, he didn't know if John lived at number 46, he didn't know about the flat in Elizabeth Street – and yet he had already searched 5 Eaton Row! How did he *know* about the mews cottage? How *could* he know about the mews cottage?

The answer to that came at the inquest. Sergeant Forsyth told the coroner he had discovered the address from a *'police source'*, another police officer, present at number 46. Now John hadn't lived at the mews for almost two years, though the 'police source' might not have known that. But how did he know about the cottage in Eaton Row at all – unless he'd *been* there, or been told about it by someone who had? Like the policeman, for example, who'd apparently spent time at the mews cottage with Veronica about two years previously – the night before she wrote her 'mugged or found dead' letter.

According to Michael Fitzpatrick, the 'Mr X' from Market Harborough, it was because his Irish friend 'didn't want to get involved with the police' that he denied the story about the 'other man' rushing out of number 46 on the night of the murder.

Let's suppose for a moment that the Irish friend *was* passing the house that evening, was bumped into by the fleeing intruder – and recognised him as a policeman. Mightn't he have considered it prudent not to go to the police – and later, when Fitzpatrick told the tale, to deny it had ever happened?

In John's final phone call to Kait from Uckfield several hours after the murder, he said he would speak to her again, and to the police, in the morning. Then he decided to 'lie doggo' instead. What made him change his mind? Was it the mention of the police? Did he realise his situation might be even worse than he'd imagined? If he remembered Veronica's fears that the police might try to rob her of her jewels ... if he added that to his belief that the intruder was a burglar ... if the thought crossed his mind that the two might be linked, how confident would he have felt at the prospect of turning himself in next morning *to* the police? Imagine the situation: all that background which might be viewed as a 'motive', his presence at the scene of the crime, no alibi to fall back on, a wife accusing him – and he turns up and says: 'It wasn't me. It was a policeman,' perhaps even: 'That chap over there!' Who would believe him?

When Chief Superintendent Ranson told me that the real murder weapon 'could be a truncheon', and that the killer 'could be a policeman', I did not take him seriously at all. I knew nothing then of Veronica's earlier fear of the police nor of her letter about police corruption which was to be handed to the Metropolitan Police Commissioner if ever she was 'mugged or found dead'. But in view of the fact that a woman *was* later found dead in the Lucans' house near the safe, how can it be ignored? If there was any link between the letter and a policeman or ex-policeman who was around on the murder night, then the whole matter warrants investigation – if only to eliminate doubt.

In the summer of 1982 when I was away from home, in the process of moving to a new address, a curious burglary took place at my house in London. A man jemmied his way in very professionally, ignored everything a thief might normally take, and concentrated his attention solely on my study, where most of my research for this book was kept. He jemmied open the study door, which was locked, and then broke the locks open on a large trunk, metal document boxes and a briefcase. Papers inside concerning the Lucan case were gone through, and a small brass casket was taken.

A neighbour who saw the man emerge gave the local police a description of the burglar, of his girl companion who sat outside in a car waiting, of the car itself and indeed the registration number. Yet, to my knowledge, the man was never tracked down or charged. But it is possible he did not find what he was looking for, and struck again. Because, shortly after, every flat at the new address I had moved to was broken into by an intruder who, mysteriously, took nothing. A coincidence? Maybe.

Over the years I have noticed newspaper reports of similar 'burglaries' to mine where state security seems the only conceivable possible link. But would the security services be interested in the Lucan case – and if so, why?

An odd reminder of this came years later when I went to visit a psychic detective. I had read an article which said she believed that Lucan was innocent and that he had been 'beautifully set up'. Out of curiosity, I took with me not only personal effects of the Lucan family but also one of my metal document boxes which had been broken open by the burglar at my house. As she held it, she said immediately: 'That's not an ordinary thief that did that – that's Special Branch.'

She repeated that she 'knew' Lucan was innocent, and said he was still alive, and that he would come forward during her lifetime.

She further suggested that Sandra Rivett had been killed because of what she knew about a big crime concerning gold, possibly bullion.

Who killed Sandra Rivett? Twelve years after I began my own inquiry, I do not know. But I am convinced beyond reasonable doubt that Lord Lucan did not murder her.

Apart from Lady Lucan's allegations, the evidence is

purely circumstantial and does not make sense. To summarise briefly:

The police case implied that Lord Lucan battered Sandra Rivett to death in a gory bloodbath of a killing, in mistake for his wife, then discovered his error and tried to kill Lady Lucan too. This despite the fact that Lucan had no history of physical violence, couldn't stand the sight of blood, is unlikely to have mistaken one woman for the other, would never have attempted such a deed while the children he was desperate to protect were in the same house, and had made no effort to establish an alibi.

The actual evidence shows the following:

* Sandra Rivett must have been killed in the basement of 46 Lower Belgrave Street on Thursday, 7 November 1974, between about 8.40 and 9.00 p.m. But at that period witnesses saw Lord Lucan outside the Clermont Club in Berkeley Square. He could not have reached the house in time. Therefore he could not have been the killer.

* Lord Lucan said he was passing the house when, through the window, he saw what appeared to be a fight between a man and Lady Lucan in the basement. He said he ran in to the rescue and the man ran off. Lady Lucan maintained that she never went down into the basement that evening. But a forensic expert who found blood of Lady Lucan's group in the basement, and blood of the murdered nanny's group on and under Lady Lucan's shoes, said it was 'a likely explanation' that Lady Lucan did go into the basement.

* The police admitted that Lady Lucan's account didn't completely add up because the times didn't fit. They explained this by saying she must have become unconscious. But if she was unconscious, Lady Lucan could not have fought the killer off. So why didn't he kill her too? If Lucan was the killer, it makes no sense. But if someone else was the killer, the answer is clear. Lady Lucan survived because Lord Lucan ran in to the rescue.

* Both Sandra Rivett and Lady Lucan had been battered with a blunt instrument of some kind. A piece of 'bandaged' lead piping found in the hall at the house was alleged to be the murder weapon. A second piece of 'bandaged' lead piping found in an abandoned car Lord Lucan had borrowed pointed to Lucan as the culprit. But the first policeman who arrived at the scene of the crime testified that when he first saw the piping in the hall, it was white. Then it turned red. If the lead piping did not become bloodstained until long after the violence, it could not have been the murder weapon. The fact that no hairs from the murdered nanny's head were found on it confirms this. Therefore the second piece of piping found in the car was a red herring.

* Evidence from a forensic expert about Sandra Rivett's injuries indicates that the murder did not take place in the way the police described. Sandra did not die immediately from one blow from behind. The forensic expert said that she met her killer face to face, that the killer lashed out first with a fist or a hand, possibly before picking up the weapon, and that he probably struggled with her before she died. This makes the chance of anyone mistaking her for Lady Lucan even less likely.

* The clothes of whoever killed Sandra Rivett and bundled her body into the US mailbag in which it was found would have become saturated with her Group B blood. The killer was probably dripping with the nanny's blood. Lord Lucan helped his injured wife upstairs and went into her bedroom, her bathroom, and up to the nursery. Yet the blood analyst on the case made no mention in her police report of Group B blood there. And Lord Lucan's elder daughter, Lady Frances Bingham, then aged ten, who saw her parents enter the bedroom, said she could not see blood on her father. If his clothes had been saturated with blood, could she have failed to notice? And why hadn't he dripped Group B blood upstairs?

* The police said there was no trace of another man

349

having been at the house on the murder night. Yet forensic experts found unexplained fingerprints and fabric fibres, and a possible unexplained third blood group at the house, which might all have been left by another person.

* Group B blood had been dripped onto leaves in the back garden. The back door was also found unlocked. If the killer hid in the garden until both Lady Lucan and Lord Lucan had fled, he could have come back through the house and out through the front door at about 9.50 p.m. Which is exactly the time when, according to one allegation, a man who was not Lord Lucan was seen rushing out of the house and away.

* The police believed Lord Lucan had borrowed the car later found abandoned as part of a plan to murder his wife. They theorised that Lucan planned to put the body in the boot and dump it. If that was the case, then Lucan needed to keep the car hidden beforehand, so that no one could connect it with him. Far from that, several people knew he had the car. It's possible he even drove a friend in the same car only about an hour before the murder. And he used to park it openly outside his flat. Only a few days before the murder, he even got a parking ticket for leaving the car too long on a meter a few steps from his front door.

* Finally, Lord Lucan had no motive for killing Sandra Rivett. And he believed he was getting nearer his aim of regaining custody of his three children legally through the courts. To have committed murder would have been to destroy everything – and I am completely convinced that he did not do so.

In 1978, the Dowager Countess applied to the Attorney-General for leave to have the inquest verdict set aside and a fresh inquest held. Unfortunately, this was refused.

I believe that the inquest verdict condemning Lord Lucan should now be quashed without delay, and that the police should launch a new investigation to find the real killer.

I hope this book will help to correct the distorted picture of Lord Lucan which has been presented for so long.

And that it will encourage him – if he is still alive – to come forward and clear his name.

33

Veronica's anxieties did not stop after the murder.

In 1978 there was The Riddle of the Missing Photograph Album – the 'mysterious theft' of one of her family albums from the mews cottage, to which she moved after 46 Lower Belgrave Street was sold.

'There were four keys to the door and I had them all,' she was quoted as saying a year later, in October 1979, when it was apparently still missing. 'The police found no sign of a break-in . . .'

The following year, in November 1980, a Sunday newspaper splashed a front-page exclusive story headlined: 'I AM POISON TARGET SAYS LADY LUCAN'. This reported that detectives from Gerald Road were investigating a new claim from Veronica that there had been 'a plot to poison' her.

In addition to the 'poison probe', the same newspaper revealed that the detectives had also 'reopened a file on an earlier Lady Lucan mystery. Drugs prescribed for her when the hunt for her husband reached its peak were said to have been tampered with . . .'

But what of John – was he dead or still alive, 'lying doggo'? Veronica said both, at different times. But in February 1979 she was quoted as saying: 'I know he is alive. I lied to everyone when I said he was dead, because I wanted to give him a chance to escape. I wanted to protect him and stop him going to prison.'

Lucan certainly wasn't known as a quitter. One friend recalled how at golf, even if he was losing, John would 'never give up, *never* give up!'

'I don't think he's dead,' his brother Hugh said. 'I just hope that he's managing to be comfortable somewhere.'

What would be in his mind – to stay away permanently, or to come back once the dust has settled?

'The drawback is that the dust won't settle,' Hugh said. 'The situation is now crystallised, it's down in the record. The coroner's court jury has given its judgement and as far as officialdom is concerned John "did" it, pending a trial. And it seems to me that this is very sad.'

Veronica had gained the sympathy of the police, the coroner, the Press and no doubt many members of the public. She was certainly a tragic figure, a suitable case for sympathy. She was also, as people recognised, a very clever woman. But what if John were to be found, or turned himself in? What if he came *back*? Veronica had clearly reviewed her position in such an event.

'I know one day that I'm going to face him again but I'm totally prepared,' she was quoted as saying. 'I even know what my first words will be: "Hello, how are you? Sit back. I've already prepared your defence."'

As the years went by, she emerged more and more as a champion of her missing husband. By October 1981 she was even implying in print that she could have been *mistaken* in thinking that her husband was the attacker. Three years before, she revealed, she had woken in the night convinced that he was in bed with her.

'It was not a dream: more an hallucination ... "It's not what you think," he was telling me. "It wasn't as it seemed" ... I only know that at the time [of the attack], I *thought* my husband had hit me ...' (My italics.)

She pointed out that there 'could quite easily' have been someone else hiding downstairs; that if John had come to murder her, he could have finished her off at any time and it was 'strange' that he hadn't.

At the end of February 1982, Veronica attempted suicide. Three months later, after leaving a psychiatric hospital, she described in graphic detail in another newspaper interview how she had cut her wrists, tried to hang herself, taken sleeping pills and drunk household bleach – but survived.

In December 1983, after Veronica was found

wandering in a confused state amid traffic near her home, she was taken to Gerald Road police station where she was deemed to be in need of attention under the Mental Health Act. She was commited to Banstead mental hospital in Surrey, where she apparently spent six months in a National Health ward.

In January 1985, a *second* Lucan nanny met a violent death – Christabel Martin, who had returned to 46 Lower Belgrave Street as temporary nanny after Sandra Rivett was murdered.

At his trial at the Old Bailey in October 1985, the court heard that her husband, Nicholas Boyce, had strangled her, dismembered her body, then roasted and boiled some of her flesh to look like 'the remains of Sunday lunch'. He dumped more than a hundred pieces of her body around London in plastic bags. Covering her severed head in concrete, he put it in another bag, and then – hand in hand with their two infant children – he walked onto Hungerford Bridge and dropped it into the River Thames. Boyce was sentenced to six years for manslaughter.

On 10 October 1985, a story in the *London Standard* shattered all hopes that the police investigation into the second nanny's death might lead to a breakthrough in the Lucan case. Under the headline 'Basement Secrets', Londoner's Diary carried four short paragraphs which read:

'One of the more intriguing aspects of the Old Bailey trial of Nicholas Boyce is the evidence it has thrown up of the unease still felt at Scotland Yard over the Lord Lucan affair.

Christabel Boyce, the dead woman, was a former Lucan nanny and naturally the police officers investigating the background to the killing asked to examine the Lucan files, still kept under lock and key in the bowels of the Yard.

Amazingly, they were told that no one under the

354

rank of Commander was allowed to see the information amassed about Lucan over the last eleven years and that in this case no access would be granted.

No reason was given. What is still being hidden?'

What indeed?

PHOTOGRAPHIC CREDITS

Lord Lucan, 14 July 1971 – Desmond O'Neill
John in the Coldstream Guards – Express Newspapers
John in his ceremonial robes – Camera Press, London
The wedding day – Portman Press Bureau Ltd
On the golf course – Express Newspapers
Sandra Rivett – London News Service
Roger Rivett – The Photo Source
Roy Ranson – Press Association Photos
Dave 'Buster' Gerring – Press Association Photos
Four of the 'murder reconstruction' pictures – Harry Dempster, Express Newspapers
Christina Shand Kydd – Express Newspapers
Kait Lucan and Bill Shand Kydd – The Photo Source
Professor Keith Simpson – The Photo Source
Dr Margaret Pereira – Press Association Photos
Lady Lucan – Press Association Photos

INDEX

Fontana Paperbacks
Non-fiction

Fontana is a leading paperback publisher of non-fiction. Below are some recent titles.

Armchair Golf *Ronnie Corbett* £3.50
You Are Here *Kevin Woodcock* £3.50
Squash Balls *Barry Waters* £3.50
Men: An Owner's Manual *Stephanie Brush* £2.50
Impressions of My Life *Mike Yarwood* £2.95
Arlott on Wine *John Arlott* £3.95
Beside Rugby *Bill Beaumont* £3.50
Agoraphobia *Robyn Vines* £3.95
The Serpent and the Rainbow *Wade Davies* £2.95
Alternatives to Drugs *Colin Johnson & Arabella Melville* £4.95
The Learning Organization *Bob Garratt* £3.95
Information and Organizations *Max Boisot* £3.50
Say It One Time For The Broken Hearted *Barney Hoskins* £4.95
March or Die *Tony Geraghty* £3.95
Nice Guys Sleep Alone *Bruce Feirstein* £2.95
Royal Hauntings *Joan Forman* £3.50
Going For It *Victor Kiam* £2.95
Sweets *Shona Crawford Poole* £3.95
Waugh on Wine *Auberon Waugh* £3.95

You can buy Fontana paperbacks at your local bookshop or newsagent. Or you can order them from Fontana Paperbacks, Cash Sales Department, Box 29, Douglas, Isle of Man. Please send a cheque, postal or money order (not currency) worth the purchase price plus 22p per book for postage (maximum postage required is £3).

NAME (Block letters) _____

ADDRESS _____

_____

_____